The Plot
to Perpetuate Slavery

The Plot to Perpetuate Slavery

*How George McClellan,
Southern Spies and a Confidence
Man Nearly Derailed Emancipation*

Phil Roycraft

McFarland & Company, Inc., Publishers
Jefferson, North Carolina

ISBN (print) 978-1-4766-9495-5
ISBN (ebook) 978-1-4766-5339-6

LIBRARY OF CONGRESS AND BRITISH LIBRARY
CATALOGUING DATA ARE AVAILABLE

Library of Congress Control Number 2024028663

© 2024 Phil Roycraft. All rights reserved

No part of this book may be reproduced or transmitted in any form or by any means, electronic or mechanical, including photocopying or recording, or by any information storage and retrieval system, without permission in writing from the publisher.

Front cover: (left to right) illustration of Daniel Mountjoy Cloud (Dickinson College); color lithographs of freed African American slave and Major General George McClellan (Library of Congress)

Printed in the United States of America

*McFarland & Company, Inc., Publishers
Box 611, Jefferson, North Carolina 28640
www.mcfarlandpub.com*

Table of Contents

Preface 1
Introduction 3

1. A Confidence Man in Manhattan 7
2. Another Grand Scheme 16
3. The Aristocracy of Slaveholding Interests 27
4. Monument Street Girls 38
5. On Mansfield's Secret Service 49
6. A Recusant Chaplain 60
7. Loudoun County Scouts 72
8. Redeeming Their Tarnished Honor 81
9. A Brighter and More Permanent Prosperity 93
10. The Curiosity Tour 103
11. Strange Bedfellows 112
12. A Fraudulent Peace 122
13. Mission to Maryland 129
14. The Church Militant 141
15. Attack of the Copperheads 152
16. A Shallow Attempt at Humbuggery 163

Postscript 175
Chapter Notes 179
Bibliography 209
Index 219

Preface

I never intended to write a book about Civil War espionage or emancipation. While researching my first book, *Valuable Hereafter*, I stumbled upon the story of John Wesley Greene, an accomplished confidence man who culminated his career with an attempt to con President Lincoln into abandoning emancipation in 1862.

Intrigued by the fact that Greene's peace initiative mirrored that of an individual named William Chase Barney, with whom he seemed to have little in common, I investigated the possible connection in my article "A Shallow Attempt at Humbuggery: Maryland and the Plot to Stop Emancipation," published in the *Maryland Historical Magazine* in the summer of 2013. The article argued that Greene's peace proposal, although a hoax, was instigated by the Confederate government, with whom Barney had met not long before. Nevertheless, details of how they coordinated such a complex plot with John Wesley Greene, a resident of Pittsburgh, remained elusive.

Ten years of exhaustive research and the use of so-called historical forensics, however, captured the true picture of the conflict over emancipation in late 1862. As one proponent of this technique says, historical forensics allows "an understanding of the bigger picture … by piecing together multiple clues and perspectives … [from] primary sources."[1] The result was a story never revealed during the war or since, which casts a new light on the dramatic events of 1862.

Hidden for more than 160 years, the clandestine chess match over emancipation became, for Major General George B. McClellan, the Lincoln administration, and the Confederate government alike, the most secret of missions. The fate of four million enslaved African Americans and the future of the nation would ride upon the outcome.

Introduction

In the wake of the Emancipation Proclamation, which President Abraham Lincoln issued days after the Battle of Antietam in September 1862, Republicans across the North were joyous. Horace Greeley, the well-known abolitionist editor of the *New York Tribune*, exclaimed, "God bless Abraham Lincoln!"[1] The *Chicago Tribune* announced, "President Lincoln has set his hand and affixed the great seal of the nation to the grandest proclamation ever issued by man."[2] In northern Pennsylvania—far from the influence of the slave states and Southern sympathizers—the tiny *Potter Journal* declared President Lincoln's proclamation "the greatest document of this century" and predicted confidently that Lincoln's name "will live in the hearts of the American people for centuries yet to come, for this, if for no other of his official acts."[3]

Despite the rejoicing, even supporters of African American freedom mused over how Lincoln would enforce the measure, given the political and military realities of the time. Journalist Joseph Scoville, who wrote editorials to the English press during the American Civil War under the pseudonym "Manhattan," expressed this frustration to his English readers in the weeks following the proclamation. "The country waits to hear of battles," he mused in a letter to them on October 17, 1862. "Alas, it will wait a long time. In my opinion, the Democratic generals have a perfect understanding with each other, and they will make this or that excuse; there will be no battles fought."[4]

Just as Scoville described, the powerful Army of the Potomac sat idle on the banks of the river for which it was named, while its commander, Major General George Britton McClellan, resisted attempts from the administration to prod it into action. Nevertheless, Americans have been loath to think McClellan a traitor, then or since. Only a week before, Scoville himself wrote of him: "I do not think he is quite an idiot in political matters, or that he will prove such a thorough traitor as to combine with … the New York Democracy to overthrow President Lincoln and the Union."[5] Unfortunately, it seems that McClellan did just that, as evidenced by a mounting collection of historical evidence.

The first significant revelation regarding General McClellan's deceit was revealed in 1915, when the unpublished diary of John Hay, Lincoln's private secretary, came to light. According to Hay, Vermont governor John Gregory Smith had come to the White House in 1864 and conveyed to Lincoln that his brother, General W.H.F. "Baldy" Smith, had told him a shocking tale. Immediately after the Battle of Antietam in 1862, McClellan had confided to him that influential Democratic New York mayor Fernando Wood and another New York politician had come to the battlefield and offered "Little Mac" the next Democratic nomination, if only he would conduct the war in a way "so as to conciliate and impress the people of the South with the idea that our armies were intended merely to execute the laws and protect their property, etc."[6]

Hay's diary would not be the only evidence of McClellan's duplicity. In 2012, historian William B. Styple published *McClellan's Other Story*, which revealed communications between McClellan and Lee's Army of Northern Virginia, attempting to broker a peace deal without involving the Lincoln administration.[7] A consummate professional, General Robert E. Lee never responded to McClellan's overtures. Nevertheless, rumors of peace offerings from the Confederacy later flooded the Northern press, propagated by two separate individuals, who claimed peace was possible—if only Lincoln would rescind his proclamation. Based on largely circumstantial but compelling evidence, I reached a series of disquieting conclusions regarding events in the fall of 1862:

- Major General George B. McClellan, shortly after the Battle of Antietam, sent former Union officer William Chase Barney across the lines to act as an unofficial peace ambassador to the Confederate government in Richmond.
- Someone within McClellan's inner circle leaked information of Barney's mission to Secretary of War Edwin Stanton, causing him to order the superintendent of the Old Capitol Prison, Colonel William P. Wood, to follow him to Richmond, ostensibly to exchange prisoners, but, more importantly, to track his movements and communications.
- Wood, at his own discretion, enlisted the aid of Thomas Nelson Conrad, a Confederate spy in Federal custody, to accompany him to Richmond, likely to better read the pulse of Confederate officials meeting with Barney.
- President Lincoln's dismissal of McClellan from command of the Army of the Potomac was based on information Wood learned in Richmond about Barney's mission, not simply because the general had a "case of the slows," as Lincoln told others.

- Thomas Nelson Conrad, while aiding Wood, covertly planned a counter mission with the Confederate government to stop emancipation and delegated it to his former college roommate, Daniel Mountjoy Cloud, who used a network of Southern sympathizers to communicate behind Union lines.
- Conrad and Cloud utilized John Wesley Greene, a former Union chaplain and likely rebel informant, to pitch a disinformation campaign to President Lincoln on the false premise that Confederate president Jefferson Davis sought peace, in the hope that Lincoln would rescind his proclamation or be forced to do so by Congress before it became effective on January 1, 1863.
- Secretary of War Edwin Stanton, convinced a fraud was afoot, had both Greene and Barney trailed from Washington by detectives, assigning the latter to chief detective Allan Pinkerton after Wood's return from Richmond.
- Although the peace plan to perpetuate slavery eventually fell apart, the 1864 Democratic nominees for president and vice president each had unique connections to it, suggesting that despite its failure, adherence to its principles remained a Democratic Party litmus test throughout the Civil War.

For his part in the plot, Mountjoy Cloud would rely on a communication chain involving pro-slavery Episcopal and Methodist Episcopal churches in northern Virginia and Baltimore to avoid detection, a technique used advantageously since the opening of the conflict. The use of Southern churches as instruments of espionage and deception is one of the more disturbing aspects of Cloud's secret mission. Proponents of this subterfuge, however, saw little to be guilty about, convinced as they were of the righteousness of their cause. It was, therefore, highly ironic that the man they chose as the centerpiece of the plot had a long history of being not only a lay minister but an accomplished confidence man as well.

If John Wesley Greene's mission to the White House in November 1862 succeeded, it would have far-reaching implications. Greene, however, was well known to certain Northern journalists, including Murat Halstead of the *Cincinnati Commercial* and George W. Matsell of the *National Police Gazette*—both of whom had already investigated him for crimes across the country, from New York to Cincinnati.

None of the active participants in the plot to stop emancipation ever revealed the truth behind their mission. The catastrophic failure of Greene's attempt to con President Lincoln virtually guaranteed that Thomas Nelson Conrad would not admit to it, as he did his other exploits in his two autobiographies, *A Confederate Spy* and *The Rebel Scout*.

Therefore, this reconstruction of the Confederacy's secret mission and conclusion that Conrad planned it while a prisoner of Union operative William P. Wood are largely based on timing, proximity, and the relationships between the participants.

This book poses numerous questions which challenge the established historical record. Was John Wesley Greene the true-life inspiration for Herman Melville's last novel, *The Confidence-Man*? Did Union major general George B. McClellan attempt to secretly negotiate peace with the Confederacy after the Battle of Antietam? Did Colonel William P. Wood travel to Richmond to trail William Chase Barney, not to exchange prisoners, as was publicly stated? Did Confederate secretary of war Judah P. Benjamin see an opportunity to stop emancipation by extending a fraudulent peace offer to the North? Most importantly, was God's *divine will* on emancipation ironically revealed in the person of John Wesley Greene, as he exercised his "confidence game" on America—an event eerily predicted by Melville in the novel published five years earlier?

Unfortunately, there are no definitive answers to these questions. The man who knew the most about the McClellan-Barney pact, journalist Joseph A. Scoville, died an untimely death at the age of 52 in 1864. With his passing, the nation lost one of the more independent voices in journalism. The Republican *Chicago Tribune* labeled his letters to the English press "a wretched compound of mendacity, filth and treason."[8] Yet, he was a frequent critic of slavery and promoted an aggressive war policy to restore the Union, leading an English journal to conclude upon his death that his letters were "on the whole more truthful than Federal dispatches."[9]

Daniel Mountjoy Cloud, the Confederate operative most likely responsible for carrying out the plot, likewise died an early death in 1871. His college roommate, Thomas Nelson Conrad, the probable mastermind, had compromised his integrity by his close relationship to Colonel William P. Wood and thus avoided the subject in his postwar autobiographies altogether. In an 1887 interview, Wood promised to reveal the truth, but never did. Thus, the complex plot to perpetuate slavery which began with the commander of the Army of the Potomac became lost to history. Thankfully, modern search engines allow us to recreate much of the jigsaw puzzle of what really happened in the fall of 1862, when President Lincoln raised the stakes of the Union war effort and established a moral justification for its cost.

1

A Confidence Man in Manhattan

> *J. Wesley Greene is of Irish parentage ... educated for the ministry of the Methodist Episcopal Church, but he early developed a perverse mind, that unfitted him for the holy calling.*[1]
> —*National Police Gazette*, 1862

On April Fool's Day 1857, author Herman Melville's publishing company released his last novel, *The Confidence-Man: His Masquerade*—a complex tale of a confidence man who sets out to defraud his fellow passengers aboard a steamboat bound for New Orleans. The book opens with a mute boarding a steamboat in St. Louis and holding up a series of signs, such as "Charity thinketh no evil," "Charity endureth all things," and "Charity never faileth."[2]

Although not apparent from the text itself, the quotes are directly from I Corinthians 13. A skeptical passenger suggests a swindle is afoot. "Charity is one thing and truth is another," he offers. "He's a rascal I say."[3] A Methodist minister intervenes and defends the mute: "But why not friend, put as charitable a construction as one can upon the poor fellow? He looks honest, doesn't he?"[4]

A dark and complex tale, *The Confidence-Man* was a commercial failure in its own time. "Mr. Melville ... appears to have adopted a quaint, unnatural style, of late, which has little of the sparkling vigor and freshness of his early works," one critic wrote. "In fact, we close this book finding nothing concluded, and wondering what on earth the author has been driving at."[5] Even Melville's brother-in-law wrote that "it belongs to that horribly uninteresting class of nonsensical books he is given to writing."[6]

Modern critics are more appreciative of Melville's deep meanings but agree that definitive conclusions are hard to come by. "Is Melville for or against Christianity, for or against democracy, for or against abolitionism, for or against Romanticism, for or against America?" questions one modern critic. "As in the novel ... you'll find someone willing to argue every side."[7] Another researcher believes Melville's first interest in the concept stemmed from the case of William Thompson, alias Samuel Powell, thought to be the original "confidence man," who preyed on New Yorkers in 1849, before he was arrested and committed to the Tombs, New York City's infamous prison.[8]

Thompson's primary means of gaining the confidence of his victims was to feign a past acquaintance or to impersonate a minor celebrity. The *New York Herald* would say that he possessed "the gift of speech to such a degree that sensible men—yes, men of business—would part with watch and money besides."[9] According to the files of the *Police Gazette*, he was eventually convicted on October 16, 1849, for grand larceny, and was sentenced to two and a half years in Sing Sing.[10]

Sometime after his release, the original confidence man was back at his trade. On April 30, 1855, the *New York Tribune* published reports that he was repeating the same frauds in Albany that had worked so well in New York. He was, however, caught once again and upon examination "shed copious tears of sorrow ... protested against intending to commit any crime, and begged to be let off."[11] This seems to have been the trigger for Melville, for scholars believe he wrote *The Confidence-Man* sometime during the months between early May of 1855 and October of 1856.[12] During this time period, however, a new confidence man hit the streets of New York—one who had personal connections to Melville.

The new confidence man first drew the attention of police on about October 5, 1855, when he worked a clever scam on Robert Rait, a jeweler at 261 Broadway, for $371 worth of goods, under the name of Benjamin Greer—directing the goods to be delivered to the publishing house of George D. Appleton. When the package arrived, he was there, "making himself very officious about the desk," having told Rait that he worked there, after which he casually wrote a bad check for the jewelry and disappeared.[13]

Ten days later, the same man wrote a false check from the Broadway Bank under the name of Thomas Bancroft for $76 worth of jewelry from Tiffany and Company at 550 Broadway. As he had with Rait, the man now calling himself Bancroft minimized suspicion by directing the goods from Tiffany's to another business—this time Peterson and Humphrey, a carpet dealer two blocks away, whom he claimed to represent. The man had carefully laid the groundwork for this confidence game by first stopping by the carpet store, selecting certain styles of carpet, and requesting his fictitious home be measured for the carpet. Thus, when Tiffany's messenger arrived at Peterson and Humphrey's, they found him, "lounging about, apparently as one of the firm or someone in authority, expecting the arrival of the goods, check in hand for the amount of the bill, and with such an air of correctness, that in most instances his check was taken without question, and the goods delivered."[14]

Starting in December, he repeated the scam with retailers up and down Broadway—most of them jewelers.[15] On December 13, 1855, it was $400 worth of watches from Jackson and Many; on December 22, jewelry valued at $200 from Foxboro Jewelry Company at 170 Broadway; on New Year's Eve, $65 worth of furs from P.W. Leak; and on January 7, 1856, $400 worth of watches from A. Morel of Nassau Street. His biggest attempt was jewelry worth over $1,000 from a jeweler named Foy, but just as he was set to accept the delivery at George Putnam's Publishing House, he "became frightened and ran out of the store."[16]

The most ingenious case of retail fraud by the new confidence man was perpetrated against Samuel St. John, a tailor at 311 Broadway.[17] St. John first met him at the Mulberry Methodist Episcopal Church Sunday school, several blocks east of Broadway, where he had introduced himself as "Mr. Greer, from the West" and helped with the children by providing a brief story and a prayer.[18] He sounded like a "real Irish gentleman" when he spoke, and some said, his accent had "just sufficient of the brogue to make his conversation interesting."[19]

Having gained St. John's confidence, Greer went to his shop on Broadway the next day, ordering a suit of clothes. Several days later, he returned, claiming to have been out of town. Interviews by the New York City police established the following conversation between Greer and St. John, as reported by the *New York Times*:

"My brother is to be married tomorrow and I want my clothes to be sent up to No. ___ Fourteenth Street," Greer told St. John, looking at up at the clock. "When do your banks close?"

"At three o'clock," the tailor replied.

"Too bad. Too bad," said Greer, pulling a small tin box from under his arm. "I have a quantity of gold dust here which I intend depositing. Will you permit me to put it in your safe till tomorrow?"

"Of course," St. John replied, and Greer went on his way, claiming to be going to collect on a debt with which he would pay for the clothes. The following day, the clothes were brought to the address he had given, where Greene accepted delivery on the front steps. Then, by an alternate route, he beat the St. John's employee back to the store.

"Mr. St. John, you need not send the clothes to my boarding house," Greene told the tailor. "That draft which I had, I did not collect yesterday."

"Your clothes have been sent sir," replied the tailor.

"Really, I'm sorry," Greer said apologetically. "I intended to pay you for the articles before they were sent."

"Oh well, sir; I don't think you'll cheat us," St. John said trustingly to the man he had just met at the Methodist Sunday School not long before. "It's all right."[20]

But it was not all right. Greer did not return to pay for the suit, and when days passed with no sign of him, St. John pried open the tin box, only to find it full of lead shavings—not gold. Under increasing pressure from merchants, Officer Joseph Keefe of the New York police focused on the case but was stymied until he began interviewing brokers who might exchange cash for jewelry. A lender named Carrol operating out of Appleton's Bookstore recognized Greer and notified the police, who promptly arrested him near the corner of Broadway and Broome.[21]

At the time of his arrest, Greer was operating under seven different aliases, including Benjamin F. Greer, James R. Treadwell, Thomas Bancroft, P.B. Bigelow, James H. Merrill, and Thomas K. Wilson. Upon his arraignment on eight counts of grand larceny and obtaining goods under false pretenses, the *New York Times* reflected on how he got away with such frauds. "Greer is evidently a man of good education, and well connected," the paper concluded. "The system of swindling which he practiced was one of a very daring character."[22]

Upon interrogation by police, Greer readily admitted to swindling thousands of dollars, but more shocking, that he posed as a Methodist minister to better gain his victims' confidence. "Greer says that he acted the part of the Methodist minister on one or two occasions," reported the *New York Herald* at the time, "and acted the part to such perfection, that the elders of several churches and the members of the congregation were completely deceived by his real character and were accordingly swindled in the most scientific and beautiful manner."[23]

While Greer was perpetrating retail frauds on Broadway and preaching the Methodist gospel, a man named J. Wesley Greene was playing another confidence game on New Yorkers: falsely representing himself as an employee of the *New York Times*, selling subscriptions he never intended to deliver. Bombarded by complaints, the *Times* published the following notice as a warning to the public on December 6, 1855:

> Caution. We have reason to believe that a person, calling himself J. Wesley Greene, is obtaining money in various ways under pretense of being connected with the DAILY TIMES. No such person has ever been connected with this establishment in any capacity. If the person whom he may next accost will put him in custody of a Police officer, and inform us of the fact, we will endeavor to secure him such board and lodging at the expense of the State as he justly deserves.[24]

Although it was not apparent at the time, the *National Police Gazette* later reported that Benjamin Greer and J. Wesley Greene were, in fact, the same man.[25]

1. A Confidence Man in Manhattan 11

Looking up Broadway, from between Grand and Broome, 1860–1880 (Library of Congress, Prints and Photographs Division). John Wesley Greene's brother-in-law operated the Cosmopolitan Art Association at nearby Appleton's Bookstore. It was here that a money lender finally recognized Greene and notified New York detectives—resulting in his well-publicized arrest in 1856 near Broome and Broadway (E. & H.T. Anthony, publisher, *Up Broadway from between Grand and Broome Sts*. [New York: E. Anthony, between 1860 and 1880]. Photograph. Library of Congress, https://www.loc.gov/item/2017651299/).

While awaiting trial, Greene was held in the Essex Market Police Court, a lockup for criminals being charged in the adjoining magistrate's court, and for those waiting to be transferred to the city prison.

He was there scarcely a week when guards discovered that he had somehow obtained a file and nearly sawed through the bars of his cell. Although Greene denied attempting to escape, he admitted being horrified by conditions at the jail. "I do not believe there is a viler prison this side of the Black Hole in Calcutta, than is that in Essex Market," he complained. "I could write a chapter of my eight days experience there that would cause our moralists and philanthropists to stand aghast with horror."[26]

The New York police, equally horrified that he had nearly escaped, transferred him to the city prison—otherwise known as the Tombs, where the original confidence man, William Thompson, had spent four months awaiting trial for similar offenses. Built almost 20 years earlier, the Tombs were modeled after the architecture of ancient Egypt. "What most forcibly strikes the visitor, is the want of some system of ventilation," one correspondent for the *New York Dispatch* wrote, on their way to visit Greene. "Its close, choking, and suffocating smell, as you enter, forcibly suggests the fancied horror of the dungeon."[27]

Many inmates passing through the Tombs were poor, uneducated, and foreign-born. Greene was a novelty. He was, by far, the most "gentlemanly and interesting individual amongst the prisoners," the visiting correspondent noted, adding that "nature did not intend for him to be a dishonest man, and if he has been so, it has evidently been only in the protracted and oftentimes unavoidable struggle for bread to feed those dear to him."[28]

Most witnesses agreed with the assessment of the *Dispatch* correspondent. Some claimed Greene could "speak four or five languages"; others offered to wager that "he was the smartest man in New York, not excepting Fernando Wood," and even his victims claimed with admiration, that he was "something of an artist."[29] During his arraignment, Greene chatted freely with both police officers and victims, all of whom declared upon his arrest that "they could not have believed it."[30] There were echoes of Melville's Methodist minister, who asked the rhetorical question "He looks honest, doesn't he?"[31]

Initially confined at the police chief's office, Greene was visited by his wife, "a beautiful woman of about twenty-two years of age" who, according to Greene, knew "nothing of his operations," and who was "weighed down with sorrow when the fact of his arrest became known to her."[32] Details of his family background, however, remained murky until the *Police Gazette* eventually discovered that Greene's wife was a sister-in-law of "one of the most eminent book publishers" in New York.[33]

Although not made public at the time, the so-called "book publisher" was Chauncey Lyman Derby, head of the Cosmopolitan Art Association, which conducted business out of Appleton's Bookstore at

348 Broadway. The family connection to Derby explains why the vicinity around Appleton's Bookstore where Derby kept his office became the epicenter for Greene's activity. His young wife—almost half his age—was probably Elizabeth Ada Flower, who would have been just 21 in 1856.[34] She may have been enamored by his charm, for one acquaintance in Cincinnati described him as "a comely looking man, then, of medium height, with coal black eyes and hair, smooth shaven face, fair complexion, and a bright, insinuating countenance."[35]

Elizabeth Ada Flower was one of four Flower sisters from western New York that included Chauncey Derby's wife, Charlotte, and Mary Jane Greene, the wife of Herman Melville's onetime shipmate Richard Tobias Greene.[36] Melville and Greene had both signed on to the whaling ship *Acushnet* as green hands in December 1840, seeking adventure. But after 18 months at sea under a disagreeable captain, Melville and Greene jumped ship together off the island of Nuku Hiva, in the Marquesas Islands of French Polynesia—where they encountered love and adventure among a people known for both cannibalism and polygamy.

Melville would immortalize their adventures in his true-life novel *Typee: A Peep at Polynesian Life,* and Richard Greene would thereafter be famous as the character "Toby"—a name bequeathed to him by the crew of the *Achushnet*.[37] The book not only put Melville on a path to become America's preeminent novelist of his time but gave Toby Greene a certain measure of immortality. He named his only son Herman Melville Greene, in honor of his famous companion, and Melville, it is said, named the novel *Moby Dick* for his old mate "Richard Toby" by simply reversing the names, exchanging "Dick" for Richard, and changing the "T" in Toby to an "M."[38]

Herman Melville and Toby Greene maintained their friendship from a distance, occasionally corresponding. "I was in New York last summer but was told you were off somewhere on a visit," Toby wrote Melville in June 1856, after visiting New Orleans. "I am engaged with C.L. Derby of the Cosmopolitan Art Association and from its connections with different publishers, I am enabled to keep the run of you."[39]

When the Cosmopolitan Art Association established an office in Chicago, Mary Jane Greene was put in charge of it. By 1860, Elizabeth Flower was living with Toby and Mary Jane in Chicago, under her birth name.[40] They likely felt responsible for her, as they were undoubtedly the ones who introduced her to John Wesley Greene back in 1854, when Toby was working as a telegraph operator in Sandusky, Ohio. A later account in the *Chicago Tribune* stated that during this time, John Wesley Greene "went to Elyria, in the same State, and … while there, he contrived to win the affections of a most estimable young lady, connected with one of the best families in town, and married her."⁴¹ Another article in the *Chicago Tribune* made clear that the "estimable young lady" was, in fact, "his brother Richard's wife's sister."⁴²

More direct evidence that the two men were siblings came in 1888, when Chicago police arrested a minister going by the name of the Rev. James S. Greene at Toby's house on West Madison in Chicago on a charge of bigamy. According to press reports, "R. Tobias Greene, his wife and Officer Tyrell ... commenced searching through the rooms."⁴³ Although Toby and Mary Jane attempted to stall and mislead him, Tyrell caught the 73-year-old minister attempting to escape out the back door.

"Oh, my dear sir," pled Greene, "I don't want to be arrested. I am old, feeble, and disconsolate. I don't see what these women want with a sickly old man."⁴⁴ One of the women, Mrs. E.G. Britton of Chicago, incensed that he had married a 35-year-old woman from Minnesota while still married to her, happily divulged his sordid history. Greene, she said, was "a base deceiver, whose real name was James Wesley Greene before he left Sing Sing Prison ... that he is not a minister of the gospel at all, having appropriated the title."⁴⁵

John Wesley Greene had attempted to avoid Sing Sing Prison altogether. When brought before the court recorder on the morning of March

Richard Tobias Greene, 1846 (Berkshire Athenaeum). John Wesley Greene's younger brother, he traveled the South Seas with Herman Melville and gained notoriety as the character Toby in Melville's first true-life novel, *Typee*. According to witness descriptions, the two bore a close resemblance. Whether Melville used the elder Greene as a model for his last novel, *The Confidence-Man*, remains a mystery (photographer unknown, *Richard Tobias Greene*, 1846. Photograph. Berkshire Athenaeum, Pittsfield, Massachusetts, https://www.pittsfieldlibrary.org/).

12, 1856, he offered a heart-rending defense, claiming he did it all for the health of his young wife:

> Your Honor, I was deeply embarrassed at the time I committed the first offense. I had brought in my wife from the West, to place her under the care of an aurist, her hearing having been very bad. I endeavored by every means to get a situation, but always found other applicants before me.... I felt almost as if I could have done anything, to enable the aurist to continue his service, and then I arranged the plan which has brought me here.[46]

The court was not sympathetic and sentenced Greene to five years—the highest term the law permitted.[47]

Whether Greene provided any inspiration for Melville's *Confidence-Man* is debatable. There is, for example, no mention of him in letters between Toby and Melville through the years of their correspondence, nor any evidence Melville ever met John Wesley Greene in New York City while he was working his confidence game on Broadway. Melville's introduction of a religious aspect to *The Confidence-Man* may simply be coincidence, as may Greene's arrest for numerous frauds in 1856, at almost the same time that Melville was actively writing it; and a freak of circumstance that Toby wrote Melville that year after journeying to New Orleans—likely on a steamboat much like the *Fidele*.[48]

In the closing line of *The Confidence-Man,* Melville warns his readers that "something further may follow of this Masquerade."[49] Never would Melville be more omniscient, for his disturbing tale of a confidence man preying on America would take on a real and dangerous aspect only five years later, when the fate of the Union and the lives of millions of enslaved African Americans hung in the balance.

2

Another Grand Scheme

He has obtained half a dozen watches. They have pocketed a half million dollars. He is a swindler.... They are financiers.[1]
—*New York Herald,* July 1849

In 1849, while William Thompson—the original confidence man—was awaiting trial in the Tombs, the *New York Herald* took the opportunity to editorialize, suggesting the tricks of the confidence man were not unlike those of corporate America. "How does it happen that the 'Confidence Man' with his genius, address, tact, and skill, sleeps at 'The Tombs' instead of reposing on softest down?" asked the *Herald* of its readers. "Listen. He struck too low! Miserable wretch! ... He should have issued a flaming prospectus of another grand scheme of internal improvement."[2]

Seven years later, while John Wesley Greene served his own sentence for grand larceny in the Tombs, others were pursuing grand schemes in Washington. After the election of Democrat James Buchanan of Pennsylvania in 1856, the city became packed with visitors, office seekers, and politicos—all anxious to profit from the incoming administration. "The plotting and counterplotting now going on here by the politicians in favor of certain gentlemen for cabinet positions is prodigious," a correspondent for the *New York Herald* wrote, the day after Buchanan arrived in Washington, "Indeed, these political hucksters are working like beavers."[3] Another noted that "politicians and office seekers are as plentiful as blackberries in June."[4]

Among the lobbyists hoping to influence the new Congress during those early days of the Buchanan administration was William Chase Barney, a man of impressive lineage and grand ideas. Born in Baltimore in 1814, he was one of several children born to William Bedford Barney and Mary Chase Barney. His maternal grandfather, Samuel Chase, had signed the Declaration of Independence, while his paternal grandfather, Commodore Joshua Barney, had fought valiantly in both the Revolution and the War of 1812. When President Andrew Jackson removed his father from his post as Customs Officer for the Port of Baltimore based on political patronage, his mother retaliated by publishing in 1831 an anti–Jackson monthly magazine—*The National Magazine* or *Ladies Emporium*—an enterprise that left her politically influential with every administration thereafter.

Barney was well educated, having attended St. Mary's Seminary in Baltimore, and studied law under some of the best attorneys of the time, including Charles Jared Ingersoll, Severn Teackle Wallis, and John Glenn. He was likely fluent in French, as the Barneys had always had a close affinity for France. His grandfather, Joshua Barney, served for eight years in the French navy after being selected to carry dispatches to Benjamin Franklin in Paris during the American Revolution and made numerous visits to Paris thereafter.[5]

William Chase Barney seems to have inherited his grandfather's affinity for France. He lived there for three years between 1840 and 1842, purportedly "enjoying the society of Lafayette, Victor Hugo and other celebrities."[6] Barney returned to New York in the fall of 1842, where he married 22-year-old Marie Felicite Le Petite of Paris on November 9, 1842.[7] Their honeymoon, however, ended in tragedy, as his young wife died in Savannah in March.[8] Barney returned her body to France, burying her in the Père Lachaise, the most prestigious cemetery in Paris.[9]

Although he spent his subsequent years in New York City, Barney's heart was in Europe. In August 1855, he returned from France on the steamship *Ariel* with the U.S. consul at Bordeaux, Levi K. Bowen of Baltimore, and announced a proposition to lower international postage prices by adding more routes to France.[10] He envisioned a line, centered in Havana, that could also carry mail from South America, the Southwest and California. When William Chase Barney approached Congress at the start of the Buchanan administration, however, he had multiple issues to lobby them about. Not only was he seeking consideration of his direct mail route from France to New Orleans, but he likely sought relief for his younger brother, Samuel Chase Barney, who had been dismissed from the United States Navy, shortly after the elder Barney returned from France.

"Chase," as his family called him, was still technically on active duty in September 1855, when the Naval Efficiency Board found him unfit for duty and abruptly retired him, as they did with 200 other naval officers that summer. The discharge was done in accordance with a statute passed by Congress earlier that year, titled "An Act to Promote the Efficiency of the Navy," which provided for the mandatory retirement of officers found unfit for duty.[11] Proponents of the act felt the act was necessary to remove "dead wood" and allow ambitious midshipmen to be promoted. Among those on the Naval Efficiency Board, or so-called "Board of Fifteen," was future rear admiral Samuel F. Dupont, who had been instrumental in the passage of the legislation.[12]

Mary Chase Barney, now over 70 years old, could not come to the defense of her son as vigorously as she had done for her husband back in 1831, when she took on Andrew Jackson. Instead, it appears his brother-in-law, William H. Rogers, a former district attorney in Delaware, took the lead to reform the statute. Samuel Chase Barney would later eulogize him as "the successful champion of the naval victims of the 'Board of Fifteen.'"[13] It appears that William Chase Barney did his share of lobbying as well. Senator Albert Gallatin Brown of Mississippi, who sponsored the Naval Efficiency Act, and Representative William Waters Boyce of South Carolina, a member of the House Committee on Naval Affairs, both acknowledged later that they "knew him in Washington City" before the Civil War.[14]

In response to a storm of controversy from dismissed naval veterans like Barney and their families, Senator Albert G. Brown declared in a speech to the Senate on January 2, 1856, that "if any man has been unjustly dismissed from the service, I am willing to hear his petition and to consider his case.... I am willing to believe that no man has been dismissed the service for base conduct of any kind."[15] Later that year, Congress would amend the statute to provide for hearings on dismissals, but Senator Brown's defense of the statute suggested that individual officers may have been dismissed for "base conduct," rather than a physical disability.

When Samuel Chase Barney's case was investigated by a Naval Court of Inquiry in November 1857, they considered both his disability and accusations of base conduct. Especially concerning to the court were various allegations of spousal abuse. An acquaintance of Samuel Chase Barney, attorney John A. Linton, later testified that he was called to their home at three in the morning to find that a drunken Barney had kicked his wife and children down three flights of stairs, leaving his wife's face and body "bruised black."[16]

Linton, who had known Barney since he was a midshipman, was appalled. "There was a double-barreled shotgun there," Linton said, "and I recommended him to load it and shoot himself."[17] It was not Chase Barney's first case of abusive behavior either. Ten years earlier, he had been arrested for "assaulting and beating" a woman by the name of Bridget Hart in Baltimore.[18]

Ultimately, there was little William Chase Barney could do to defend his brother or promote his steamship line to France, other than lobby Congress. Despite his grand ideas, Barney represented neither the U.S. government nor a steamship company and had control over neither. If he had any hope of success, he would have to sway Congress by lobbying influential senators, like Judah P. Benjamin of Louisiana, who represented the port of New Orleans. By 1857, Barney had convinced Benjamin to present a memorial to Congress for the new mail route, arguing, "France is a large consumer of American cotton and New Orleans, and the Southwestern States are large consumers of French goods."[19]

The House Committee on Post Offices and Roads apparently supported the proposal, concluding that such a route would "save the commissions and freights paid to agents."[20] Despite the support from Senator Benjamin and the House committee, Barney's proposal stalled, as the desire of legislators to protect slavery overshadowed all else. Most influential Southern leaders had already agreed to oppose subsidizing the American merchant marine industry, as a strong fleet of mail steamers could easily be used against the South in the event of secession.[21] Senator Robert M.T. Hunter of Virginia led the push to end steamship subsidies and succeeded in ending all existing contracts, effective September 30, 1859.[22] A select committee led by Representative William Waters Boyce of South Carolina recommended a series of free trade reforms, including one that allowed foreign vessels equal access to American ports.[23]

Senator Judah P. Benjamin of Louisiana, ca. 1856 (Library of Congress Prints and Photographs Division). Benjamin was a sponsor of William Chase Barney's bill to establish a direct mail route from France to New Orleans. Benjamin and Barney had both married women from France. Barney would lobby Benjamin again five years later in Richmond, when the latter was the Confederate Secretary of State (*Judah P. Benjamin, Senator from Louisiana, half-length portrait*, ca. 1856. Photograph. Library of Congress, https://www.loc.gov/item/2004666306/).

Faced with such opposition, Barney produced his own prospectus for internal improvement, in an article he published in the pro-slavery periodical *DeBow's Review*. Barney's "Steamships at the South" advocated the direct line from Bordeaux to New Orleans as an economic boon to the South. Despite modest support for his plan, however, it is unlikely that most congressmen took him seriously. Later questioned about Barney, William H. Davidge, president of the Pacific Mail Steamship Company, was blunt. "The circle in which I move in New York have not much confidence in Mr. Barney," he would say. "I do not know who his friends are, he may have friends who think better of him."[24]

As Davidge revealed, Barney had a well-established reputation as a huckster. In the early 1840s, his uncle, former Congressman John Barney of Maryland, sent one or more letters to the U.S. minister to France, Lewis Cass, charging his nephew with "frauds and rascality of various grades," as well as being an illegitimate child—and not the blood of Commodore Barney at all.[25] The allegations resulted in Barney suing his uncle for libel, claiming some $50,000 in damages. A jury found in favor of young Barney and awarded him $800, far less than what he had sought, but a significant sum nevertheless.[26]

Despite John Barney's legal defeat, there is substantial evidence that his fraud allegations were true. Colonel John Hull of Virginia advised Henry Ledyard, the U.S. *chargé d'affaires* in Paris, that he first met Barney in London in 1839, and that Barney had swindled upwards of $1,000 from him, writing a worthless check in return for cash.[27] Both men were staying at Long's Hotel there, where "the fastest and best men in London lounged in and out of the coffee room from breakfast time till well on in the afternoon, and smoked, drank champagne ... and swore loudly."[28]

The practice of the hotel was to place incoming mail in the coffee room, where patrons would retrieve it. One day, however, mail containing a substantial check came up missing. The proprietor, W.J. Markwell, later ascertained by a handwriting comparison that Barney had attempted to cash the check, and only caution by Coutts Bank of London prevented him from doing so. Colonel Hull confronted Barney in a private room, during which the latter "reluctantly confessed" to taking the check.[29] Hull advised him to pay his bills and leave town or face prosecution, which he promptly did, returning to the States destitute. Barney's own obituary 50 years later corroborated the tale: "When he went to London, Mr. Barney thought he had sufficient money to support him for a year, but the extravagant life of the capitol soon exhausted his funds and in three months, he was compelled to return."[30]

Hull openly shared Barney's misbehavior, revealing that he "was told in Balt[imore] that he had committed frauds so gross that if they had

[been] practiced on any but his relations would have sent him to the penitentiary."[31] These "frauds on his relations" were later revealed during a trial over the estate of his grandmother, Hannah Kitty Chase, with the most damning testimony coming from his own mother. Mary Chase Barney testified that Hannah Chase had educated and taken care of young Barney in her twilight years, but that rather than help her, he instead "resorted to every means to obtain her property."[32]

Mrs. Barney would testify that he took virtually all her mother's income and stocks and squandered what he got, spending $8,000 a year—a lavish amount in the 1840s, but consistent with the cost of living in London and Paris. She had numerous examples of how her son swindled his grandmother out of thousands of dollars and boasted about it. When he would get $500 from her, he would give her back five or ten dollars of her own money, and she would be delighted at what a "generous fellow" he was.[33]

Often, Hannah Chase would cry to her daughter and swear not to give in to him, but then always relent to his wishes. Barney's sister, Catherine Oldfield, testified that he employed "animal magnetism" on his grandmother; that he had various means to extract cash and promissory notes from her and if she refused, he would speak "soothingly" to her until she relented.[34] When Hannah Chase died in 1848, virtually all her assets were gone, save her furniture, which sold for a mere $300.[35]

Amid the libel trial against his uncle, sometime during 1844, William Chase Barney began courting young Elizabeth Booth of New Castle, Delaware, the 22-year-old daughter of Delaware's chief justice, James Booth, and purportedly "an heiress of considerable property."[36] According to friends of Barney, the two were engaged for some time, but postponed the wedding because of her father's reservations. Even after the court found in Barney's favor, however, Judge Booth still refused to allow the marriage, forbidding Barney to ever visit again—likely concluding that at least some of John Barney's allegations were true.

As one journalist noted, Barney was "a fine, handsome fellow, well thought of by everyone except his uncle and ... heir to the estate of the late Com. Barney."[37] Likely for these reasons, Elizabeth Booth slipped away with him, despite her father's objections, and the two were married in a private ceremony on June 20, 1845, by a Catholic priest in Wilmington. As a witness, they used Barney's brother, Lieutenant Samuel Chase Barney of the United States Navy, who had allegedly assaulted young Bridget Hart only a week before.[38]

Although the priest that married them, Father Reilly of St. Peter's Church in Wilmington, issued a statement that he had received Elizabeth Booth's "full and deliberate assent to the obligations of the marriage

James Booth, Jr., House, New Castle, Delaware, 1936 (Library of Congress Prints and Photographs Division). Judge Booth reportedly banned William Chase Barney from visiting his daughter here after learning that Barney's uncle, former congressman John Barney, had accused him of "frauds and rascality of various grades" (Historic American Buildings Survey, creator, *James Booth House & Office, 216 Delaware Street, New Castle, New Castle County, Delaware*, 1933. Photograph. Library of Congress, https://www.loc.gov/item/de0079/).

contract," she returned to her father's home rather than consummate the marriage.[39] In January 1846, the Maryland legislature formally divorced them, determining after careful consideration, that "the grievance ... was altogether on the side of the lady," as she thought that she was "merely taking a pledge to become his wife, in case he should succeed in wiping from his character charges of a dishonorable character."[40]

William Chase Barney's messy personal affairs did not dampen his ambition. The year after his divorce, he moved to New York and began a weekly journal titled the *Aristocratic Monitor*—a magazine dedicated to following the social elite of New York. He bluntly advertised that he did not "write for the people, his paper is for the aristocrats."[41] He charged the exorbitant price of six cents per issue and filled the classifieds with notices for "foreign fiddlers and French dancing girls."[42]

For a time, the magazine was all the rage. "I find the *Monitor*, 'The Aristocratic Monitor,' is everywhere," noted one columnist. "If I go into a fashionable drawing-room, there is the *Monitor*; if I go into bank to have a check cashed, there is the *Monitor*; if I go into a store, there lies the *Monitor*; the people go through the streets reading—what? Why, '*The Aristocratic Monitor*.'"[43] According to one source, the subscription list for the *Aristocratic Monitor* accelerated by the thousands, faster than any journal of the era.[44]

The Catholic Church, however, was critical of the *Monitor*'s scurrilous content. A review by the *United State Catholic Magazine* recommended "the omission of those flaming descriptions of private soirees" and "everything that gives encouragement to theatrical performances."[45] The personal gossip that they lamented, however, is likely what made the *Monitor* so popular. Although the *Catholic Magazine* review acknowledged that "the character of the *Monitor* has been much improved" since early issues, the change did not improve circulation.[46]

By the end of that year, the *Aristocratic Monitor* was discontinued, and Barney took time out to marry 17-year-old Ada B. Franciscus of Baltimore on November 18, 1848.[47] She was one of the first students at Baltimore's Eastern High School, which had been established in 1844 for girls "who may have manifested superior abilities and attained suitable acquirements in the Primary Schools."[48] Frustrated by his fortunes in New York, Barney started a new weekly in 1849 titled *The Court Journal*, published in Washington.

The Court Journal prospectus advertised it as "devoted exclusively to the amusement of the Ladies ... such as announcements of marriages, parties, balls, and dinners, and ... accounts of all fashionable gatherings."[49] The man who once eloped against his fiancée's father's wishes gave this advice on umbrella etiquette in an early issue: "If you meet a lady without an umbrella in the rain, it is not proper to lend an umbrella to her, but you ought to escort her home, but if you meet two ladies, you should give them your umbrella."[50] The *Philadelphia Public Ledger* noted humorously that there was no advice on how to get your umbrella back. The *Boston Post* thought the paper harmless; another critic, however, deemed it a "ridiculous absurdity," and it seems not to have lasted beyond the year.[51]

By 1850 Barney was living in Hackensack, New Jersey, where he listed his occupation as a "government agent."[52] Despite the use of this title, he did not work for the government. Rather, he procured passports from the State Department on behalf of clients not wishing to do so themselves. It was not long, however, before Barney was mired in controversy once again. Joseph B. Nones, a notary public authorized to provide the same service, filed a formal complaint that Barney had sent in forged passport applications and issued false passports. William C. Riddell, the local passport clerk, promptly issued notices in New York papers, advising the public that the State Department would no longer process applications sent in by Barney or the Berford and Co. Bookstore, through which he worked.[53]

Barney promptly sued Nones for libel and sought $5,000 damages, claiming the charges were "false and malicious, and calculated to injure his reputation."[54] Simultaneously, he filed complaints against Riddell for "abuse of office" and demanded the *New York Tribune* discontinue the public notices. The *Tribune* did so, but only after publishing Barney's letter under a bold headline: "Passports—Alleged Frauds—W. Chase Barney," which was far more damaging than Riddell's original notice.[55]

The State Department's refusal to accept his applications abruptly ended Barney's passport sales. Instead, he became the New York City agent for the Berford and Company express mail service, which carried letters, newspapers, and packages to California, undercutting the cost of the U.S. mail. "No law of the United States is violated," they argued, "inasmuch as they do not pass over any mail route in the United States."[56] Rather than simply sell express mail services, Barney sold passenger tickets to California—a more profitable venture, for gold fever had struck the East Coast and tickets fetched nearly $200 per passenger.[57]

Over the next three months, Berford let Barney go—reportedly because of the alleged forgery allegations by Nones.[58] In a familiar pattern, Barney filed a lawsuit, charging Berford with libel and seeking damages of $50,000.[59] He also formed a partnership with 24-year-old Alexander H. Pride to compete directly against them, but the scheme backfired when both men were arrested in April 1852 for allegedly defrauding some 30 travelers to California.[60]

The controversy began when Barney sold 33 vouchers in New York and sent Pride to Panama to purchase tickets to California on the SS *Monumental City*. However, the ship broke down before arrival, stranding his passengers on the isthmus with worthless vouchers.[61] When Barney's clients returned to New York seeking refunds, he denied them, claiming that under their contract, he was only required to pay their expenses in Panama until alternate arrangements were made—a clause rendered void as soon as they returned to New York. Livid, several clients filed charges.[62]

Barney denied any wrongdoing, and as in the passport case, claimed that the complaints were "false and malicious for the purpose of obtaining money for black mail."[63] Unable to post the $10,000 bond, Barney spent several days in "the Tombs" before procuring it. "It is seldom that one of the [editorial] fraternity is charged with a serious crime," bemoaned one New York correspondent, remembering Barney's *Aristocratic Monitor*. "Pride, the other member of the firm, is quite a young fellow, but old enough, it seems, to swindle."[64] The partnership with Pride was dissolved by mutual consent, with Barney agreeing to settle the claims.[65]

From 1853 to 1855, Barney continued in the express mail business in New York City, albeit with a lower profile, first as a partner in "Chase & Co" and later as manager of the "European Express" agency, where he advertised worldwide express mail service "at greatly reduced rates."[66] It was likely through this express mail business that he conceived the idea of a new steamship route to New Orleans with the U.S. consulate at Bordeaux.

Barney's failure to convince Congress to establish the new route did not prevent him from speculating on others. In June 1858, for example, he obtained a mail contract from the Postmaster General for the routes between New York, New Orleans, and Havana, on behalf of the New York and New Orleans Steamship Company. This was a straightforward arrangement, as they had an established passenger route between these ports. Things became more difficult when Barney began bidding on mail routes to California.

The Postmaster General advertised for bids on the San Francisco route in April 1859, from both New York and New Orleans. They received four bids from Barney and one from an individual named Daniel H. Johnson—who as the low bidder, won the contract. Johnson, however, was a speculative bidder, just like Barney. When he predictably defaulted, the Buchanan administration turned to Cornelius Vanderbilt—a man who unquestionably had the ability to complete the contract but had not bid, as two other companies had previously paid him $40,000 per month "to lie idle" rather than compete with them.[67]

By seeking a mail contract without direct control over ships to service the West Coast, Barney was once again promising a service he had no power to control. Nevertheless, he was livid that his bids were ignored. "Whoever had the mail contract, had the power to control the Isthmus [of Panama]," he later testified to Congress. "...Four-fifths of the passengers who go from New York want to go by the mail line, for they know that the mails are bound to go through, and they want to go with the mails."[68] He thought the mail route was worth some half a million dollars to the one clever enough to control it.

The following year, Barney would take his complaints about the Buchanan administration to the so-called "Covode Committee" of the House of Representatives, where his true motivation for establishing a new route from Bordeaux to New Orleans became apparent. He had secured a $400,000 loan from a shipping family in France, and if he secured a contract with the United States government, they were to provide the ships. With the free trade initiatives spearheaded by Representative Boyce, the ships would not even need to be American owned or operated.

Despite Barney's ambitious dreams, others saw him as simply a huckster. A correspondent for the *Cincinnati Gazette* would later describe

William Chase Barney as "dependent largely on shape and talent ... well educated, glib with the tongue, good looking, a man of the world, but celebrated for being reckless of truth, and void of those delicate moral refinements which beget confidence in human character."[69]

3

The Aristocracy of Slaveholding Interests

> *The leading ideas of the Republican party ... would incite a servile population to murder and rapine.*[1]
> —William H. Norris, December 1860

Although William Chase Barney had few financial resources to compete with the likes of Cornelius Vanderbilt, his proposal for a direct mail route to France was more likely doomed by Senator Jefferson Davis' fear that steamships would be used against the South in the event of war. As the pivotal election of 1860 neared, it became clear that Southerners were becoming increasingly reluctant to compromise over the slavery issue. Rejecting Illinois Democrat Stephen Douglas, Southern Democrats instead nominated the sitting vice president, John C. Breckinridge of Kentucky. In Barney's native state of Maryland, Breckinridge was particularly popular, largely based on his advocacy of Southern rights.

The political strength of John Breckinridge in Maryland was fully displayed on October 22, 1860, when his supporters held a mass meeting at Monument Square in Baltimore. Prominent attorney William Henry Norris presided over the event, while his vice presidents included fellow attorney J. Mason Campbell, former Maryland representative James Carroll, industrialist Thomas Winans, and police commissioner Charles Howard. The highlight of the rally was the appearance of a group called the "Democratic National Volunteers" who held a torchlight parade through the city streets, while a band played "Ever of Thee," a popular Southern tune.[2]

Norris called the upcoming election the culmination of an "irrepressible conflict," against which Democrats must respond, to block what he called the "aggressive power" of Republicans.[3] The inflammatory rhetoric of Norris was a stark contrast to the actual Republican platform, which was remarkably moderate when the party met in Chicago in April 1860 to choose a candidate. They denied any intention to interfere with slavery in states where it existed and supported the right of each state to decide its legality. Party leaders had chosen the obscure Abraham Lincoln from Illinois, concerned that well-known Republican voices like William H. Seward and Salmon P. Chase were "too conspicuous."[4]

Despite the strength of Breckinridge in the South, the split in Democratic ranks virtually assured a Republican victory. The polls had barely closed on election day, November 6, 1860, when South Carolina representative William Waters Boyce addressed a crowd in Columbia and advocated secession. "In all human probability the nominee of the Black Republican party is at this moment elected President of the United States.... I think the only policy for us is to arm as soon as we receive authentic intelligence of the election of Lincoln."[5]

As Senator Jefferson Davis had foreseen when he refused to support the construction of American commercial steamers in the 1850s, Southern states began seceding from the Union almost immediately after the results from the polls showed that Lincoln had won a majority of electoral votes. The Baltimore National Volunteers sent a letter to South Carolina governor William H. Gist, promising that in the event of that state's secession, they would provide "a light horse regiment, thirteen hundred strong" for the purposes of preventing coercion by the "accursed league" of Republicans.[6]

Emotions escalated still further when the South Carolina Secession Convention voted to withdraw from the Union on December 20, 1860. In Maryland, the legislature was adjourned, and many wished to keep it that way. Maryland's governor, Thomas H. Hicks, was sympathetic to the South, but abhorred the type of violent conflict advocated by the National Volunteers, arguing that "if the Union must be dissolved let it be done calmly, deliberately."[7] Others, however, were anxious for Maryland to take a formal position in support of the South immediately. Towards this end, a public meeting was held at the Universalist Church in Baltimore. The church was more than full, with men standing in the aisles and passages; and among them, men of high standing and no less than 49 vice presidents, including attorneys J. Mason Campbell and William H. Norris, who had acted in the same capacity for the Breckinridge campaign.[8]

After the reading of formal resolutions, the audience then called out loudly for attorney William H. Norris, who proceeded to give a lengthy argument in support of slavery. "Free speech and free press, as entertained by the North, were but another name for murder, outrage and robbery," he reasoned. "They will commit these by the grace of God. They will commit these as French revolutionists.... They were the same class of men, visionaries, idealists, and infidels."[9] Norris was interrupted time and again by thunderous applause, an indication that the crowd's pro-slavery sentiment was stronger than their commitment to the old Union.

As Maryland vacillated, states in the Deep South quickly followed the example of South Carolina. Even before South Carolina seceded, however, some Marylanders were plotting to ensure the president-elect would never take office. As early as December 12, 1860—a week earlier—the *Washington Evening Star* had reported that the National Volunteers intended to waylay Lincoln before he ever reached Washington, based on information that a *Richmond Dispatch* correspondent obtained from "the man, who beyond a doubt, carried Maryland for Breckinridge."[10] The anonymous man was likely William H. Norris, whom Breckinridge supporters chose to preside over their mass meeting at Monument Square, for he controlled the most virulent anti–Republican forces in Baltimore.

Chicago detective Allan Pinkerton investigated the assassination allegation by sending operatives to various points along the route, posing as Southern secessionists, with Pinkerton himself going to Baltimore. "It was not long before I received undoubted evidence of the existence of a systematized organization whose avowed object was to assist the rebellious States, but which was in reality formed to compass the death of the President and thus accomplish the separation of the States," Pinkerton later wrote in his autobiography.[11] Whether this organization was the National Volunteers or another militia organization is unclear from Pinkerton's account. He soon found, however, that Barnum's Hotel at Monument Square was the epicenter of Southern sympathizers. The law office of William H. Norris was conveniently next door—at 72 West Fayette Street.[12]

Among the most vocal of secessionists at Barnum's was the hotel barber, a 38-year-old man from Corsica named Cipriano Ferrandini. "This hireling Lincoln shall never be President," Ferrandini swore at a secret meeting of them, in the presence of a Pinkerton operative. "My life is of no consequence in a cause like this and I am willing to give it for his. As Orsini gave his life for Italy, I am ready to die for the rights of the South and to crush out the abolitionist."[13] Ferrandini may have been influenced by Breckinridge supporter Thomas Winans, who, it was later found, issued a $2,000 mortgage to him for his wife's house, a debt which was not released until 1869.[14]

The first leg of Lincoln's journey—that from Harrisburg, Pennsylvania, to Philadelphia, was uneventful. Traveling through Baltimore would be more difficult. Pinkerton, therefore, arranged for the president-elect to pass through the city in the dead of night, arriving at the Baltimore and Ohio depot in Washington at 6 a.m. on February 23, 1861. Mary Todd Lincoln and the Lincoln children stayed on the original schedule and arrived in Baltimore early in the afternoon, where they were entertained at the home of banker John S. Gittings, president of the North Central Railroad, on Mount Vernon Place, near the Washington Monument.

The Lincolns' hostess for the day was Mrs. Charlotte Ritchie Gittings, daughter of former *Richmond Enquirer* editor Thomas Ritchie, who, before he passed away in 1854, was one of the South's most-quoted Democratic Party spokesmen. Despite her obvious Southern bias, Charlotte Gittings was the most gracious of hostesses. It was, however, ironic that on Lincoln's first day in Washington, his family was entertained by a Southern sympathizer. Charlotte Gittings was by no means the only secessionist-minded resident in the Mount Vernon neighborhood. Not slaveholders themselves, they represented what Allan Pinkerton would later call "the aristocracy of slaveholding interests."[15] These interests were closely aligned with Virginia and included banking, shipping, law, and international commerce, all of which, Democrats argued, were in danger of collapse in the event of mass abolition.

The rift between Southern sympathizers in Maryland and the Lincoln administration grew wider in the wake of the firing on Fort Sumter by South Carolina forces and Lincoln's subsequent call for 75,000 volunteers on April 15, 1861. Two days later, William H. Norris hosted a secret meeting at his home on Monument Street. According to the part owner of the *Baltimore Daily Exchange*, William Wilkins Glenn, the purpose of the meeting was "to organize an armed resistance to the passage of troops through Maryland" and obtain verbal commitments "to carry the State out of the Union."[16] Severn Teackle Wallis and Frank Key Howard had advised Glenn not to attend the meeting at all, telling him that he risked his integrity by associating with "so extreme a party."[17] Although only 13 attended, the small gathering would have lasting implications.

The man Glenn called "Billy Norris" seemed an unlikely rebel. The youngest son of wealthy Baltimore merchant William Norris, Jr., was sent to Yale by his father, who had specified in his will that "no expense or trouble be spared in giving to my dear children excellent educations."[18] He graduated in 1829 and returned to Baltimore, where he was admitted to the bar in 1834.[19] He represented the Baltimore and Ohio Railroad in the so-called "Extra Dividend Case" in the 1850s and was one of their "private directors" in 1854–55.[20] He even represented Rachel Parker, a free African American, who had been wrongfully abducted from her Pennsylvania home in 1853 in an attempt to enslave her.[21]

Despite his resume, there were signs that William Henry Norris had the capacity to be a political fire-eater, even early in his career. As a young attorney, he served as the judge advocate in the court-martial of Captain Alexander Slidell MacKenzie of the United States Navy after Mackenzie hung three purported mutineers aboard the brig *Somers* in December 1842. When Mackenzie was subsequently acquitted, Norris claimed the trial was a "fraud" and a "virtual conspiracy."[22] He then started a clandestine correspondence with writer and novelist James Fenimore Cooper, which resulted in Cooper's 80-page "Elaborate Review" of the trial. As one historian concluded, having lost his case in court, Norris "wished to recoup it in the press."[23] Although seemingly inappropriate, these traits would make him a fitting leader of the rebel underground in Baltimore in 1861.

Like many of his neighbors on Monument Street, Norris was a member of Emmanuel Episcopal Church at the corner of Reed and Cathedral. At the close of 1859, the congregation had brought in the Rev. Noah Hunt Schenck from Chicago, who had given up a budding law career in Cincinnati almost ten years before to join the ministry. Schenck was likely recruited by influential church member Charles Howard and his wife, Elizabeth Phoebe Key Howard.

Born in 1802, Howard was the son of Revolutionary War hero Colonel John Eager Howard, while his wife, Elizabeth Phoebe Key, was the daughter of Francis Scott Key, author of "The Star-Spangled Banner." Key had died at their home in 1843, "within the shadow of the first monument erected to George Washington."[24] Another of Key's daughters, Mary Alicia Nevins Key, had married Schenck's brother-in-law, George H. Pendleton of Cincinnati—a sitting U.S. congressman.

The Rev. Noah Schenck's introductory sermon at Emmanuel Episcopal on January 8, 1860, delivered the simple and eternal message that through faith, the congregants could "overturn the kingdom of darkness and establish an earth wide empire of light and peace and salvation."[25] To Schenck, these sentiments were not just words, for under his leadership, the congregation quickly established what they called a "Christian Labor Union" to effect positive change in Baltimore.[26] His vice presidents in the union included Howard, former congressman James Carroll, and Isaac R. Trimble, superintendent of the Potomac and Ohio Railroad. Mrs. Richard Snowden Andrews and Mrs. William H. Norris oversaw the congregation's two chapels, and Thomas S. Rhett of the Union Bank managed financial affairs. Miss Nora Latrobe, daughter of civil engineer Benjamin Henry Latrobe II, taught Sunday school for people of color.[27]

Although only 16, Nora Latrobe was also deeply rooted in America's first families. Her grandfather, architect Benjamin H. Latrobe, took over the construction of the United States Capitol Building in 1803, and her father was involved with the Baltimore and Ohio Railroad for decades—a period during which the railroad went "from very small beginnings to be an immense power."[28] Nora Latrobe's uncle, attorney-inventor John H.B. Latrobe, was also integral to the Baltimore and Ohio, while simultaneously sitting on the board of directors of Baltimore's Union Bank and serving as grand master of the Masonic Order in Maryland. According to his principal biographer, John H.B. Latrobe "had a pew" at Emmanuel

Episcopal.[29] He held no official position with the church, however, for he was also an active member of Grace Episcopal in Elkridge, south of Baltimore, where he maintained his country house.[30]

His obituary noted that John H.B. Latrobe was "personally acquainted" with the last living signer of the Declaration of Independence, Charles Carroll of Carrolton, and was "on terms of social intimacy with the family of the signer."[31] Carroll was one of the largest slaveholders in the country, enslaving between 300 and 400 people—but also a believer that the practice was inherently evil.[32] "Why keep alive the question of slavery?" Carroll rhetorically asked in 1820. "It is admitted by all to be a great evil."[33] Nevertheless, he never freed his own slaves. Instead, he became an early president of the of the Maryland branch of the American Colonization Society at the age of 91, an organization dedicated, in Latrobe's words, to "the removal of the free people of color, with their consent, to Africa."[34]

The American Colonization Society had founded the nation of Liberia on the west coast of Africa in 1822, based on what Latrobe described as "the conviction that the two races must forever remain separate."[35] John H.B. Latrobe was an early proponent of colonization, fueled by his relationship with Carroll. To accomplish this purpose, the Maryland branch of the American Colonization Society, under Latrobe's direction, established a settlement of its own in Africa and named it "Maryland in Africa" in 1834. His obituary credits the establishment of Liberia to "his individual efforts."[36]

Latrobe became president of the American Colonization Society in 1853, after spending 28 years advocating the voluntary colonization of Africa by free African Americans.[37] Although Latrobe stressed that emigration was in the best interest of free African Americans, others revealed the true motivation of most members: the belief that "the presence of the black man in the state of freedom is injurious to society."[38] The belief became even more widespread after John Brown's failed raid on the Harpers Ferry arsenal in October 1859, with the intent of inciting an uprising of the enslaved—a thought which mortified slaveowners across the South.

Ironically, at the same time as the fear of racial violence was increasing, the success of African colonization was waning. At the American Colonization Society annual meeting on January 17, 1860, chaired by Latrobe, the society reported that only 300 emigrants went to Africa the preceding year, with the society's contract steamer, the *M.C. Stevens*, running at barely over half its capacity.[39] "Can any farce be more ridiculous than keeping up a society as this?" the *New York Herald* asked rhetorically after the meeting. "Its object was to encourage the emancipation of negroes, with a view to send them out to Africa.... But if the Colonization Society cannot furnish emigrants in greater numbers than three hundred per annum ... no effect whatever will be produced."⁴⁰

The *New York Herald* sarcastically labeled the annual meeting of the American Colonization Society in 1860 "an old fogey affair."⁴¹ Slave-owning Maryland delegate Curtis Jacobs expressed similar sentiments after he proposed a package of repressive bills that would prohibit manumission, require free African Americans to register themselves, so as to be removed from the state—all while eliminating subsidies for colonization.⁴² When a colleague suggested an amendment restoring support for the Colonization Society at the same time, Jacobs flew into a rage. "Hope for a change of affairs in Liberia is dead," he pronounced. "There is no longer any room for it. There is no vitality in it. In this state of affairs, it is astonishing that any gentleman should get up in this House and hope for anything from the dead carcass of the Society."⁴³

Latrobe's counterpart at the Maryland Colonization Society, Charles Howard, was forced to beg

Emmanuel Church, Baltimore, 1864 (Library of Congress Prints and Photographs Division). Emmanuel Church was led by former Chicagoan Reverend Noah Hunt Schenck; the *Chicago Tribune* called it the "church militant." The congregation before the war included future Confederate general Isaac Trimble, future rebel artillerist Richard Snowden Andrews, William and Mary Norris, and former congressman James Carroll, at whose house the song "Maryland! My Maryland" was conceived (D.R. Stiltz, photographer, *Emmanuel P.E., Cathedral and Reed Streets*, Baltimore, Maryland, 1864. Photograph. Library of Congress, https://www.loc.gov/item/2022630701/).

the Maryland legislature to continue the $10,000 per year appropriation to support the society, rather than repeal it, while ignoring the repressive amendments. "The officers and managers of the Colonization Society have seen with regret some of the proposed enactments introduced ... in reference to the colored population, deeming them to be more stringent and coercive than there is any occasion for adopting," Howard wrote the legislature, hoping they would continue his appropriation.[44]

Although most of the Emmanuel Episcopal congregation were not themselves slaveholders, they were, nevertheless, very Southern in their outlook. William Wilkins Glenn, who kept an office next to Norris, called him "not only very Southern but very extreme."[45] The election of Abraham Lincoln in 1860 did nothing to allay his extremism. In a speech on December 22, 1860, Norris raised the specter of a race war because of Lincoln's election, arguing that abolitionists would "preach insurrection as a sacred duty" and disseminate documents which would "incite a servile population to murder and rapine."[46]

Glenn never revealed the other twelve attendees at Norris' secret meeting on April 17, 1861. However, the results were seen immediately, for

Attorney John H.B. Latrobe, 1860–1890 (Library of Congress Prints and Photographs Division). President of the African Colonization Society, Latrobe felt that mixed races could never coexist. Although he was ostensibly a Unionist, his three sons fought for the Confederacy, including his son Osmun, an aide to Major General James Longstreet. The attorney was the trustee of Grace Episcopal Church in Elkridge and kept a pew at Emmanuel Episcopal in Baltimore—locations which would prove highly strategic for a secret mission (*J.H.B. Latrobe*, 1855–1865. Photograph. Library of Congress, https://www.loc.gov/item/2017897766/).

the National Volunteers of Baltimore held an impromptu open-air rally the following morning at Monument Square. "I do not care how many Federal troops are sent to Washington," 32-year-old attorney and Emmanuel Church member Wilson C.N. Carr told the crowd. "They will soon find themselves surrounded by such an army from Virginia and Maryland, that escape to their homes will be impossible; and when the 75,000 who are intended to invade the

3. The Aristocracy of Slaveholding Interests 35

South shall have polluted that soil with their touch, the South will exterminate and sweep them from the Earth."[47] The fiery speech was met by wild applause.

Predictably, a Baltimore mob attacked the 25th Pennsylvania and Sixth Massachusetts Infantry on their way to Washington the following day, hurling rocks and paving stones at soldiers while they changed trains. The troops were to have been transported in rail cars pulled by horses, but the mob blocked the rails by obstructing the tracks. Forced into the street, the raw troops were serenaded with lusty cheers "for the South, for Jefferson Davis, South Carolina, and secession" and, eventually, were "greeted with a volley of stones."[48] Although Glenn claimed in his diary that "everyone was taken by surprise" by the attack of the mob, it appeared to be at least somewhat organized.[49] According to one report from the *Philadelphia Press*, "the mob were commanded by a party of young men, well-dressed, apparently gentlemen's sons."[50]

That these young men could have quickly organized such violence was not far-fetched, for many had as much military training as the troops they were facing. Attorney Wilson C.N. Carr, who had delivered the incendiary speech the day before, was an officer in the Maryland militia, as were Charles Howard's son, McHenry Howard, and William H. Norris' stepson, Samuel H. Lyon.[51]

The first documented casualty of the riot was "Nick" Biddle, a 65-year-old African American orderly to Captain James Wren of Company H, 25th Pennsylvania Infantry. A longtime member of the Washington Artillery of Pottsville, Pennsylvania, Biddle was in uniform—a sight which enraged the angry crowd. Shouts of "N____ in uniform! N____ in uniform!" rang out, followed by a volley of heavy paving stones, pulled from the street.[52] Biddle was struck full in the face, a wound which bled profusely. "Poor Nick had to take it," Captain Wren later said sadly.[53] He was the first Union volunteer wounded in action.

At the corner of Pratt and Gay Streets, someone fired a shot. Nervous officers had the men present arms and fire a volley, scattering the crowd, but several with pistols returned fire. Marshal of Police George P. Kane organized a detachment of officers to seal off Camden Station, which successfully got the remainder of the regiment out of the city. When it was over, eight rioters, one innocent bystander and three soldiers were killed in what would be the first casualties of the Civil War.

Among the seemingly innocent victims was Robert W. Davis, a merchant with the dry goods firm of Pegram, Paynter and Davis. According to a witness, he was standing near the tracks when Northern troops fired indiscriminately into the crowd. "Davis, are you hurt?" a companion asked, as he fell to the ground. "Yes," Davis replied. "I am killed."[54] His

Attack on the Sixth Massachusetts at Baltimore, April 19, 1861 (Library of Congress, Prints and Photographs Division). Among the rioting crowd, dry goods merchant Robert W. Davis was killed when troops on a train fired in response. The merchants on West Baltimore Street would become the staunchest of secessionists and include Nelson Conrad, father of future Confederate operative Thomas Nelson Conrad (William Momberger, *Attack on the Massachusetts 6th at Baltimore, April 19, 1861* [Hartford: Hurlburt, Williams & Co., ca. 1862]. Steel engraving by O. Pelton. Library of Congress, https://www.loc.gov/item/2004680236/).

death reportedly created "an intense feeling in this community, especially among the merchants."[55] His funeral was held at the Emmanuel Episcopal Church, where the Reverend Schenck conducted the service and where "a large concourse of sympathizing friends … followed the remains to the grave."[56] A local inquest found that he was "ruthlessly murdered while enjoying the privilege of a peaceable and quiet citizen."[57]

In the aftermath of the Pratt Street Riot, President Lincoln telegraphed Baltimore mayor George Brown, requesting he travel to Washington to discuss how to keep peace in Maryland. Accompanied by attorneys George W. Dobbin, John C. Brune and S. Teackle Wallis, Brown made the trip by a "special train" and met Lincoln and his cabinet at the White House. Brown lobbied against bringing more troops through Baltimore, while Lincoln acknowledged his desire and duty to avoid the "fatal consequences" of a conflict between Federal troops and the people of Baltimore. Lincoln stressed, however, that he must move troops through Maryland to protect the capital.[58]

3. The Aristocracy of Slaveholding Interests

On Brown's heels was a peace delegation of the YMCA, led by the Rev. Richard Fuller, a slaveholder from South Carolina and pastor of the Seventh Baptist Church in Baltimore. The delegation presented President Lincoln with a petition on April 22, 1861, requesting that Lincoln recognize the Confederacy, demilitarize the capital, and stop the transport of troops through Maryland—all to prevent further bloodshed.[59] Among the 50 members of the YMCA delegation was the president of the Baltimore branch, John W. Selby, a trustee of the Strawbridge Methodist Episcopal Church.[60] The delegation may also have included one of Selby's vice presidents at the YMCA—attorney Wilson Carr, who just days earlier was inciting a riotous crowd at Monument Square.[61] President Lincoln apparently detected a level of sincerity in Selby that he did not detect in the others. After the peace petition was presented, Lincoln placed his hand gently on Selby's shoulder. "Young man you display a noble spirit, but you have no idea what you are asking."[62]

Despite his sympathy towards Selby, Lincoln was incensed by the hypocrisy of the committee. "You gentlemen, come here to me and ask for peace on any terms, and yet have no word of condemnation for those who are making war on us," Lincoln retorted, in response to their petition. "You express great horror of bloodshed, and yet would not lay a straw in the way of those who are organizing in Virginia and elsewhere to capture this city."[63] Lincoln's aide, John Hay, was even more blunt in his diary entry for the day, when he referred to the committee as "whining traitors."[64] Hay's rhetoric was not simply bluster, for as Selby was appealing for peace, others like him were actively preparing for war.

At the Emmanuel Episcopal Church, the Rev. Noah Hunt Schenck's vision of an "empire of light and peace" quickly evaporated.[65] Of those signing on to his Christian Labor Union in 1860, many were gone by summer. Vice President Isaac Trimble became a colonel in the Provisional Army of Virginia, architect Richard Snowden Andrews organized the Maryland Flying Artillery, while many others, like attorney Wilson Carr, also joined the Southern ranks. Many more, like William H. Norris, Charles Howard, and John H.B. Latrobe, had multiple sons flee Baltimore for Virginia. Little wonder that the *Chicago Tribune* joked in July 1861 that former Chicagoan Noah Hunt Schenck was now leading the "church militant."[66]

4

Monument Street Girls

These young ladies [of Baltimore] gathered their young friends ... all were in sympathy with the Southern cause.[1]
—Rebecca Lloyd Post Shippen, 1908

At the same time as the YMCA peace committee was meeting with Lincoln, General George H. Steuart of the Maryland militia was writing to the commander of Virginia troops in Harpers Ferry, Major General Kenton Harper, asking him to transfer 1,000 Virginia troops to the Relay House on the Baltimore and Ohio, to block the passage of Federal troops.[2] Situated strategically between Washington and Baltimore, the Relay House was where the Baltimore and Ohio branched west towards Pittsburgh, just north of the Patapsco River—directly across the river from tiny village of Elkridge. Only the arrival of Federal troops in Annapolis deterred Harper from taking the critical location.

Within days, Colonel Benjamin Butler's Massachusetts troops pushed inland to the Relay House from Annapolis, securing both the railroad junction and the viaduct over the river. It was a strategic victory for the untested Northern troops; the *Baltimore Exchange*, however, was dismissive of the feat. "On Saturday last, as our readers will remember, General Butler assaulted and carried the heights surrounding the Relay House by forced march in a railway train with twenty-four hundred men ..." the *Exchange* noted sarcastically. "The watchman on the viaduct was speedily overpowered; the landlord, the barkeeper and stable boys, who were posted on this side of the river, shared the same fate, and the three lawyers—who held the key of the position were also forced to surrender."[3]

Although the *Exchange* did not identify the "three lawyers" holding the viaduct, one of them was likely John H.B. Latrobe, for his residence on what was dubbed "Lawyer's Hill" strategically overlooked it. The other two may have been his son Osmun Latrobe, also an attorney, and George W. Dobbin—who had convinced Latrobe to move there in the 1840s. Dr. James Hall,

4. Monument Street Girls

who had purchased the African property that became Liberia, also lived nearby, at his residence "Claremont," designed by Baltimore architect and Emmanuel Church member Richard Snowden Andrews.[4] As Latrobe maintained a law office near Monument Square in Baltimore, he became one of the East Coast's first railroad commuters, riding the Baltimore and Ohio rails daily into the city.[5] Upon the outbreak of the war, Dobbin became "very active in the Confederate effort, assisting southerners trying to escape to the north and arranging for medical supplies to be transported to the south."[6]

Latrobe, like many others in Maryland, was against secession, but thought the solution to the national crisis was further guarantees to protect slavery and restrict abolitionists. In January 1861, in the wake of Lincoln's

Union soldiers of Cook's Boston Light Artillery overlooking the Thomas Viaduct, 1861 (Library of Congress, Prints and Photographs Division). Other sources indicate this battery was posted on John H.B. Latrobe's property near Elkridge—the location of his idyllic country house, "Fairly Knowe," from which he commuted to Baltimore (*Unidentified Union soldiers of Cook's Boston Light Artillery Battery 1st Massachusetts Light Artillery Battery, with two cannons, at the Baltimore & Ohio Railroad viaduct on the Patapsco River, Maryland. United States Maryland* [between 1861 and 1865]. Photograph. Library of Congress, https://www.loc.gov/item/2022631302/).

election, he had urged Pennsylvania to abolish its own state laws protecting fugitive slaves to prevent border states from seceding. "Remove the causes which threaten dissolution of the Union," he urged them. "Not only must she (Pennsylvania) repeal the personal liberty laws and the like unconstitutional legislation, but she must declare the terms on which she is willing that the whole question that is now agitating the land shall be settled once and forever."[7] The thought of Federal troops encamped on Lawyer's Hill must have galled him, for he once poetically described the hill as a "very lovely spot which has grown to its present beauty from the end of the spur of a Chestnut ridge overlooking the Patapsco."[8]

The three attorneys did not literally surrender; they did, however, lose the use of much of their property, for Butler installed several military positions on the hill, including a two-gun battery near the railroad right-of-way and a two-gun battery at Claremont, commanded by Captain Asa M. Cook.[9] The presence of Federal troops near Baltimore elicited so much interest that some 500 civilians rode the train from Camden Station on Saturday, May 11, to view them in person. The visitations were cordial, and one visiting party, deemed "roughs" by the *Exchange*, even presented the regiment with an American flag.[10] Two days later, at eight o'clock on the evening of May 13, the regiment quietly arrived in Baltimore and secured Federal Hill, the most prominent point in the city.

Upon hearing the news of Butler's arrival in Baltimore, secessionist partisans quickly prepared for war. "About eleven o clock on the night of May 13 we were quietly summoned by our sergeants ... to the Armory at Carroll Hall," recalled McHenry Howard. "We found the place dimly lighted and the guns being carried off singly and by twos and threes or more by any members of the Battalion who would undertake to hide them. I took and carried home three muskets, but did not attempt to hide them specially, for I apprehended that my father would be arrested as President of the Board of Police and his house on Cathedral Street next to Emmanuel Church would be searched."[11]

Butler's aim was unambiguous. He issued a proclamation the following day from Federal Hill, prohibiting the shipment of any goods to the South:

> A detachment of the forces of the Federal Government under my command have occupied the city of Baltimore.... No transportation from the city to the rebels of articles fitted to aid and support troops in the field will be permitted; and the fact of such transportation after the publication of this proclamation will be taken and received as proof of illegal intention on the part of the consignors and will render the goods liable to seizure and confiscation.[12]

Butler's proclamation to the citizens of Baltimore was unmistakably clear, but Baltimore secessionists attempted to smuggle war material south anyway. In mid–May, Butler's men captured a device called a "steam gun," assembled in the Baltimore machine shop of Latrobe's colleague, Ross Winans.[13] Secessionists were clandestinely hauling the unique cannon to Harpers Ferry along the tracks when they were arrested near Ellicott's Mills by Captain Robert H. Han, one of Butler's aides. A man following in a wagon protested bitterly and questioned under what authority his property was being seized. "By the same authority under which I now arrest you," Han replied, leveling a revolver at the man's head. "That of the United States!"[14]

With Union control of the Baltimore and Ohio Railroad, Maryland, secessionists instead migrated across the Potomac River at Harpers Ferry, where Virginia troops had seized the federal arsenal. James R. Herbert, captain of the Baltimore Independent Greys secretly organized his men and took the railroad to Harpers Ferry from Sykesville, Maryland. Many of them, however, traveled unarmed, as the risk of being caught increased dramatically otherwise.

Seventeen-year-old George Wilson Booth rode the train from Baltimore to Harpers Ferry on May 18 with nothing but the clothes on his back.[15] William Key Howard, son of Charles Howard, did the same, as did several of his brothers, who enlisted at Harpers Ferry on May 23 in what would become the First Maryland Infantry. McHenry Howard, the youngest of the Howard brothers, lingered in Baltimore, as he explained later, "partly because it was not clear that more could not be accomplished in Maryland, than by leaving it."[16]

McHenry Howard's later admission revealed a truth regarding Baltimore residents who stayed behind—they often fought in the shadows, by providing supplies, intelligence, and recruiting—and were every bit as dangerous as men shouldering a gun. Nevertheless, Howard and two companions headed south on June 1, 1861. Hearing the trains were to be searched, they instead traveled the so-called "lower route" to Virginia, traveling down the Patuxent River to Millstone Landing in St. Mary's County. Although they were unarmed, they had packed their Maryland Guard militia uniforms, which they donned at the landing. Howard later recorded that when they arrived at Millstone Landing, they "enquired for the home of George Thomas, at whose house, a couple of hundred yards off, we intended to spend the night and enquire how to proceed further."[17]

George and Richard Thomas were known secessionists. The latter had attended West Point but did not graduate—instead joining Garibaldi in the Italian War of Independence in 1859, where he adopted the unique name "Zarvona." He had intended to enlist in the Confederate cause immediately, but an invalid mother and his own sensitivity to sun exposure caused him to delay. Nevertheless, he was happy to aid other

Marylanders to reach the Confederacy. Staying two nights in St. Mary's County, Howard and his companions proceeded south with Thomas as a guide, stopping at an Episcopal church, where Howard noted that they were "shown much attention by the congregation, there being no necessity of keeping up any disguise in this country."[18] The church may have served as a waystation for supplies and Southern recruits heading to Virginia. A Union general in Tennessee later declared that "the clergymen of this state, especially the Protestant Episcopal Church, are the most disloyal and mischievous of all the citizens."[19]

The lower route to Virginia described by McHenry Howard was used by numerous Maryland secessionists making their way to Richmond. Howard would enlist in Captain William H. Murray's company of Marylanders, as would Wilson Carr. Murray had been captain of the Maryland Guard militia, and hoped to raise a company in Baltimore, but fearing arrest, had fled south. He became a captain of a company in the First Maryland Regiment in June, when sufficient men arrived from Maryland.[20] From his hometown of West River, in Anne Arundel County, acquaintances of Murray could easily have made the same journey as Howard down the Patuxent River to Millstone Landing.

Another West River native who did not join Murray but made repeated undercover trips to Baltimore on supply missions was 23-year-old Henry A. Steuart, the eldest son of Dr. William Frederick Steuart, later chief surgeon of General George H. Steuart's brigade.[21] Steuart's nephew, historian and journalist Richard D. Steuart, later wrote that "not long after the victory at Manassas, young Steuart was selected as a special agent of the Confederate States with the rank of captain" and that he made "several trips through the lines carrying medical supplies, fuses and musket caps."[22] Steuart's preferred route, according to family history, was through St. Mary's County and by ferry across the Potomac—presumably the same route that McHenry Howard had used months before. As an intermediate stop on his way to the Patuxent River, he used Mount Airy, the family estate of the Calvert family to whom he was related. There he could safely eat, rest, and obtain "relays of horses" for the next leg of his journey.[23]

On October 29, 1861, Captain Steuart relayed an urgent note to Confederate Secretary of War Judah P. Benjamin by special courier. "The gentleman who will hand you this comes on very important business with the Navy Department. Anything that I can do for you here let me know immediately." Steuart advised. "General Dix has announced his intention of hanging me as a spy if he can find me."[24] The fact that he was communicating directly with the Confederate Secretary of War is indicative of the size and importance of his operations.

The following year, Benjamin revealed that he had entrusted Steuart with some $30,000 in Confederate bonds, "to be used in the purchase of revolvers for the Army."[25] Steuart left Richmond for Baltimore on November 15, 1861, intending to supply the Third Maryland Artillery, then being organized in Richmond by Captain Henry B. Latrobe, the eldest son of attorney John H.B. Latrobe—the man who had spent a lifetime attempting to remove free African Americans from the continent by shipping them to Liberia through the American Colonization Society.[26]

Steuart traveled from Richmond to Maryland with the bonds in hand, but never made it back. Family tradition says that he left Baltimore with a wagon loaded with "medical supplies and military stores" and was near Annapolis when halted by a detachment of United States cavalry.[27] Abandoning the wagon, he "charged through the lines of the cavalry" and fled south towards the safety of secessionist friends in St. Mary's County. He reportedly took refuge at "Susquehana," the family estate of Henry J. Carroll on the Patuxent River near Millstone Landing, where he was captured on December 12, 1861. Steuart was taken to the Old Capitol Prison in Washington, where he was charged with supplying goods to insurgents.[28] The Confederate bonds, however, had disappeared.

The experiences of Booth, Howard, and Steuart reflected a continuing difficulty for Maryland secessionists: the task of supplying and

Susquehana, near Millstone Landing in St. Mary's County, Maryland, 1933 (Library of Congress Prints and Photographs Division). Henry Steuart was captured here in December 1861 by Federal cavalry while running supplies to Virginia for Captain Henry B. Latrobe's Third Maryland Artillery. Missing from the capture was $30,000 in Confederate bonds (Historic American Buildings Survey, creator, E.H. Pickering, photographer, *Susquehanna, Lexington Park, St. Mary's County, MD.*, 1933. Photograph. Library of Congress, https://www.loc.gov/item/md0816/).

maintaining troops in the field when the entire state was under Union control, a problem exacerbated by the fact that the Confederacy was just that—a confederation of states without a strong central government to rely on for support. From the start, Maryland troops would have to fend for themselves.

Of the 500 men from Maryland who assembled at Harpers Ferry and the Point of Rocks on May 23 to join the Confederacy, none of them came armed—excepting Company A, which had come from Washington with antiquated carbines. According to George Wilson Booth, they were issued flint-lock style muskets, converted to percussion caps, after arriving in Harpers Ferry, but still had no cartridge boxes, uniforms, or camp equipment and "presented a sorry sight compared with troops of other states."[29] The Maryland men at Harpers Ferry were not only largely unarmed, but were lacking clothing, tents, and camp supplies as well.

Colonel Bradley T. Johnson's wife, Jane Claudia Johnson, took it upon herself to arm the regiment. Leaving her comfortable home in Frederick, Maryland, she traveled to her home state of North Carolina and using her political connections in Raleigh, returned with enough rifles for every recruit. Jane Johnson stopped in Richmond long enough to obtain uniforms and camp supplies from Governor Letcher, so that by the time they were brigaded with other regiments, the Marylanders were at least "presentable."[30]

In Baltimore, a group of women residing in the affluent neighborhood west of the Monument Square also worked to supply the men of the First Maryland Regiment by sewing uniforms and smuggling medicine. Called the Brown Veil Club for the secrecy they practiced, or simply the "Monument Street Girls," they often met at the home of James Carroll, former Director of the Baltimore and Ohio Railroad, at 105 West Monument. The unsuccessful Democratic gubernatorial candidate in 1844, Carroll was once described by the *New York Tribune* as "a highly respectable old Federalist of great wealth" and even his Whig Party opponents had to admit that if nothing else, Carroll was "amiable."[31] By 1860, he listed his occupation as a "gentleman" and he held over $200,000 in real estate assets.[32]

The Monument Street Girls had a particularly close affiliation with men in the Maryland Guard like McHenry Howard, even before the war started. Maryland Guard member Isaac F. Nicholson noted some 50 years later that members of the Maryland Guard would select certain girls to be "daughter of the company" and honor them accordingly, "pledging loyalty and devotion."[33] Among them were the Cary sisters, Hettie and Jenny; Rebecca Chapman Gordon, daughter of Union Bank president John Montgomery Gordon; Alice Wright, 18-year-old daughter of coffee merchant Robert Clinton Wright; and Ida B. Winn, niece of James Carroll's oldest daughter, Sophia Carroll Sargent.[34] Many of them lived in the 100 block of West Monument Street, near James Carroll.

Carroll's daughter, Sophia Sargent, and her husband, the Rev. Thomas B. Sargent, lived just next door. Sargent had presided over the wedding of his younger daughter, Prudence Gough Carroll, to William T. Winn in 1840. By 1860, Prudence Gough Winn and her three teenage daughters, including Ida, still lived at Carroll's home.[35] Union Bank president James M. Gordon and the Norris family lived just down the street at 101 and 92 West Monument, respectively.[36] Although the group were labeled the "Monument Street Girls," their leader appeared to be William H. Norris' wife, Mary Norris—not a girl, but rather, a middle-aged woman with extensive social connections across Maryland and Virginia.

Mary Norris was 52 years old in 1861 and had already buried one husband—James E. Lyon, who died in 1838 at only 33. She had borne him two sons, James William Lyon and Samuel H. Lyon, and after she married William Henry Norris in 1843, they added another son, Kennedy Owen Norris, two years later.[37] Mary Norris was one of four Owen sisters, who besides herself, included Rebecca, who married James J. Grogan; Anne, who married Algernon Sidney Allen of Virginia; and Sarah, who did not marry, but helped raise three of Rebecca Grogan's four sons after they were orphaned at an early age.[38] In 1860, the three still lived down the street from Mary Norris, at 100 West Monument.[39] The fourth son, Robert Riddle Grogan, appears to have been adopted by the Allens, for he was living with them at their estate "Clifton," near Berryville, Virginia, in 1850, together with their three sons—Robert Owen Allen, David Hume Allen and Algernon Allen, Jr.[40]

William H. Norris also had sisters who married into influential families. His sister Charlotte married Charles B. Calvert, who maintained a large family estate, Riversdale, in Prince George's County, where he founded the Maryland Agricultural College in 1856. Calvert was also a significant slaveholder, as some 44 people of all ages were enslaved there in 1860.[41] Another Norris sister, Eleanor, married Thomas A. Spence, a judge in Worcester County, Maryland. Just among their direct relations, William and Mary Norris had connections in several strategic locations—connections they would use in coming years to support the Confederate war effort.

The so-called Monument Street Girls became famous for taking the nine-stanza poem "Maryland, My Maryland" by native Marylander James Ryder Randall and converting it to a song. Randall, living in Louisiana at the time of the Pratt Street Riot, but disturbed by the events, authored the poem in the middle of the night on April 26, 1861, and soon thereafter had it published in the *New Orleans Sunday Delta*. One day in July 1861,

Baltimore attorney Henry Rozier Delaney arrived at the home of James Carroll, excited about the poem someone had shown him.[42]

According to Rebecca Nicholson, it was Mary Norris who suggested the poem be made into song. "Mrs. William Henry Norris had come in to chat ... for she was deeply interested in the Southern cause," Nicholson recalled. "One of the girls sat at the piano, on which lay a book of Yale songs and one tune after another was tried."[43] After settling on the German version of "Tannenbaum, O Tannenbaum," the "enthusiastic crowd of girls sang the song with a will," and "as soon as quiet was restored, Mr. Norris suggested that Mr. Dulaney should have it published as a song."[44] It was so wildly successful among the Southern-minded element that "many times did the boys sing this song ... before they crossed the Potomac."[45]

Many members of the Brown Veil Club were also members of the Emmanuel Episcopal Church at the corner of Cathedral and Read, where Mary Norris and James Carroll exerted considerable influence. The marriage of Carroll's daughter Sophia to the Rev. Thomas B. Sargent also created a unique religious alliance—for although Carroll was an active Episcopalian, Sargent was a Methodist, having led John W. Selby's Strawbridge Methodist Church from 1856 to at least 1858.[46]

The two denominations had a spirited rivalry. Carroll, however, encouraged cooperation, as he had a family interest in doing so. When the standing committee of the Episcopal Church formally sent a letter of condemnation in 1853 to the rector of the Emmanuel Church, Dr. Henry Van Dyke Johns, for preaching in a Methodist church, the otherwise amiable James Carroll offered a series of resolutions at the Episcopal Convention that year to "expunge the obnoxious letter," resulting in a protracted debate which lasted all afternoon and "was continued with great acrimony."[47]

The Rev. Thomas B. Sargent's close relationship to the Brown Veil Club of Monument Street put him in a distinctive position of influence, for he had also served many years in the Baltimore Conference with Reverends Dabney Ball and John Landstreet, both of whom rode with Colonel J.E.B. Stuart's First Virginia Cavalry, ostensibly as chaplains.[48] Ball's role with Stuart unquestionably extended beyond that of chaplain even from the outset, for his mother reported on July 25, 1861, that Ball had informed her that was "neither a lieutenant or chaplain in the Southern army, but was living in his own quiet home, and preaching to a Presbyterian congregation."[49] Confederate records, however, clearly show Ball was appointed chaplain of the First Virginia Cavalry on July 1, 1861, well before his mother reported his neutral status to the press.

The message was clearly a ruse, to conceal Ball's true activities, which undoubtedly involved both espionage and smuggling out of Maryland.

Ball himself recognized Maryland as the potential supply depot of the Confederacy before he ever donned a uniform. "The South is Maryland's chief market," he wrote a friend in the wake of the Pratt Street Riot in April 1861. "She buys of the North *but sells* to the South."[50] Ball's initial success at trafficking goods from Maryland was evident when Stuart promoted him to chief of brigade commissary later that year, likely because of his extensive connections across Maryland.[51]

Among the young men who stayed in Baltimore, but immediately became involved in smuggling goods to the Confederacy, was Mary Norris' son, 25-year-old attorney Samuel H. Lyon. He became engaged with Zarvona's lieutenant, George W. Alexander, in a scheme to ship rifles south from Maryland's Eastern Shore. The plot went awry when citizens in Cambridge, Maryland, grew suspicious over several large, heavy boxes the men had among their baggage. When one was opened, it was found to contain firearms—rifles with bayonets, by one account, pistols and cutlasses by another. Unfortunately for Lyon, the local judge was his Unionist uncle, Thomas A. Spence. Recognizing his nephew and suspecting something nefarious, he requested permission from Governor Hicks to have them arrested.[52]

Only two weeks before Alexander's arrest in Cambridge, he and Zarvona had pulled off one of the most audacious feats of the war when they captured the steamer *St. Nicholas* in Chesapeake Bay on June 28, 1861, as part of a complex naval operation approved by Virginia governor John Letcher. Zarvona had boarded the ship as a passenger in Baltimore, dressed not as himself, but as a "French Lady." He had tried out the disguise days before by walking into Severn Teackle Wallis' law office in Baltimore dressed as a woman and starting a conversation. Neither Wallis nor Zarvona's own cousin, John Thomas, recognized him. "Well, if neither of you know me, I think I am safe," Zarvona finally said, pulling off his wig and revealing his identity.[53]

Once aboard the *St. Nicholas*, Zarvona played his part as if he were a stage actor, openly joining others for supper, jabbering profusely in French and overall "making quite a scene."[54] Zarvona's disguise was effective, although the captain of the St. Nicholas had his suspicions. "She sat next to me at the table, so close our knees touched," he confided later. "I fancied she looked mighty queer; but I'll be hanged if I thought she was a man."[55] Alexander and eight accomplices boarded the ship at Point Lookout, disguised as laborers bound for Washington. According to one account, the French lady retired to her stateroom after dark, only to emerge with "her wig and petticoats doffed, in full military costume, with revolvers and cutlass by her side."[56] Supported by Alexander and the other "passengers," Zarvona took control of the ship, with which he subsequently captured two other vessels, laden with coffee and ice.

Returning to Richmond, Zarvona became an instant celebrity. "Vast numbers of citizens of Richmond called to make his acquaintance, and to pay their respects to him—to express their thanks—and tender their congratulations," Governor John Letcher later recalled. "His room at the Executive Mansion was generally crowded with visitors from the city and the country."[57] Zarvona and Alexander did not rest on their success. Instead, they were quickly back in Maryland—Alexander obtaining guns on the Eastern Shore and Zarvona, with six or seven comrades, heading for Baltimore aboard the steamer *Mary Washington*. By chance, Lieutenant Thomas H. Carmichael of the Baltimore police boarded the *Mary Washington* at Fair Haven, and recognizing Zarvona and his associates, redirected it to the Fort McHenry dock, where Federal authorities quickly charged them with treason and piracy.[58]

Zarvona was imprisoned in Fort McHenry, together with Lyon and Alexander. Among these, Alexander was especially committed to escape, and with the help of his wife, he developed a plan to do so. On her weekly visits, she smuggled in a map of sentry locations, a Federal uniform and a makeshift life preserver fashioned from a waistcoat. Jumping from the ramparts, he eluded the sentries and braved a two-and-a-half-hour swim to the mainland—despite being badly injured from his leap to the ground. Rescued from the shore by a man and his daughters, he convinced the girls to take him to Baltimore in their buggy, concealing him under their hoop skirts. According to his lengthy obituary in the *Baltimore Sun*, "he was taken first to the house of W.H. Norris ... then taken in a carriage by [Kennedy] Owen Norris to Hoffman Street, where he saw his wife for a moment, and thence to the home of E. Law Rogers, where, at 4 P.M., he had the services of a surgeon."[59]

On October 2, 1861, Alexander belatedly wrote Secretary of War Judah P. Benjamin from Richmond, where he had successfully returned: "Stretched on a bed of pain I have neglected to report my escape and return.... I am nearly convalescent. When fit for duty I will report in person."[60] His successful rescue was due, in large part, to the Norris family. Not only were they the leaders of the so-called Monument Street Girls—composing songs and sewing clothes—but were also at the epicenter of secessionist activity in Baltimore, including intelligence, supply and recruiting.

5

On Mansfield's Secret Service

... of all my family, I alone stay true to the Government.[1]
—William Chase Barney, 1862

The case of Richard Thomas Zarvona highlighted the fact that, in the spring of 1861, rebel spies were acting with impunity across the District of Columbia and southern Maryland. For this reason, General Winfield Scott appointed Colonel Joseph K. Mansfield as chief of the Military Department of Washington, consisting of the District of Columbia and the state of Maryland as far as Bladensburg, effective April 28, 1861. Mansfield immediately recognized the need for undercover agents to conduct counterintelligence—men who were both above suspicion and familiar with Washington and Baltimore. He found such a man in native Marylander William Chase Barney, serving with the 71st New York State Militia, the so-called "American Guard," stationed at the Washington Navy Yard.

Barney had been in Paris during the winter of 1861, but hurried home in April, after he saw, in his own words, "the danger that menaced my country."[2] His obituary suggests he joined Major Philip Kearny on the voyage back to New York.[3] Like Barney, Kearny was living in Paris when the war broke out and, according to one biographer, shipped out for the United States "early in the spring of 1861, on receiving the first reliable intelligence of his country's peril."[4] Barney arrived in New York City on April 18, 1861, and joined the ranks of the American Guard three days later, as they marched down Broadway. "I stepped from the sidewalk and joined the ranks of the first N.Y. regiment I saw on its way to Washington," Barney wrote in a letter the following year. "I did not tarry to say adieu to my wife and children, and they knew not of my departure."[5]

Although Barney's enlistment may have been spontaneous, his choice of the American Guard was not likely coincidental. The regimental adjutant was his former business partner, Andrew H. Pride, whose influence Barney undoubtedly used to enlist, for the regiment had already refused "over two hundred applicants," several of them "on account of their advanced age."[6] By Barney's own admission, he was the oldest man in the regiment at age 45 and had never before shouldered a musket.[7] The American Guard was, at the outbreak of the Civil War, one of the premier militia regiments in the country, and aside from his relationship with Pride, it's hard to see how he would have been accepted.

The regiment arrived in Washington on the morning of April 27, 1861, having sailed to Annapolis and marched some 30 miles inland to catch the railroad south. A correspondent of the *Washington Star* thought them "a fine-looking specimen of the American soldier ... and their powers of endurance admirable."[8] Its arrival, together with the other regiments from Annapolis, could not have been more welcome. Just the day before, General Winfield Scott was so alarmed with secessionist activity near Washington that he issued an order stating that an attack upon the city was imminent.[9]

Scott ordered the regiment to one of the most strategic points in the capital—the Washington Navy Yard, where they supported naval operations to secure points along the Potomac River. One of these was the bridge across the Anacostia River near the Navy Yard. On the night of Friday, May 10, sentries of the American Guard stopped a lone African American man attempting to cross from Virginia and were obliged to arrest him. The man made no attempt to conceal himself or his purpose. He was escaping north from enslavement and had walked sixty miles to do so—twice the distance the American Guard had marched from Annapolis. They sent him to confinement, having to do so under the Fugitive Slave Law still in effect at the time.[10]

The arrest left a bad aftertaste, for the New Yorkers did not relish the job of returning fugitives. "Humanity speaks louder here than in a big city," one of them wrote. "I do not think it strange that the ones who objected the most strenuously to the arrest of fugitives were the old-time Democrats ... they gladly seize the opportunity to show that they think it is a mean business."[11] Yet, Union troops arriving in Washington in May 1861 found numerous incidents like that confronting the sentries at the Anacostia bridge.

For Northern soldiers disgusted by the prospect of returning fugitive slaves back into captivity, there were small victories. Such was the case when Union troops, including Elmer Ellsworth's Zouaves and a contingent of the First Michigan Infantry, entered Alexandria, Virginia, at the end of May and captured a squadron of rebel cavalry quartered in the slave pen of Price, Birch and Company. It was a dreary structure containing a

Slave pen, Alexandria, Virginia, 1861–1865 (Library of Congress Prints and Photographs Division). Union troops captured it in May 1861. In most cases, though, they were obliged to return slaves to their owners (*Slave Pen, Alexandria, Va.* [Hartford: War Photograph & Exhibition Co., between 1861 and 1865]. Photograph. Library of Congress, https://www.loc.gov/item/2011646199/).

literal "pen"—described by one correspondent as "fifty feet square, open above, and surrounded by walls twenty feet high, with brick flooring and dungeons underneath."[12]

Although most of the African Americans held in the slave pen had been spirited off before the capture, one remained, locked inside the structure. "He was liberated by the Zouaves, who picked the lock, and has been adopted by the Michiganders as their cook," the correspondent reported. "He likes cooking but says he must have a musket if fighting is to be done."[13] It was an early indication that having gained their freedom, former slaves were willing and able to fight.

Even in 1861, Union regiments were happy to take on free African Americans for camp chores. Such was the case with the 71st New York State Militia, who took on Ignatius Smallwood, described as "a young man, apparently not more than twenty-five years of age and withal, very intelligent."[14] Census records show Smallwood was actually 35 years old, with a wife and five children, all of whom lived together in the neighborhood west of the Navy Yard.[15] Smallwood was undoubtedly happy for the work—but risked everything when the American Guard went up against the forces of the Confederacy later that summer.

The regiment's three-month term of service was to expire on July 20, 1861. Four days short of their expiration date, orders were received to cross into Virginia as part of General Ambrose Burnside's brigade. Although William Chase Barney had been detached from the regiment "on special secret service" with General Joseph K. Mansfield, as soon as the regiment was ordered to Virginia, he "applied for orders to join it."[16] General Mansfield declined the request but upon Barney's "urgent solicitation" was granted a leave of absence to do so.[17]

Burnside's brigade became one part of General Irwin McDowell's Grand Union Army, which was to crush the rebellion in one quick stroke. The Union advance was slowed by obstructions, which according to one regimental commander, were "placed on the road by the rebels, who had felled trees at several points, and through which we had to cut our way."[18] As the regiment approached Fairfax Courthouse, journalist George W. Wilkes, embedded with the American Guard, astutely observed that such obstacles were evidence that "Confederate troops seemed to have been, to some extent, appraised of our intentions."[19]

Despite the apparent forewarning, the rebels fled Fairfax Courthouse as McDowell advanced, leaving members of the 71st with four fresh quarters of beef and 50,000 good cigars. On July 18, as the Union army approached Blackburn's Ford on the Bull Run branch of Opequon Creek, the rebels put on a better show, repulsing the troops attempting to cross. One observer, however, thought the setback simply "served to stimulate the ardor of our troops."[20] The real action would come three days later, when McDowell chose to attack rebel positions south of the creek, in a two-pronged attack.

Burnside's brigade, as part of the flanking column, was awake at two that morning, to be in position by midmorning. Confronting them were elements of General Nathan Evans and General Barnard Bee's brigades on Henry House Hill. Wilkes described rebel fire as "doubly hot" at this moment, but just as the regiment wavered, a Union flag appeared on the crest of the hill from regiments attacking the opposite slope—encouraging the New Yorkers to press forward. Confederate general William R. Terry, then with the Second Virginia Infantry, later said that when Burnside's brigade filed out of the woods, "it was the most magnificent sight that I saw throughout the war."[21]

As Burnside's men came up over the hill, the Fourth Alabama Infantry mounted a furious counterattack. "At one point the rebels seemed determined to risk all rather than retreat," said a correspondent of the *New York Tribune*. "The 71st New York regiment, literally mowed down and annihilated double their number."[22] Convinced the day was won, Colonel Burnside ordered them back to the protection of the woods, reasoning that "the brigade had done its full portion of the day's work."[23] According to the commander of the American Guard, Colonel Henry Martin, "General

McDowell with his staff rode around the field in rear of our brigade, waving his glove in token of victory and we all considered the day was ours."[24]

Congratulations were premature. Unknown to the Union command, rebel reinforcements had arrived via the railroad at Manassas Junction and landed squarely on the right flank of the Union line, where the artillery batteries commanded by James B. Ricketts and Charles Griffin had pushed forward south of the Henry House to enfilade the Southern line. Although the New York Fire Zouaves had gone forward to support them, a counterattack from their rear by Colonel J.E.B. Stuart's First Virginia Cavalry quickly scattered them. "I have no hesitation in saying that if other regiments, the NY Fire Zouaves specifically, had done their duty that day, instead of inglorious flight from the battle ... our arms would have captured the entire rebel army," Barney would later conclude.[25]

Among Stuart's cavalry was the former Methodist Episcopal minister from Baltimore, the Rev. Dabney Ball. Appointed chaplain of the First Virginia Cavalry on July 1, Ball did not restrict his duties to the pulpit, but

Colonel Burnside's brigade at Bull Run, July 21, 1861 (Library of Congress Prints and Photographs Division). William Chase Barney's 71st New York State Militia was one of three regiments in the brigade. He later sought to raise his own brigade of Catholics based on his one-day experience in battle (Alfred R. Waud, artist, *Colonel Burnsides brigade at Bull Run, First and Second Rhode Island, and Seventy-First New York Regiments, with their Artillery, Attacking the Rebel Batteries at Bull Run.* Sketched on the spot by A. Waud. Bull Run, Virginia, 1861. Photograph. Library of Congress, https://www.loc.gov/item/2004660449/).

waded into the desperate fray with relish. One observer saw Ball at the height of the conflict, south of the Henry House, "sit on his horse ten paces from the line of the New York Zouaves and empty every barrel of his pistol as deliberately as if he was practicing at a target."[26]

Although the Union batteries were reportedly captured and recaptured three times, the fresh Confederate troops from Manassas Junction won the day and collapsed the Federal line. With broken regiments fleeing past, Burnside's brigade covered the retreat. According to Burnside's official report, "The Seventy-first regiment, New York Militia, was formed between the columns and the enemy by Colonel Martin."[27] Months of drill at the Washington Navy Yard now came into play, as the exhausted New Yorkers retreated slowly among the chaos.

Among those caught in the confusion was Ignatius Smallwood, who was captured by Virginia cavalrymen with 74 other Union prisoners and taken to the rear. There, according to Smallwood, "a major of the eighth Louisiana regiment took possession of him and carried him to Beauregard, who, after hearing the statement of his capture ... told the major to take him."[28] The Louisiana major was likely Major John B. Prados, a 25-year-old New Orleans native who had been given responsibility for Union prisoners.[29] The Confederate commander at Manassas, General P.G.T. Beauregard, reportedly remarked that the major had "done a good day's work, as the d___d Yankee n___r was worth $1,500."[30] On the day after the battle, the major advised Smallwood that "he need not think of getting free again, for he was his slave for life."[31]

At Beauregard's headquarters, Confederate officers interrogated Smallwood extensively. He answered their questions faithfully and in return, simply asked if he could "send to his family and let them know what had become of him." The officers scoffed. "Boy, we are going to Fairfax today and tomorrow we will take Washington and hang old Abe Lincoln."[32] Luckily for Smallwood, Major Prados was preoccupied with Union prisoners. Left largely unattended, Smallwood followed the Eighth Louisiana to Fairfax Courthouse and then "took to the thicket," returning to Washington only after a "severe walk" through the countryside.[33]

Some believed that had Beauregard attacked Washington in that moment, as rebel officers had told Smallwood, the War would have quickly been over. Northern correspondent Joseph Scoville agreed, telling his readers that "had the rebels not been stupefied, or scared at their own success—had a single regiment started in pursuit with fifty or a hundred drums, they would have driven the panic-stricken troops out of Washington."[34]

Washington socialite and rebel spy Rose O'Neal Greenhow also thought an attack on Washington in the wake of the battle would have succeeded. "Our gallant Beauregard would have found himself right ably seconded by the rebels in Washington had he deemed it expedient to advance on the city," she wrote. "Measures had ... been taken to spike the guns in Fort Corcoran, Fort Ellsworth and other important points, accurate drawings of which had been furnished to our commanding officer by me."[35]

Greenhow was in a unique position to know the weakness of Washington. Confederate president Jefferson Davis attributed Southern success at Manassas not to strength of arms, but to military intelligence she had provided. Greenhow had successfully conveyed news of the Federal advance with enough accuracy to allow General Joseph E. Johnston to shift his troops by rail to Manassas Junction at the critical time.[36] A native of Virginia, Rose Greenhow was the widow of former State Department employee Robert Greenhow, who had died unexpectedly in California in 1854, leaving her with four children and no apparent means of support.

Representative William "Extra Billy" Smith of Virginia, a future Confederate general, advocated a special appropriation on her behalf, arguing that Robert Greenhow, while at the State Department, had "attached himself to a lady as lovely as a houri, and the result of that connection was a cluster of little ones."[37] Smith's description of Greenhow as a houri—the seductively beautiful maiden said to be the reward for faithful Muslims in paradise—became an accurate description for how otherwise sober Union officers viewed the middle-aged widow.

In April 1861, Greenhow was the perfect choice to glean military intelligence from unwitting Union officers and government officials, a fact that Colonel Thomas Jordan of Confederate general P.G.T. Beauregard's staff quickly recognized. A former quartermaster in the United States Army, Jordan supplied her with a military cipher and instruction on how to communicate with him before he left Washington to join the Confederacy.[38] According to detective Allan Pinkerton's later assessment, "Her long residence at the capital, her superior education, her uncommon social powers, her very extensive acquaintance among and her active association with the leading politicians of this nation, has possessed an almost superhuman power, all of which she has most wickedly used to destroy the Government."[39]

Federal authorities arrested Greenhow on August 23, 1861, for conducting treasonable correspondence with the enemy. The *Washington Evening Star* concluded her arrest was no surprise, for "her secession proclivities have long been the subject of popular conversation."[40] Even after her arrest in August 1861, however, she left what Pinkerton described as "secret and insidious agents" throughout the city of Washington.[41]

Although not directly associated with Greenhow, one of the most cunning of Confederate agents in the Washington area was schoolmaster Thomas Nelson Conrad, who operated the Georgetown Institute on Dumbarton Street, together with his younger brother, John S. Conrad.[42] He was born to wealthy merchant Nelson Conrad of Fairfax, Virginia, but a devastating fire there in 1853 caused the family to migrate to Baltimore, while young Tom Conrad attended Dickinson College in Carlisle, Pennsylvania.

Founded in 1783 by Dr. Benjamin Rush, a signer of the Declaration of Independence, Dickinson College was the first college founded in the new United States of America, with a vision of promoting freedom of thought and freedom of action. Financial troubles and debates regarding curriculum caused Dickinson to close temporarily until the Methodist Episcopal Church took it over in 1833. Despite its location north of the Mason-Dixon line, Dickinson College attracted many students from Virginia, Maryland, and Southern states as far as Georgia. Nevertheless, Conrad later said that his four years at Dickinson convinced him that "the mind of the masses of the North was so poisoned and inflamed against the South and Southern people and institutions, that it would be impossible to restrain them by legal processes, constitutional exactions or moral influences."[43]

Conrad tried to get a former classmate at Dickinson, Horatio King, to help teach at the Georgetown Institute by what King called a "Methodist minister trick"—he listed King as an "assistant" in a school circular, despite King not yet agreeing to the job. "Tom must 'hoe his own row,'" King confided in his diary. "I will probably teach a few months, and then do myself the honor to resign."[44] Unable to enlist King, Conrad recruited his younger brother, John S. Conrad, instead.

The Conrad brothers first attracted significant attention from Federal authorities when commencement exercises for the Georgetown Institute in June 1861 were culminated by the band playing "Dixie" to what Conrad called "cheer after cheer" from the audience.[45] The celebration resulted in his arrest that evening, but he was released in a few days to await parole, under the condition that he not "leave the capital until regularly exchanged ... pending the trade of prisoners."[46] Upon his release, however, Conrad admitted that he "proceeded to get into more mischief without delay."[47]

Conrad later noted that "few towns of its size south of Mason and Dixon's line had as many Confederate sympathizers as did Georgetown," and according to a contemporary historian, "no one in Georgetown was more defiantly pro-Confederate than Thomas Nelson Conrad."[48] Conrad had a multitude of sources inside Washington. "There were prominent clerks in the War Department," he later revealed, "who had been my warm personal friends and whose loyalty to the South was unquestioned."[49] He reportedly passed intelligence gleaned from the War Departments to rebel forces across the Potomac River by simply "raising and lowering his window shades."[50]

Sometime after the Battle of Bull Run, Conrad was paroled and sent south—where he was formally sponsored by Stuart's chaplain, the Rev. Dabney Ball. This was likely not coincidence, for Ball had only resigned from the Columbia Methodist Episcopal Church in Baltimore a scant few weeks before.[51] Located on Baltimore's west side, Columbia may have been Nelson Conrad's home church, for he lived on South Greene Street in 1860, only a few blocks away.[52]

Like Conrad, Dabney Ball had been born in Fairfax County, Virginia, of strongly Methodist parents. Aspiring to the ministry, Ball served in a multitude of churches across the Baltimore Conference of the Methodist Episcopal Church, including two churches in Baltimore and two in Washington.[53] As tensions increased over slavery, Ball found himself at odds with others of his faith—especially in the Baltimore Conference. In a letter to Confederate president Jefferson Davis, Ball opposed a proposal to allow Bishop Ames from visiting Union prisoners in Southern captivity, arguing that Ames was "an uncompromising antislavery man not to say abolitionist…. For many years the Methodist Episcopal Church, of which I am a humble minister, has been fearfully agitated and cursed by the same class of fanatics that have now brought this terrible disaster upon the nation."[54]

Tom Conrad's parole later that summer left his brother John alone in Washington. When not himself teaching, he attended the Columbia University medical school in Washington and functioned as an assistant surgeon at the Georgetown Hospital. After John Conrad expressed the sentiment that "all those who opposed the secession of the southern States were abolitionists," a colleague asked him why he did not instead go south.[55] Conrad replied that "he could do the north more harm by obtaining a medical position in the United States army, than he could by joining the southern army."[56] He likely had numerous connections in not only Washington, but Baltimore as well, for he had attended school there at the Newton and Union academies before the War.[57]

Rebel agents like Rose Greenhow and the Conrad brothers were just the type of underground operatives that William Chase Barney was to root out in his role on Mansfield's secret service. A native of Baltimore, he had lived in the South and was outside the normal age of active service, making him the perfect mole to investigate treasonous activity in Maryland. As he said himself, he "was born and reared south of Mason & Dixon's line, in the midst of that 'peculiar institution' which is the cause of this accursed rebellion."[58]

Barney was likely unaware of the Conrad brothers' activities in Georgetown. He may, however, have shadowed Rose Greenhow, for her residence on 16th Street West was within blocks of his mother's home on 17th Street West, north of Lafayette Square. The Barney home was itself a hotbed of secession sentiment. His mother, Mary Chase Barney, was said to have "hung in her parlor a Confederate flag" and according to one of her daughters, Maria "Rosa" Barney, even "old [General Winfield] Scott saw it there."[59] Although she was "often told to take it down," she never did.[60]

William Chase Barney later bemoaned the fact that "of all my family, I alone stay true to the Government."[61] Barney's involvement, if any, in Greenhow's arrest is unclear, but he took an active role in the arrest of former Minister to France Charles J. Faulkner of Virginia that same month. On August 16, 1861, Barney gave a deposition stating that he was present in Paris when Faulkner read a letter from Senator James M. Mason of Virginia advising Faulkner to not leave France, for Virginia intended to secede on February 20, 1861, and to take possession of Washington on the night of March 3—the night before Lincoln was to be inaugurated. Faulkner had been arrested on Washington on August 12, 1861, and Barney's deposition was undoubtedly designed to help support charges against him.[62]

Barney's assistance in Faulkner's arrest may have prompted Secretary of State William H. Seward to recommend him as an additional army paymaster, with the rank of major, on August 21, 1861.[63] His secret service duties did not end after his commission, however, for the following month, he seems to have been used to garner evidence against Charles H. Winder, a Washington attorney with Southern connections. In August 1861, the Union Provost Marshall's office had received an anonymous letter warning Federal authorities of the threat Winder posed to Washington. "C.H. Winder of this city is an avowed secessionist," the informant wrote. "He has a brother [John H. Winder] who ... is now a Brigadier General in the Confederate Army."[64]

An agent of detective Allan Pinkerton, D.G. McKelvey, was shadowing Winder as early as August 20, 1861.[65] What Federal authorities needed to arrest him was more evidence. To do so, they apparently lured him to Barney's quarters in Washington on Sunday, September 8, 1861, on the pretext that Winder was to help Barney with "something relative to his children."[66] It was not an odd request, since Winder was one of several attorney's representing Barney's brother on similar matters.[67] Barney's two children, Mary and William, had been born in 1854 and 1856, respectively, but Barney and his wife, the former Ada B. Franciscus of Baltimore, appear to have largely separated by 1861, for during the war years she taught in the Brooklyn schools and, even in 1865, she was living with her sister and the children without him.[68]

The day after meeting Barney, Winder was brought in for questioning by detective Allan Pinkerton, who asked him if he knew on what charge he was brought in. Winder provided the following answer:

> I only imagine it may be upon information provided by an English letter writer whom I met at Major Barney's quarters last night where I had gone to see the Major.... The Englishman and myself got into a violent discussion about the War, he taking the side of the North and I of the South. I don't disguise the fact that I am all over for the South, from the crown of my head to the sole[s] of my feet.[69]

Although Winder denied corresponding with family and friends in the South, he was arrested anyway, on a charge of "treasonable practices," but was released on a conditional parole on October 15, 1861, after Pinkerton failed to produce any substantive evidence.[70]

Although he suspected the "English letter writer" of turning him in to Federal authorities, it was likely Barney who had set him up for arrest. The so-called "English letter writer" was likely journalist Joseph Alfred Scoville, the former editor of the *New York Picayune*, who wrote for English periodicals under the pen name "Manhattan." In a letter to Assistant Secretary of State Frederick Seward the following year, Barney would complain of a "traitorous" letter to the *London Times* and instead recommend "several letters written by Joseph A. Scoville of this city, which were published in the London Morning Herald."[71]

He enclosed Scoville's card and address—an act that suggests Scoville and Barney had an active and ongoing correspondence. However, Scoville's letters in 1862 would reveal that Barney's allegiance to the government was not nearly as strong as Barney once claimed.

6

A Recusant Chaplain

The Methodists preach falling from grace, and seldom miss an opportunity to practice it.[1]
—Colonel William P. Wood

Charles H. Winder and Rose O'Neal Greenhow were not the only secessionist sympathizers arrested in the wake of the Union disaster at Bull Run. Realizing that the southern shore of Maryland was a sieve through which supplies were pouring into northern Virginia, Union detective Lafayette Baker attempted to close off the contraband trade by arresting prominent secessionists in Charles and Prince George's County east of Washington. On Monday, August 29, 1861, Major Innis N. Palmer and a detachment of the Second U.S. Cavalry arrested six men near the White Horse Tavern in Prince George's County, on the charge of providing aid and comfort to the Confederates.[2]

The arrested men included the owner of the tavern, slaveholder Henry Culver Thorn; George W. Smith, the former sheriff of Charles County who kept a hotel in Bryantown; and three men of the Kirby family, who owned extensive properties in Prince George's County.[3] Smith would later admit in a written statement that he aided in the transport of at least 200 boxes of guns from Anne Arundel County to the mouth of Pope's Creek on the Potomac, from whence they were conveyed by boat to Virginia. He had done so, he claimed, only because others had convinced him "that there was no wrong in what he did."[4]

Major Palmer took the six men to the county jail in Washington, known derisively as the "Blue Jug" for the dull blue color of its walls. Located at Judiciary Square, the Blue Jug had been "fouling up" the neighborhood there since 1838.[5] "It stands forth an architectural abortion," commented a journalist for the *Evening Star*, who visited the Prince George's County prisoners there. "It's repulsive appearance outside fitly shadowing forth the lack of comfort and convenience within."[6] The building's abhorrent appearance was exacerbated by wooden enclosures over the windows, which were added to prevent prisoners from hurling obscene verbal epithets against pedestrians on the street.[7]

Although jail conditions were poor, the newly arrested men were not unlike their jailers. The deputy marshal, George W. Phillips, was a staunch Democrat and had sympathies virtually identical to theirs.[8] Before the election of 1860, Phillips reportedly said that "the election of Mr. Lincoln was or would be a sectional matter and that the south would not and ought not to submit to it."[9] Jailer Amon Duvall later testified that Phillips would, against orders, authorize visitor passes for secessionists, in one case for three prisoners from Alabama, who were "taken with arms in their hands fighting against the government."[10]

Duvall was one of the few jailers at the Blue Jug who wasn't a Southern sympathizer. Despite this, he was promptly fired when he reported the incident regarding the Alabama prisoners, an action Marshal Ward Lamon attributed to his "incessant opposition to Deputy Marshal Phillips and his friends."[11] These so-called "friends" included former Washington mayor James G. Barrett and prominent Democratic attorney John E. Norris.[12] Barrett had been arrested on the suspicion of treason, but had been released upon giving an oath of allegiance; Norris, on the other hand, had written a letter sometime after Lincoln's election, debating whether he should remain in Washington, or "go back to Virginia and join the confederacy."[13]

John E. Norris' decision to stay in Washington was likely due to family considerations and his established law practice, rather than any loyalty to the Union. A measure of his support for slavery was a speech he made at a mass meeting of conservative Washington Democrats in 1867, when he predicted a future race war in which "the colored race would be swept from the face of the country," to the wild applause of his peers.[14]

Ironically, the five secessionists were confined adjacent to rooms full of African Americans, both free and enslaved, many of the latter being caught during failed bids for freedom. Although they welcomed the journalist from the *Star* with "broad grins," their smiles belied their condition, for as a Senate investigation later revealed, African Americans were routinely tortured there for trivial offenses or no offense at all, by a practice called "cobbing"—a punishment inflicted by tying the victim face down to a barrel, stripping off their clothes and then beating them with a heavy board.

"I have known as many as thirty odd blows administered at one time, with the whole strength of the person inflicting the punishment," Duvall later testified. "The superintendent sometimes inflicts the punishment, or some one of his deputies who may choose to do so, for there being no law for it they are not compelled to act."[15] No rules defined the offenses punishable by cobbing, nor were there any records kept of such punishments, once inflicted.

The conditions for African Americans at the county jail were so poor that the superintendent of the Old Capitol Prison, Colonel William P. Wood, advised several of them incarcerated there to stay with him, even after their release, for fear the civil authorities would rearrest them as fugitives. "I questioned several of them before I released them and warned them about the probability of their being recaptured by the civil authorities." Wood said of the matter. "They requested their discharge, as ordered, and were released. I believe that all of the said contrabands so released were taken and recommitted to the county jail in less than twenty-four hours after we released them."[16]

Wood was cut from a different cloth than Deputy Marshal George W. Phillips, despite having been born in Alexandria, Virginia, and resided in the conservative atmosphere of the District of Columbia. A cabinetmaker and inventor by trade, Wood was an early adherent of the Republican Party and an operator on the Underground Railroad before the war. He had gained the trust of attorney Edwin Stanton on a patent case involving the McCormick reaper in 1858, and Stanton undoubtedly remembered it when appointing him superintendent of the Old Capitol Prison in July 1861.[17]

William P. Wood was a funny sort of liberal. In 1847, at the outbreak of the Mexican War, Wood enlisted in a company of mounted rifles raised by Captain Samuel H. Walker.[18] Walker's company was stationed at Castle San Carlos de Perote to counter Mexican guerrilla activities, and as the war progressed, the fighting became increasingly brutal. According to John Jacob Oswandel of the First Pennsylvania Volunteers, Walker's mounted rifles had little compassion for their opponents. "Should Captain Walker come across guerillas, God help them, for he seldom brings in prisoners," Oswandel recorded in his diary. "The captain and most all of his men are very prejudiced and embittered against every guerila in the country."[19]

On October 5, 1847, Walker left Perote with General Joseph P. Lane to escort a supply train to Mexico City. Learning from spies that an enemy force was near Huamantla, Mexico, Walker attacked the village, capturing two artillery pieces. The Mexicans counterattacked, with anywhere from 2,000 to 3,000 lancers, and in the melee that followed, Walker was killed—reportedly shot twice by men in hiding. According to Oswandel, Walker's men resolved that after this, "they would take no prisoners, and death to all Mexicans found with firearms in their hands."[20] According to other sources, they did not confine the slaughter to armed Mexicans, but also took their revenge on the local population, raping and killing dozens of civilians in the wake of the battle.[21]

6. A Recusant Chaplain

Wood never blamed the horrors of the Mexican War for his loss of faith, but at some point, abandoned his Catholic faith in favor of being a committed atheist. "Bad hearted men wish to make falsehood pass for truth," he wrote in a letter to the *Washington Evening Star* in 1857, arguing that Christian communities were infested with "villainous vagabonds and cutthroats."[22] Choosing an alternative to traditional Christianity, Wood chose to live by the maxim of Thomas Paine, who once said "to do good is my religion."[23]

Wood's position as superintendent of the Old Capitol Prison allowed him to do just that. The Old Capitol was essentially a military prison, holding rebel prisoners, citizens suspected of disloyalty and so-called "military contrabands"—African Americans who were fugitives from military labor details. With assistance from Duvall, Wood "succeeded in having fifteen or sixteen released by an order from the provost marshal and obtained employment for them."[24]

Unlike the Old Capitol, the county jail held a variety of prisoners. At the time it was visited by the journalist of the *Evening Star*, it held not only the six secessionists and numerous African Americans, but a Union soldier who had shot and killed a regimental teamster two weeks before; another Union soldier thought mentally ill; a rebel surgeon named

Old Capitol Prison, Washington, 1866 (Library of Congress Prints and Photographs Division). Colonel William P. Wood supervised a variety of inmates here and still acted as Secretary of War Stanton's confidential spy. In 1861 he would often incarcerate escaped African Americans to protect them from being returned into slavery (Wm. R. Pywell and Alexander Gardner, photographers, *Old Capitol Prison*, Washington, D.C., ca. 1866. Photograph. Library of Congress, https://www.loc.gov/item/2007685827/).

Fleming; and two women from Maine, who had been arrested as prostitutes, despite their pleas of innocence. The most unusual of the lot, however, was the Rev. John Greene, the regimental chaplain of the Tenth Pennsylvania Reserves—described by the *Star* journalist as a "gentlemanly looking person, dressed in black cloth, with a blue cord down the seams of his pantaloons."[25]

Greene pled innocence and begged to have his name kept out of the paper. It was too late, however, as his arrest had already been reported elsewhere. "A clergyman in prison on the Sabbath day, charged with a criminal offence, was a sad sight," the *Evening Star* lamented.[26] The Reverend Greene had been arrested the day before near Georgetown at the direction of Washington postmaster Lewis Clephane, for pilfering the regimental mail.[27] Clephane had been alerted to Greene's activities by a shoe dealer, who reported that Greene came to his shop on High Street in Georgetown on August 20, professing to want a shoe repaired. After using the backyard privy, Greene was "in a hurry to get off," and left, claiming the shoe did not need much repair anyway.[28] Suspicious, the man checked the privy, only to find several opened envelopes, addressed to members of the Tenth Pennsylvania Reserves and Tenth Massachusetts Infantry.

Seeking more evidence, Clephane planted "decoy letters" with money enclosed on two consecutive days that week.[29] District police allowed Greene to pick up the mail in Washington on Saturday, August 24, but arrested him outside of Georgetown and returned him to Washington for questioning. Asked whether he had any mail for regiments other than his own, Greene replied that he had no letters at all. A search of his pockets, however, produced newspapers and several letters. Officer Aquilla R. Allen asked if that was all, to which Greene replied, "Yes," but when Allen searched his pockets, more letters appeared.[30]

"Do you have any letters back at camp other than those of your own regiment?" Allen asked.

"No," Greene replied.

"I will go and search your tent," Allen retorted.

"Gentlemen, I see you intend to carry this thing to the farthest extent.... Just name the amount of money, if it's a hundred dollars, I will raise it and give it to you, if you will let me return to my regiment and not to prison."[31]

Allen ignored the bribery attempt and ordered a search of Greene's trunk at Camp Tennally, which again found open mail to both regiments. Two of the decoy letters were found, two were not, but based on the evidence, Clephane was confident of a conviction. Greene was equally confident of an acquittal—telling Clephane that he thought there was not much of a case, given that "he didn't work for the Post Office Department."[32]

6. A Recusant Chaplain

Journalists reported that despite the damning evidence against him, Greene had "the admiration and respect of the entire regiment, and they were astounded at his arrest."[33]

Typical of his regiment's reaction was that of Private James D. Chadwick, who visited Greene at the Blue Jug, and wrote his father of the encounter:

> I visited Mr. Green as I told you I would.... Poor man! He was in great agony of mind. As soon as he saw me through the door, he called me to him. I went up to him and he reach[ed] out his hand through the iron bars and grasped mine with the energy of a drowning man. He said he was glad to see me, glad to know he had friends to sympathize with him in his trouble. He declared that he was *innocent* of the charge laid against him and appealed to God to witness the same. He talked about his wife and innocent babes that he had left behind him.[34]

Up until the day of his arrest, Greene had given members of the Tenth Pennsylvania Reserves no reason for suspicion. Shortly after Lincoln's call for 75,000 volunteers, Greene had helped form the West Middlesex Rangers, a unit which mustered on April 23, 1861. Although initially rejected because Pennsylvania had met its quota, the unit later became Company B of the Tenth Pennsylvania Reserves.[35]

At the outbreak of the war, Greene was pastor of the West Middlesex Methodist Episcopal Church and under his care had begun construction of a substantial brick structure for worship in 1861.[36] Characteristic of Greene's congregation was village postmaster David Farrell, a "consistent member of the Methodist Episcopal church" who, politically, was "always a Republican ... active in party circles and campaigns."[37]

On the strength of his success in West Middlesex, Greene was appointed Chaplain of the Tenth Pennsylvania Reserves, a commission announced at the Erie Annual Conference of the Methodist Episcopal Church, which met in July 1861 in Warren, Pennsylvania.[38] Private James D. Chadwick wrote home to his father about the appointment on August 2, 1861: "Rev. John Green is here; he preached in camp last Sunday; he has been chosen as Chaplain to Hays Regiment, but I do not know how long he will stay."[39] Chadwick trusted Greene implicitly, informing his father to send letters "direct to the care of Capt. Ayer or Chaplain Green, 10th Regiment, P.R.C."[40]

The Tenth Pennsylvania Reserves mustered at Camp Wilkins, established at the Pennsylvania Fairgrounds outside Pittsburgh, where residents of the city treated them as honored guests. According to one officer there, "The Ladies of the Liberty Methodist Episcopal Church on Saturday evening presented the Erie Regiment at Camp Wilkins with 500 pies which were distributed at a rate of fifty to each company."[41]

On the hot march from Washington to Camp Tennally in August, young Private Chadwick thought Greene's conduct exemplary. "Mr. Green, the Chaplain, walked along with the regiment all the way, ministering to the wants of the sick and thirsty soldiers," he wrote his father on August 8. "He is esteemed by every man in the regiment."[42] Thus, when Washington authorities arrested Greene later that month, Chadwick and other members of the regiment were shocked. "As Col. McCalmont had told me there was something wrong with the mail some way and rather seemed to think Mr. G[reene] might possibly be guilty, I thought he was, likely—guilty," Chadwick wrote his father. "It was hard to think so. But when I saw him and talked with him, the explanation which he gave of the affair compelled me to believe him innocent."[43]

There was one man in Washington who was not surprised at Greene's arrest—Murat Halstead, editor of the *Cincinnati Daily Commercial*, who was in Washington covering the war, recalled Greene from his early days as a journalist in Cincinnati a decade earlier. Halstead would later verify that Clephane's evidence was credible and that testimonials from Camp Tennally supported the conclusion that Greene was rifling through the regimental mails. "A poor boy in the regiment received from his poor widowed mother a letter inclosing a gold dollar which she said was all the money she had," Halstead recalled later. "The boy received the letter, but not the dollar."[44]

Despite his uncomfortable stay in the Blue Jug, Greene was released on bond by not one, but two Washington attorneys: John E. Norris and W.R. Woodward.[45] It was a curious event, as Norris and Woodward were not law partners, but rather, political opposites. Norris, as Amon Duvall later testified, was an ardent secessionist from Virginia, while Woodward was friendly enough with the new administration that he was appointed clerk of the District of Columbia in 1862.[46] Woodward may have been hired by officers of his regiment, but the appearance of Norris suggests that Southern sympathizers had an interest in Greene's defense.

Norris largely avoided the suspicion of authorities during the war, but his potential connection to the Confederate underground was revealed afterward, when his daughter Emma married former rebel scout Frank Hume in 1870.[47] Frank and his older brother, Charles Conner Hume, were both Washington natives—living a scant three blocks from Norris' house on Seventh Street West. When Charles Hume was killed by members of the Maryland Potomac Home Brigade in 1863 while working undercover for General J.E.B. Stuart, Frank Hume took his place.[48] Norris also welcomed former rebel spy Thomas Henry Harbin into the conservative Jackson Democratic Association in 1876, a group one historian later called "a militant political organization of Southerners."[49]

Although the evidence against Greene was compelling, the men of the Tenth Pennsylvania were unwilling to testify against their own chaplain. The regimental commander, Colonel John S. McCalmont, and ten other officers testified in court that they once thought money was missing, but then determined it was not. With no apparent victims, Greene was quickly acquitted.[50] Ironically, while newspapers were reporting his acquittal, the *Warren (PA) Mail* published a letter from a member of the regiment complaining that he had mysteriously received no mail from home. "I thought there was something in the wind," John G. Brower of Company H wrote from Camp Tennally on September 2. "I have not received a letter from home since I returned to camp; perhaps they were directed to the *dead letters office*."[51]

Private Chadwick explained the unusual situation with Chaplain Greene to his father in a letter home on September 9: "Mr. Green has left us and gone home, I guess. I rather think he has been dismissed from his position, although, as I stated in my last, he was acquitted.... There is something mysterious about him."[52] Although Private Chadwick thought there was something *mysterious* about Greene, no one at the time suspected him of espionage—even the police. There is, however, circumstantial evidence that he was not only stealing for himself but spying for the Confederacy simultaneously.

Greene would later admit that despite his enlistment in the Union army, he aided the Southern cause to satisfy his wife and in-laws:

> My wife's friends lived in Maryland and Virginia, and were, almost to a man, for John C. Breckinridge, and directly thereafter for secession. The first caused a coolness between us; the second almost an open rupture. At that time, a pro-slavery man, I was not however, a rebel. I advocated "peaceable secession"... I denounced the government at Washington for the bungling manner in which it attempted to coerce the South.... I said many hard things against the government; tried to prevent enlistments; found myself getting into trouble.[53]

Greene's enlistment in the Tenth Pennsylvania Reserves undoubtedly contributed to his marital distress. Unwilling to resign a position carrying the generous salary of a major, Greene may have chosen instead to work against the Federal government from within—just as Dr. John S. Conrad was doing at the Georgetown Hospital.

Had Greene simply been after the money, it would have been a simple matter to either dispose of the letters or deliver them; the fact that he hoarded them suggests there was potential value in the letters themselves—regimental strengths, troop movements, and strategic plans—the same intelligence Rose O'Neal Greenhow had conveyed to win the Battle of Manassas. Obtaining strategic information about Federal strength through seemingly innocent activities was nothing new when Greene arrived in Washington in August 1861. On June 24, 1861, John S. Emerson of Alexandria, Virginia, was arrested by order of General Mansfield for posing as a fictitious Lieutenant Hill of the Sixth Massachusetts. According to the arresting officer, "He mingled with the officers and men, talking with the sentinels and seemed desirous of ascertaining the position and strength of the Union forces in and about Alexandria."[54]

Greene's wife was the former Frances A. Cullison of Baltimore. Although her lineage is not well documented, she was likely the daughter of Micajah Cullison of Carroll County, for Greene admitted later to using her brother's name, M.M. Cullison, as an alias.[55] If so, she was also the sister of Jesse M. Cullison, a feed dealer who lived on West Biddle Street in Baltimore and owned substantial property near Hampstead.[56] In 1862, Jesse Cullison was likely an active member of Baltimore's Strawbridge Methodist Episcopal Church. His daughter Laura was married there in 1876 and the Cullisons had been active Methodists since early in the century, when they established the Cullison Meeting House in Carroll County, an old log church which was used for decades, until it was abandoned during the war because of the slavery issue, which caused a "schism among the members."[57]

The identity of Frances Greene's secessionist friends in Baltimore is unclear, but one of them was likely John W. Selby, who lived near her brother on West Biddle, and represented Strawbridge when the YMCA presented Lincoln with a peace memorial at the outbreak of the war.[58] Despite his pleas for peace, however, Selby was actively supplying the Confederate war machine. He was a principal in the dry goods firm of Lanier Brothers and Company of Baltimore—who throughout 1861 were providing supplies to the Confederate government via Harpers Ferry. The Lanier brothers had outfitted an entire company earlier that summer, the so-called "Lanier Guard" who became Company B, 13th Virginia Infantry.

One of the members of the Lanier Guard, F.M. Burrows, admitted later that many of them participated in the Pratt Street Riot.[59] The revelation by Burrows suggests that dry goods merchant Robert W. Davis, killed in the melee, may not have been as innocent as his inquest determined, for his firm of Pegram, Paynter and Davis was virtually next door to the Lanier Brothers store on the 200 block of West Baltimore Street.[60] Many of them had close personal and professional ties to Virginia and could not wait to join the rebellion below the border.

To get out of Baltimore en masse after the riot, members of the Lanier Guard feigned a funeral procession, hiding their firearms in the coffin. When safely out of the city, "the coffin was opened, and quickly each man was armed ... to join the young Confederacy."[61] Selby's brother, Joseph

Selby, was one of the company's lieutenants, while another brother, James Selby, served in the ranks. John Selby, acting on behalf of Lanier Brothers, supplied them—as evidenced by numerous receipts from the Confederate War Department.[62]

Greene had ample opportunity to visit his in-laws in Baltimore on his way to Camp Tennally, for according to Private James Chadwick, the regiment had "gone to Washington, via Baltimore" sometime before July 24, 1861.[63] If Greene became an intelligence operative for the Confederacy, it was then, as there were numerous connections between the Methodist Episcopal Church in Baltimore and partisans in Virginia. Strawbridge member John W. Selby traveled south from Baltimore on behalf of Lanier Brothers at the same time as Greene and could have personally introduced him to rebel operatives in Washington—including the Conrad brothers, as Nelson Conrad, like Selby, was a dry goods merchant who lived just blocks from the Lanier Brothers' store on West Baltimore Street before the war.[64]

Selby made his journey south on behalf of Lanier Brothers via Washington in late July or early August 1861, after which he ventured on to Richmond "for the purpose of attending to the settlement of some business affairs."[65] According to Tom Conrad's autobiography, he was living with his parents in Georgetown at that time, so a meeting between them and Selby was entirely possible—as Nelson Conrad, like the Lanier Brothers, had numerous business connections in northern Virginia which he undoubtedly wished to maintain with the help of an intermediary like Selby.[66]

Upon returning home, John Selby was arrested by Federal authorities at Sandy Hook, Maryland, across the river from Harpers Ferry, on the charge of treason, apparently on the basis that he was carrying letters from Richmond back to Baltimore.[67] After a short stay in Fort McHenry, he was released after agreeing to take the oath of allegiance, which he did on August 16, 1861.[68] Despite his oath, Selby later joined the 21st Virginia Infantry, while Lanier simply moved his headquarters to Richmond and continued to supply the Confederate government on a contract basis from there.[69]

Nelson Conrad moved his business to Leonardtown in St. Mary's County, where he advertised "quick sales and small profits."[70] The move to Leonardtown, located on the so-called "lower route" to Virginia, may have been designed to facilitate continued business with Richmond, just as Lanier Brothers had done, for as one newspaper noted in December 1861, "A very extensive trade has for a long time been carried on by that county and Virginia."[71] He was arrested briefly by military authorities in 1864, but released unconditionally after authorities declared there was a "misapprehension of facts" associated with his arrest.[72]

Whether John Selby introduced Greene to the Conrad brothers or other members of the Confederate underground while on his way to Richmond is speculative, but the shoe store on High Street near Bridge, where Greene hastily opened letters to his regiment, was only a stone's throw from the Conrad's Georgetown Institute on Dumbarton Street. Greene, however, clearly chose the wrong privy at which to open letters. Despite its convenient location on the way to Camp Tennally, the owner was a serious-minded man who had almost lost a hand ten years earlier from mishandled explosives.[73]

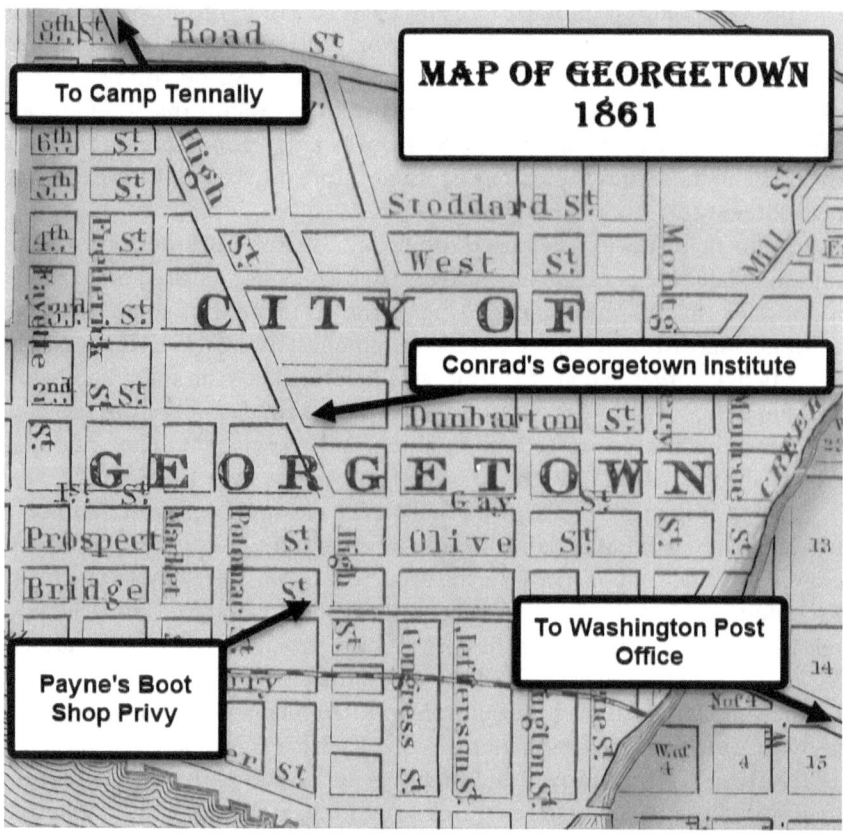

Georgetown, 1861 (1870 base map from Library of Congress, Geography and Map Division). The map highlights the proximity of Thomas Conrad's Georgetown Institute to the privy of boot maker Lewis Payne, where John Wesley Greene chose to rifle through the regimental mail on his way back to Camp Tennally. The location, in addition to Greene's later admissions, suggests Greene was acting as a rebel informant in addition to lining his own pockets (A.J. Johnson, *Johnson's Washington and Georgetown* [New York: A.J. Johnson, 1870]. Map. Library of Congress, https://www.loc.gov/item/88693476/).

6. A Recusant Chaplain

The Georgetown shoemaker was Lewis Payne. Today, his name is infamous as the alias of another figure, Lewis Thornton Powell, who together with John Wilkes Booth engaged in the conspiracy to kill President Lincoln in 1865. The coincidence suggests the Confederate underground selected Payne's name as the alias to exact revenge for his ratting on Greene to Lewis Clephane in 1861. Clephane, after all, was no ordinary postmaster.

Six years earlier, Clephane and four other men had met secretly in Washington and conceived of the idea of forming a national club to oppose slavery, which they christened the "National Republican Association of Washington." Consisting variously of Democrats, Whigs, Know-Nothings, and members of the so-called Free-soil Party, the group held that slavery should not be extended to any territory of the United States and that the power of the Federal government outside states already committed to slavery should be to exert "life, liberty and the pursuit of happiness to all men."[74]

The idea of excluding slavery from the territories and limiting its reach was so radical in 1855 Washington that Clephane, the "moving spirit" of the group, would later admit that the original signers risked "perpetual ostracism" by the community in which they lived, just for putting their name to such a platform.[75] Nevertheless, they became the nucleus of the Republican Party which occupied the White House in 1861. Since there was only one Lewis Payne in the Washington-Georgetown area during the war, it seems unlikely that the use of his name as an alias was mere happenstance, especially since John Wesley Greene reemerged in Washington a year later, professing to be the unofficial ambassador of Confederate president Jefferson Davis.[76]

7

Loudoun County Scouts

[Reverend] Averitt went to Winchester yesterday.... He is a very clever gentleman ... but I fear is too tender for a soldier's life.[1]

—Captain Nathaniel Dawson, 1861

At the Georgetown Institute, Thomas Conrad had gotten the name nickname "the Reverend" for his dual duties as instructor and evangelist.[2] He was, therefore, entirely comfortable impersonating a chaplain as he crossed the Potomac to gather or deliver intelligence. Among his wardrobe, he kept not only a Confederate uniform, but a Union chaplain's uniform—not unlike that worn by John Wesley Greene in the Blue Jug. In his autobiography, Conrad suggests that he was appointed chaplain of the Third Virginia Cavalry "at Major Ball's suggestion" soon after his arrival within rebel lines.[3] Confederate service records, however, show that Conrad wasn't formally appointed to that duty until September 30, 1863—suggesting that in his autobiography he attempted to legitimize his nefarious use of chaplain's garb early in the war.[4]

Tom Conrad used two routes to slip into Washington, crossing the lower Potomac below Washington and crossing at the upper fords near Poolesville. There were two ferry crossings near Poolesville—Conrad's Ferry, which dated back to 1786 and operated with a flatboat attached to a 300-yard cable stretched across the river, and Edwards Ferry six miles east, on the direct road from Poolesville to Leesburg, Virginia.[5] Parallel to the river on the Maryland side ran the Chesapeake and Ohio Canal, which allowed goods to travel downriver despite the numerous rapids.

Conrad knew the area well and often used it to cross from Maryland to Virginia. One of his first missions was to smuggle two Europeans through the lines to negotiate a loan for the Confederacy, using a "farmer friend" who lived on the river near Poolesville to guide them across a ford in the night.[6] Conrad never revealed the man's identity, but the description aptly fits Samuel C. Young, who owned a large farm near Edwards Ferry, including the property between the canal and the river.

Young, who held 13 people enslaved near Edwards Ferry in 1860, had no love for the federal government.[7] In June 1861, Federal forces set up camp on three acres and confiscated several outbuildings for their use. Then in October, as Federal forces prepared for what would become the Battle of Ball's Bluff, an African American named Henry Warren escaped from him, and according to a fugitive slave advertisement taken out by Young, was "supposed to be in some of the Federal encampments."[8]

Brigadier General Charles P. Stone later testified to the Joint Committee on the Conduct of the War about the probable fate of Henry Warren. According to Stone:

> One slave came into my camp announcing himself as a slave and stating that he had been employed on some fortifications on the other side.... Shortly after, the son of the man who had this slave in his employ came and wanted to withdraw him, and I refused, on the ground that I had no jurisdiction over the man; that he came under the rules that he had been employed on rebel earthworks, as I was informed, and the man was not given up.[9]

The Young family remained so bitter that, in 1909, the heirs to his property successfully sued the Federal government for the value of the property they "leased" from the family, almost 50 years before.[10]

Despite not giving up Henry Warren, Federal forces allowed Young's family an extraordinary degree of freedom. Since Young owned and cultivated a portion of Harrison's Island in the Potomac River, a Union officer later testified that General Stone had given Young a pass "giving him the right to pass to the island and back again whenever he pleased without any questions being asked."[11] Young was a known secessionist with a son in the Confederate army, yet there was virtually nothing to keep him from smuggling arms or intelligence into Virginia on the authority of his pass. Under low flow conditions, the officer testified, it was possible to ride from the island to Virginia "on horseback, in wagons or any way they see fit."[12]

Across the Potomac River from Poolesville lies Loudoun County, Virginia—a domain controlled in 1861 by Colonel Turner Ashby's Seventh Virginia Cavalry, an elite unit made of the best horsemen northern Virginia could produce. "Ashby had not to deal with conscripts," one biographer wrote after the war. "His command was made up of those who, sharing his enthusiasm, followed him from love of the cause of which they regarded him the faithful representative."[13] Ashby and his men held a picket line some 75 to 80 miles along the banks of the Potomac which Ashby would inspect in a single day, and after a night's sleep, "be as fresh as ever."[14]

The nucleus of Ashby's regiment was the Faquir Mountain Rangers, a Virginia militia company which Turner had led since at least 1859, when they responded to the John Brown raid on Harpers Ferry.[15] Even before the war, his men held him in the highest esteem. In March 1860, they presented him with a service of silver, "as a testimonial to their high appreciation of his ability as an officer, and his worth as a gentleman."[16] Shortly after Virginia seceded, Ashby offered the services of his company to Major General Kenton Harper of the Virginia militia and was quickly assigned to guard the fords and crossings of the Potomac near Harpers Ferry. His men often acted as spies during this period, entering the city of Washington "disguised in citizens dress."[17] One of these may have been Private Thomas Benton Gatch, who had attended medical school with John Conrad before the war.[18]

When Colonel Angus McDonald sought to form a regiment to defend the Virginia border along the upper Potomac, Turner Ashby's "Mountain Rangers" were his first choice. They became company A of the Seventh Virginia Cavalry on June 17, 1861, together with nine other companies from northern Virginia. McDonald soon drafted an Episcopal minister serving as a private in the Fourth Alabama Infantry to be his regimental chaplain. "Rev. James B. Averitt of the Episcopal Church has been induced by me to accompany the command as acting Chaplain of the regiment," he explained to the Confederate War Department. "Aside from the positive good to the command, the charges of land pirates and other unenviable sobriquets already preferred against us as parties to this partisan warfare may be the more fully met and refuted."[19]

As a result of McDonald's request, Averitt would be the first commissioned chaplain in the Confederate army. More importantly, it was a signal that in an ugly partisan war along the border, rebel chaplains would be used not only to save souls, but as a tool of propaganda and subterfuge. The 26-year-old Episcopal minister was perfect for this role, for as his friend and former commanding officer, Captain Nathanial Dawson, once confided, Averitt was "a very clever gentleman."[20]

Raised in North Carolina, Averitt had practiced law before joining the ministry in Alabama in 1859.[21] A prolific author after the war, he always wore his Confederate uniform when he made a speech and, according to one contemporary, "was a Confederate first and a Confederate last."[22] Like Ashby, he viewed slavery as a blessing to African Americans, rather than a curse—a position he advocated in his postwar book *The Old Plantation*, extolling the virtues of the antebellum South. "In no time in the history of our race has there ever been seen a peasantry so happy and in every respect so well to do, as the negro slaves of America," he would later write.[23]

The day after McDonald wrote to the War Department seeking a commission for Averitt, a vicious little skirmish highlighted his usefulness. It started with Ashby's decision to arrest a Union man who lived near the Baltimore and Ohio Railroad who reportedly had given him "considerable trouble."²⁴ Splitting his small command, he assigned a squad of seven men to his brother, Captain Richard Ashby, who didn't find the man but did find a troop of the Eleventh Indiana Infantry, known as Wallace's Zouaves, hidden in the gorges along the railroad. The troop consisted of 13 mounted scouts under the command of Mexican War veteran David B. Hay.

A running fight ensued over a mile of the railroad grade until Hay's horse was shot from under him. The momentum of the Hoosiers waned, as Hay himself was shot in the shoulder and hip, with a saber cut across the head.²⁵ They fell back and regrouped on Kelley's Island, an island in the Potomac River which afforded them natural protection. Turner Ashby, alerted by the sound of the guns, sprinted to his brother's aid and together they charged, "fording the river under a destructive fire."²⁶ Once on the island, a desperate hand-to-hand melee ensued.

According to Indiana scout Thomas Wise Durham, Richard Ashby was about to run one of his comrades through with a bowie knife when another of them swung his rifle like a club with such force that the gun stock shattered against Ashby's skull and "drove the hammer into the captain's head."²⁷ The Indiana Zouaves were forced to withdraw but Turner Ashby was dismayed to find his brother nearly dead. "Dick Ashby was terribly cut up, one of his eyes being shot out, and his head and neck badly cut by balls," wrote a member of the regiment to the *Baltimore American*. "I received the above account from two of Ashby's own men who were in the fight. As their accounts tally, I suppose them to be correct."²⁸ Ashby's eye was likely not shot, but rather, ruined by the effect of the gun hammer as it crashed into his head—a result closely matching Durham's version of events.

Regimental chaplain James B. Averitt would have heard the same account, for the trooper who wrote the *Baltimore American* noted that "upon hearing of the fight I immediately started for the scene of action, asking the chaplain [Averitt] to accompany me, which he willingly did."²⁹ Despite the firsthand account by two of Ashby's own troopers, Averitt recorded a quite different story of the wounds in his postwar biography of Turner Ashby. In this alternate version of events, a wounded and helpless Richard Ashby, surrounded by the enemy, receives a "bayonet thrust by the hand of a creature, whom to call a man were inhuman."³⁰ Accounts in many Southern newspapers reported something similar, the *Richmond Enquirer* reporting that he was "bayoneted twice."³¹

Ashby was carried on a litter to the mansion of Colonel George W. Washington near Romney, Virginia. He lingered for a week under a surgeon's care, until he died on July 3, 1861. "We all believed a part of the time that he would recover, at one time he thought so too," Turner Ashby wrote their sister after his death. "But the exposure without attention for several hours upon the battlefield so prostrated him as to make it hard for reaction to take place, which kept him from having any appetite."[32] As bayonet wounds are almost always fatal, it is difficult to imagine his recovery if he had been run through, as Averitt claimed.

Averitt's allegation that Union soldiers bayoneted a helpless Ashby may have originated from the fact that his own men had perpetrated the same atrocity. The Indiana Zouaves had been forced to leave a scout named Hollenbeck behind, shot through the bowels, when they retreated from Kelley's Island. Returning later with reinforcements, they discovered his fate. "His body was found about a mile and a half from the [battle]ground, with seven gun shot and bayonet wounds in him," recorded a correspondent for the *Indiana Journal*. "His body was yet warm when found—There is no doubt that he was murdered after being taken prisoner."[33]

Colonel Angus McDonald's prediction to the War Department that Ashby's Rangers would be accused of piracy was quickly coming true. As McDonald had alluded, Averitt's job was to refute them. In this regard, he acted more as lawyer than chaplain. Captain Nathaniel Dawson divulged to his fiancée that Averitt was not entirely well suited to the conventional ministry. "He is extremely fickle and impressible and lacks many of the elements to make a successful man," Dawson offered, shortly after Averitt's appointment as chaplain. "Mr. A. is unstable, was in love with Miss Washington, a young lady at Lynchburg, and with Miss Williams all at once."[34]

Ashby's command would be joined in September by an enthusiastic recruit named Harry Gilmor, who had been arrested by Federal authorities after the Pratt Street Riot but who traveled south not long after his release.[35] The 23-year-old Gilmor had been raised at his father's magnificent estate, Glen Ellen, in Baltimore County—where Federal authorities arrested him on July 5, 1861, for what Gilmor himself called his "secessionist activities."[36] He had been a member of the Baltimore County Horse Guards, a militia company which trained in the yard next to the courthouse in Towson and which reportedly burned three bridges after the riot to prevent the movement of Federal troops.

Upon crossing the upper Potomac on August 31, 1861, Gilmor sought out Ashby, whom he found at Camp Turner near Charlestown, "lying on the lawn surrounded by his men, among whom I recognized several who had been comrades in Captain Charles Ridgeley's company of Baltimore County Horse Guards."[37] Ashby joined Company G, commanded by Dr. John Francis Mason of Loudoun County, Virginia—who had among his company a significant number of Marylanders. Among them was First Lieutenant Thomas Sturgis Davis of Towson, Maryland, who would be elected captain by the end of the year, perhaps in part because he was a "tall, well-proportioned and strikingly handsome man."[38] Because of men like Davis, Company G maintained an identity of being a "Maryland command" within a Virginia regiment.[39]

In a traditional command, serving with men from your hometown might be the primary attraction for recruits like Harry Gilmor. In Ashby's regiment, however, command structure meant little, for the regiment covered miles of the upper Potomac. The greater attraction was the freedom of action as a partisan ranger. On the night he arrived, in fact, Gilmor went on a "scouting expedition" led by Private Elijah Viers White, a native of Poolesville, Maryland, where Thomas Nelson Conrad crossed the Potomac with loan officers from Europe. Although he was attached to Frank Mason's company of Marylanders under Ashby's command, the man called "Lige" White by his friends became "a most valuable scout" during the summer of 1861, operating primarily in Loudoun County under Brigadier General Nathan "Shank" Evans.[40]

Elijah White was the son of Mary Elizabeth Viers and Dr. Stephen Newton White of Montgomery County, Maryland.[41] According to his obituary in 1860, his father "engaged in the practice of medicine in Medley's District for a number of years and endeared to a large number of its inhabitants by acts of friendship and kindness."[42] The 1850 census lists him simply as a farmer, but by the time of his death, Stephen White had "acquired an ample competence of fortune."[43] He was, in fact, wealthy enough to have as many as 36 African Americans enslaved to work his farm near Edwards Ferry but, preoccupied with his medical practice, left the management of it to an overseer. One of the enslaved, Phillip Johnson, was interviewed in the 1930s about his childhood at the Whites'. "We all liked the missus," Johnson said, but added that the overseer was "so cruel.... I promised him a killin' if I ever got big enough."[44]

In 1861, members of the White and Viers families populated much of the countryside north of the Potomac near Poolesville. "Most of the people about here were known to be secessionists," Union officer William B. Lapham noted about the area. "Many of the families here furnished men for White's marauders and were in almost constant communication with the guerilla chief. White's father lived within a short distance of our encampment and rockets were sometimes sent up from his house in the night, doubtless as signals to his son on the other side of the river."[45]

Despite spending four years at colleges in the North, "Lige" White was an enthusiastic proponent of both maintaining slavery in the South and extending it to the western territories. He had travelled to Missouri in 1855 to fight with a pro-slavery militia in the Kansas-Nebraska border war, was a corporal in the "Loudoun Cavalry" in 1859 when John Brown raided Harpers Ferry, and proudly claimed to have captured the first Yankee of the Civil War.⁴⁶ On his return from Kansas, he purchased a 355-acre estate north of Leesburg in Loudoun County—across the Potomac from where he had been raised.⁴⁷ "It is in the midst of a fertile and picturesque country," the *Loudoun Mirror* would later write about the area, noting that from nearby Mount Gilead, "you can take in a panoramic view of nearly all of Loudoun County, with the views of the Cobler Mountains in Fauquier and the Sugar-loaf in Maryland."⁴⁸

There were few men who knew the terrain of the upper Potomac River as well as White. This knowledge would prove priceless when Union forces under Brigadier General Charles P. Stone conducted a reconnaissance in force near Harrison's Island in October 1861, an action which would culminate in the Battle of Ball's Bluff, a fight which would catapult White's career but ruin others—including Stone's. Although Confederates named it the Battle of Leesburg, it was Ball's Bluff—a 600-yard-long cliff rising from the floodplain of the Potomac—that would help them inflict a disastrous defeat upon Stone's forces.⁴⁹

Upon taking command of Union forces near Washington in August 1861, Major General George B. McClellan allowed Stone the flexibility to cross the Potomac into Virginia, if he saw "the opportunity of capturing or dispersing any small party by crossing," but stressed that "great discretion is recommended in making such a movement."⁵⁰ With this conditional

Looking up the Potomac River from Fort Sumner, near Washington, D.C., 1861–1865 (Library of Congress Prints and Photographs Division). In 1861, Turner Ashby's forces kept a close watch on the upper fords across the river and recruited men from lower Maryland, assets that would prove useful later in the war (Andrew J. Russell, photographer, *Looking up the Potomac River, from Fort Sumner* [between 1861 and 1865]. Photograph. Library of Congress, https://www.loc.gov/item/2004680103/).

authorization, Stone set about preparing for such a crossing by constructing several flat-bottomed scows and constructing limited entrenchments on Harrison's Island, near Conrad's Ferry. Unfortunately for Stone, he vastly overestimated the capacity of the boats and grossly underestimated the strength of Confederate forces opposite Harrison's Island—as well as the difficulties of crossing the river adjacent to the island, where the channel was narrow and the current fast when the river was high.

Ironically, Elijah White was home on furlough when he heard the first sounds of a battle along the Potomac River. Finding General Evans hopelessly drunk, he volunteered to serve as a scout to individual regiments and was "assigned the duty of placing commands in advantageous positions."[51] If one man could be credited with the Confederate victory, it was White. "Mr. White of Colonel Ashby's cavalry volunteered his services during the day," Col W.H. Jenifer recorded in his official report. "I never witnessed more coolness and courage than this young gentleman displayed, being exposed to the heaviest fire of the enemy. He rode in front of a part of the Seventeenth Mississippi cheering and encouraging the men."[52]

Near dusk, the Union line collapsed. Unable to recross the river with any semblance of order, many men threw their rifles in the river and swam to the Maryland shore. Others huddled along the riverbank. Colonel Epa Hutton of the Eighth Virginia Infantry, wary of what might transpire in the darkness, requested White help man his forward picket line. "He did so," Hutton reported later, "and by his intimate knowledge of the country and daring courage rendered great service."[53]

Guiding a band of 40 men in the darkness, White forced 325 exhausted Union soldiers along the river to surrender. Although the men were commanded by Captain William N. Berkeley, White was the true leader of the little band—despite not being a part of the unit and holding no rank. According to his chief biographer, Frank M. Meyers, White "posted Lieut. Berkeley on top of the bluff, just over the Yankees, while he moved the remainder down to the edge of the river and charged ... yelling like demons."[54]

The aftermath of the battle was sobering. A reporter riding across the terrain described the scene:

> The limbs of trees all around are marked by bullets, the decaying and odorous carcases of dead horses lay in frequent and unpleasant proximity to us, tattered hats, pieces of clothing, bits of equipment, rooting hogs and browsing cows were scattered here and there in all directions, while the hoarse cawing of the ill-omened crow formed a fitting accompaniment to the dismal panoramic view.[55]

The disaster for Union arms proved a windfall to rebel quartermasters, and weapons of all sorts were quickly scavenged from the field.

Elijah White was quickly recommended for an officer's commission and found recruiting in Leesburg to be effortless. As his biographer Frank Meyers later noted, many members of the local militia were busy constructing fortifications, and "it was natural to suppose that many of them would prefer ranging service on the border to wielding the shovel and the hoe in the breastworks."[56] White also garnered a significant number from the Maryland side, where he had been raised. Union officer William B. Lapham later recorded that "there was a mixture of rebel and Union people along the Maryland side…. Many of the sons of the rebel families were in Lee's army and oftentimes the head of the family would serve with White's guerillas. It was known that they occasionally visited their homes, arriving after dark and leaving before day."[57]

The success of White's charge along the south shore of the Potomac at Ball's Bluff undoubtedly caused him to replicate the maneuver on numerous occasions, thereafter, giving rise to his command being labeled "White's Comanche's." Frank Meyers admitted as much when describing an attack by White's Battalion at the Battle of Brandy Station in 1863, when they charged their opponents with "yells that a 'Comanche' might envy."[58] The Confederate army would fall back from the Potomac River position in the months following the Battle of Ball's Bluff, but Elijah White would always feel at home crossing the Potomac into Maryland in the countryside where he was raised and where numerous families supported him. This familiarity would prove valuable in 1862, when the Confederate government engaged in surreptitious missions to Washington and Baltimore.

8

Redeeming Their Tarnished Honor

I beg that instead of being thrust out in disgrace, I may be permitted to redeem the tarnished honor of names which brighten the pages of our history from '76 to 1815.[1]
—William Chase Barney, 1862

The Battle of Ball's Bluff catapulted Private Elijah V. White to command of a battalion of Confederate cavalry; for many Union officers, however, it resulted in ignominious disgrace or death. How and why the battle happened at all was the subject of acrimonious debate in Washington for months. The battle was precipitated by Union brigadier general Charles P. Stone, who commanded three brigades in what was called the Corps of Observation, responsible for guarding the ferry crossings near Poolesville, Maryland.

A West Point graduate and Mexican War veteran, Stone had come out of retirement on January 2, 1861, to prepare the defense of Washington—a task he performed admirably, given that militia companies like the National Rifles of Washington were populated by what he called "openly declared secessionists" when he took command.[2] Despite his early success fortifying Washington, Stone seems to have been ill-prepared to cross the Potomac and his efforts to do so resulted in not only the rout of Union forces, but the death of Colonel Edmund Dickinson Baker of the 71st Pennsylvania Infantry, who was in the unique position of being both a regimental commander and a sitting United States senator, having been elected to the Senate from Oregon in 1860.

Baker had befriended Abraham Lincoln in Springfield, Illinois, during the 1840s and the two were so close that Lincoln named his second son Edward Baker Lincoln in his honor. Baker, in turn, helped establish the Republican Party in California and Oregon and proved to be one of Lincoln's most enthusiastic supporters. When Lincoln was inaugurated earlier that year, Baker gave the introduction to his inaugural address.³ Baker had intended to raise his regiment on behalf of the State of California—thus it became known as the "California Regiment," even though it was populated largely by men from Philadelphia.

Although a lawyer and politician by profession, Baker had led Illinois troops with distinction in the Mexican War and Stone considered him a "gallant and energetic officer."⁴ Perhaps for this reason, Stone ordered him to assume command of Union forces at Ball's Bluff, giving him the discretion to move troops across the river or to withdraw them, as he saw fit.⁵ Stone had cautioned him that "no advance [be] made unless the enemy be in inferior force," but Baker knew little about what confronted him on the Virginia shore.⁶

When Baker fell in the subsequent firefight, his shattered body was turned over to Lieutenant Francis G. Young, his regimental quartermaster and personal aide. It was not a pleasant task. By one estimate, the body contained eight gunshot wounds, including "one large wound in his left temple" which, according to Young, caused the battle orders Baker had put in his hat to be covered in his "blood and brains."⁷

Over the next three days, Young bore the body back to Washington with the aid of several members of the Third New York Cavalry. Coincidentally, Young met a friend on the road to Washington, the war correspondent Edmund C. Stedman of the *New York World*. "I had started for Edward's Ferry this evening," wrote Stedman from Washington on October 23, "but meeting the procession, have returned with my friend Capt. Young, from whose lips I take down the following terrible summary of Monday's events."⁸ Stedman rode no further, recording in his diary that he had come down with what he described as "bilious remittent fever."⁹

Stedman's written report of the battle, taken from the lips of Francis G. Young, provided a chilling account of the Union debacle and recovery of Baker's body:

> I got the Colonel's body to the island before the worst of the rout, and then looking to the Virginia shore, saw such a spectacle as no tongue can describe. Our entire forces were retreating, tumbling, rolling, leaping down the steep heights; the enemy following, murdering, and taking prisoners.... A thousand men thronged the bank. Muskets, coats, and everything were thrown aside, and all were desperately trying to escape. Hundreds plunged into the rapid current, and the shrieks of the drowning added to the horror.¹⁰

Young's narrative was so graphic that government telegraph operators refused to transmit it, but Stedman recorded in his diary that it was "the only accurate and synthetic account [of the] late battle."¹¹

Unfortunately for Young, a correspondent for the *New York Herald* embellished the story. "It should be stated that the safety of the remains of

8. Redeeming Their Tarnished Honor 83

Death of Colonel Baker at Ball's Bluff, 1861 (Library of Congress Prints and Photographs Division). Baker's quartermaster, Lieutenant Francis G. Young, took possession of Baker's body at the Potomac River and escorted it back to Washington. Young was an attorney by profession, and his battlefield accounts aggressively defended Baker but conflicted with other accounts. Although he reportedly rode with President Lincoln in Baker's funeral procession, his acquaintance with the president didn't prevent his dismissal for disobedience of orders early the following year (F.O.C. Darley, *Death of Col. Baker at Ball's Bluff near Leesburg, Va. in the Civil War*, ca. 1862. Steel engraving by H. Wright Smith. Library of Congress, https://www.loc.gov/item/2003663456/).

General Baker was owing to the timely and self-sacrificing exertions of the Quartermaster of his brigade, Captain Young," crowed the *Herald*. "Captain Young was near General Baker when he fell. He seized his body, and was carrying it off, when he was encountered by a party of five rebels, who attempted to take the remains from him. He used his two navy revolvers, and four of the rebels bit the dust."[12]

The *Herald* account earned Young nothing but the enmity of his colleagues. Lieutenant Colonel Wistar of the California Regiment later called Young "a coward and a liar who was at no time within 2 miles of the battlefield," while Lieutenant Henry Livermore Abbott of the Twentieth Massachusetts urged his father to "disbelieve all ridiculous yarns about a certain

California Capt."[13] Young himself attributed the retrieval of Baker's body to others in his later testimony before Congress, stating, "Captain Bierol, Captain Hicks, and others, ran up and got the body, and brought it back to where I was; and I went down the hill with it and came across the river.... I got over on the Maryland side and put the body in an ambulance and ... went on to Poolesville with the body; gave it over to the undertaker there."[14]

While in Poolesville, Lieutenant Young took the extraordinary step of telegraphing President Lincoln personally with the news of Baker's death, before bringing the body to Washington.[15] Years later, in a letter to a friend, Young recalled Lincoln's reaction at viewing the body of his old friend and colleague. "Baker has gone," Lincoln reportedly exclaimed in grief, "and my heart will go down into his grave with him, and I don't care what comes next!"[16]

At the funeral that week, the *Washington Evening Star* noted that "the grief of such members of Col. Bakers immediate command as were present seemed to know no bounds."[17] Lieutenant Young sat near the president and Mrs. Lincoln during the funeral ceremony, and noted that Mrs. Lincoln was "sobbing audibly," while she "whispered some incidents regarding her last meeting with Baker, just a few days before."[18]

Despite his brief intimacy with the president, Young was soon under arrest. Stationed at Camp Observation near Poolesville, he had applied to his new commanding officer for a pass to travel to Washington. After the request was denied on the basis that his quartermaster duties were being neglected, Young applied twice more with the same result. Finally, he left anyway, allegedly telling a fellow office that he had "run away" and was going to New York.[19]

A general court-martial of Lieutenant Young was held in accordance with Special Order No 153 from the Headquarters of the Army of the Potomac, dated November 22, 1861. Pleading not guilty on three separate charges, Young quickly appealed to the president. Lincoln, in turn, wrote to Major General George B. McClellan, commander of the Army of the Potomac, asking if "the past, whatever it is, cannot be waived and he placed in service, and given another chance?"[20] Young was copied on Lincoln's letter, but rather than being grateful for the president's extraordinary intervention in a military court-martial, he was instead offended. "You have deemed me to be an obscure and friendless person, seeking your favor through your affection for Col Baker," he complained. "I did not then know that you thought me untruthful and unworthy of your friendship."[21]

Admitting that his relations with most of the California Regiment were hopelessly ruined, Young begged the president for an appointment as a brigade quartermaster elsewhere, based on Baker's verbal promise to promote him. "I had been regularly appointed by Col Baker and he promised me to see to my commission," Young pleaded to Lincoln. "Two days before he was killed, he told me and several officers that he intended to write a private letter to Secretary of War and have me appointed."[22] Predictably, neither Lincoln nor McClellan intervened further in the court-martial, but Young would thereafter refer to himself as a captain, to reflect the rank he thought he deserved.[23]

He pled not guilty to the charges against him, on the basis that Baker authorized him to travel with no restriction before his death. Nevertheless, he was found guilty on two of three charges and was promptly cashiered from the army, effective January 2, 1862.[24] Although Young should not have been surprised by the verdict, he was crestfallen. "By order of General McClellan, I am cashiered and dismissed from the service of the United States," he wrote Lincoln on January 7. "My overzeal for my Regiment and in defending the memory of Col Baker are the real causes of my trouble.... Mr. President, as God Knows all things, I am not deserving of this terrible punishment upon me and all those who bear my name."[25]

Young had one more chance to redeem his reputation. On January 16, 1861, he testified at length before the Joint Committee on the Conduct of the War, which was investigating the entire Ball's Bluff debacle. During the proceedings, he stayed at Willard's Hotel in Washington and conversed with a variety of officers and legislators. Through these discussions, Young became convinced that his termination was due to his criticism of Union leadership and "unkind things" said by Lincoln—rather than his own direct disobedience of orders, which he characterized as but "technical."[26]

Feeling betrayed, Young wrote Lincoln a fourth time on February 7, 1862, from the Brevoort House in New York, to express his dismay over rumors being circulated about him by McClellan's staff. "I beg you will cease to speak of me as you have done to many persons," he wrote. "Already have I suffered greatly by reason of your remarks."[27] Young felt particularly hurt by the perceived snub from the president because of his long involvement in Republican politics, arguing that "long before I ever met you, I did you good service."[28] Once again, such complaints helped him little. Discouraged, he seems to have placed his faith in another former officer dismissed from the service—William Chase Barney.

Exactly how and when Barney and Young first met is unclear. A native of Geneva, New York, Young graduated from Hobart College there in 1848 and by 1853 had established a law practice in New York City.[29] An early adherent to the Republican Party, he was a member of the Young Men's Republican General Committee in New York City in 1856—one reason why Baker may have appointed him regimental quartermaster on June 28, 1861.[30] Despite their political differences, Young, like Barney, seemed obsessed with the accumulation of wealth, observing in his youth that "the poor have but few joys."[31]

During the 1850s, both Barney and Young maintained offices in lower Manhattan, where in 1859, Young became the agent for Hector Jennings of Ohio, a reputed heir to the William Jennings fortune in England, estimated to be worth as much $200 million.[32] By the mid–1850s, however, most experts recognized that there was no fortune left to be had. When a woman from Newark, claiming to be the daughter of William Jennings, posted a notice in the *New York Dispatch* in October 1854, seeking information on how to claim her fortune, a sympathetic and knowledgeable reader responded that the "chances of coming into possession of his property are exceedingly slim…. The scheme of setting this claim on foot was gotten up by starving lawyers in London who are in the habit of 'raising the wind' by squeezing retainers and fees out of simple but ambitious clients."[33]

Francis G. Young was likely one of these ambitious clients. Later in life, he strongly advised against the folly of pursuing such claims. "In some cases, this insane belief in foreign possessions comes, I believe, from no other source than daydreams and cheap novels," Young advised in 1880. "In a great many instances, however, the victims are the victims of legal knaves."[34] Despite this experience, there is evidence that Young himself was something of a legal knave. One acquaintance, for example, expressed the opinion that he would not trust him "with a dog case."[35] There is also evidence that he may have used his position as quartermaster of the California Regiment for personal gain, by selling regimental supplies back in Washington. On October 19, 1861, General Charles P. Stone's assistant adjutant general, Captain Charles Stewart, was forced to warn Colonel Baker that Young had "no right to order sales of public property, but that it must be turned over to the nearest Quartermaster."[36]

The first wartime meeting of Barney and Young may have been a month earlier, in September 1861, when Barney found himself attached to Captain Charles Griffin's "West Point" battery at the Chain Bridge south of Washington. Griffin was helping to support Brigadier General "Baldy" Smith, who had been ordered by General George B. McClellan to push his brigade toward Lewinsville, Virginia, on September 11, 1861.[37] Although attached to the California Regiment, Young claimed to have been "acquainted with Maj. Genl W.F. Smith," and "have served with him," sometime before his dismissal in January 1862—possibly during this same period.[38]

Barney wrote Assistant Secretary of State Frederick William Seward an encouraging note from Lewinsville on September 29, 1861, after encounters with Confederate cavalry there on September 11 and September 18. "I have the honor to report that I have been with Capt. Griffin's battery at the Chain Bridge, and I trust if we meet the rebels to give a good account of myself," he wrote Seward.[39] His short letter suggests that he was angling for some appointment of prominence and was attempting to keep his name at the forefront. If so, it seems to have worked, for some time after writing Seward, Barney was transferred, by order of the Secretary of War, to the State Department, as a "special envoy."[40]

There is no formal record of Barney's service for the State Department during the next three months, but Joseph Scoville later revealed in a letter to the English press that it involved the so-called "French princes" on McClellan's staff—Prince Philippe of Orléans, Count of Paris, and Robert J. d'Orléans, the Duke of Chartres—who had obtained commissions

Major General George B. McClellan and staff, March 1862 (Library of Congress Prints and Photographs Division). From left: Lieutenant Williams, A.D.C., Surgeon Walters, General G.W. Morell, Lieutenant Colonel A.V. Colburn, A.D.C., General G.B. McClellan, Lieutenant Colonel N.B. Switzer, François d'Orléans, Prince of Joinville, and Prince Philippe of Orléans, Count of Paris at Miners Hill, Virginia, March 1862. William Chase Barney was transferred from paymaster duties in the fall of 1861 to be an unofficial liaison to the French princes but was transferred to Fort Leavenworth two months later (*Major General George B. McClellan and staff*, Virginia [photographed March 1862, printed between 1880 and 1889]. Photograph. Library of Congress, https://www.loc.gov/item/2013647713/).

as additional aide-de-camps to McClellan in September 1861, while they were touring America.[41] Their uncle, François d'Orléans, the Prince of Joinville, was the son of King Louis Philippe, the last king of the Orléans dynasty and, according to Scoville, had hosted Barney in Paris some 15 years before.

The French princes had been guests of McClellan at one of his grand military reviews in Washington on Saturday, September 21, 1861—inspecting the 10,000 troops of Brigadier General George A. McCall's Pennsylvania Reserve Division.[42] The following week, they were suddenly members of the United States Army themselves. "The Count de Paris and the Duke of Chartres enter our service with great enthusiasm," declared a Washington correspondent. "They are for the Government, and in their sympathies, are against slavery and the slaveholding rebellion."[43]

The spontaneous nature of the appointments may have led to Barney's reassignment, as he was both fluent in French and personally familiar with the French princes. Joseph Scoville would later simply say that the Prince de Joinville and Barney "renewed an acquaintance commenced under happier auspices," one that according to Scoville, was "approved of by M'Clellan."[44]

In the wake of the Bull Run fiasco, McClellan had become the de facto general-in-chief of Union forces and had inspired a new confidence in the Union army. Joseph Scoville wrote his readers in London the following optimistic assessment of McClellan as early as August 3, 1861:

> All see that we have got the right man in General M'Clellan. He has already an army—not a mob. Now newspaper complaints are silent. Spies are arrested. Correspondence with the rebels has ceased. The army in every respect is being entirely remodeled. Every abuse is being corrected.... Now, when the army marches, it will crush everything before it.[45]

The appointment of the French princes was not without controversy. Even before they joined McClellan's staff, newspapers were buzzing about perceived slights to Emperor Napoleon III by the administration. "The newspapers are filled with suggestions as to the cause of Seward ordering their baggage to be passed free, a courtesy he did not extend to Napoleon," Joseph Scoville wrote on September 17—a week before the princes were commissioned. "One journal thinks the Emperor will regard the courtesy to the Prince as hostile to himself."[46] The issuance of actual commissions to the French princes heightened the controversy, both in Washington and Europe. A correspondent of the *New York Herald* explained it this way:

> Both inside and outside the diplomatic corps, it has been pronounced inexpedient, if not also indecorous, in our government to adopt among their military proteges the two French princes in question, because these princes represent

the Orleans dynasty, which is said to be the most popular in France after the House of Bonaparte, and is, therefore, regarded, if not with hostility, certainly with keen and restless jealousy by the reigning Emperor.[47]

As for the Orléans princes themselves, they displayed little care for international intrigue over their appointments. Rather, one of the brothers frankly admitted that he simply "could not resist this opportunity, unique, perhaps, of acquiring as a soldier a practical experience of which, more than anything else, he felt the desire and need."[48]

Unfortunately for the French princes, the next three months were sorely lacking in the practical experience they were seeking. Except for the debacle at Ball's Bluff, General George B. McClellan's Army of the Potomac stayed close to Washington. At first, the public appreciated the drill, discipline and professionalism McClellan was infusing in the new army. As the months wore on, however, their impatience grew. "General McClellan seems to have come to the conclusion that his duties are to make a fuss generally, have a couple of French princes trotting after him, and get up a review every week to show off his horsemanship before a few women," Joseph Scoville declared in December. "The people are getting heartily sick of such nonsense."[49]

The Orléans brothers were likewise weary of inaction. Joseph Scoville wrote the English press on December 31, 1861, announcing that they were back in New York City, having "left the army at the bequest of their mother," and were "on their way to Niagara Falls."[50] Although they would return to the army the following year, their departure over the holidays doomed William Chase Barney's career as a special envoy. By December 24, 1861, he was back in New York City, awaiting orders from the chief paymaster. Barney himself had little to say about his dismissal—only that he was "relieved from duty" on orders from the Secretary of War on Christmas Eve, 1861.[51]

As Major General George B. McClellan launched his Army of the Potomac against Richmond in the spring of 1862, Barney must have felt great humiliation at not being part of it. His idol from Paris, General Philip Kearny, was now leading a division; the Orléans princes were back on McClellan's staff; and many of his comrades from the American Guard were now officers in other regiments.[52] After being relieved from duty on Christmas Eve, Barney was ordered on December 29, 1861, to the remote post at Fort Leavenworth, Kansas, to resume his duties as a paymaster.

After a grueling cross-country trip in January, Barney arrived at Leavenworth on February 3, 1862.[53] Almost immediately, he began lobbying Assistant Secretary of State Frederick Seward for a transfer, telling him on February 18 that he would "cheerfully exchange my present position for ... one in the field, or for one of diplomacy."[54] His wish for change was granted three weeks later, when his appointment was negated by the U.S. Senate on March 11, 1862.[55] Barney later claimed his dismissal was due to his service with the State Department on behalf of McClellan. "Congress passed a law to reduce the number of Paymasters and upon a call from the Senate Committee for a statement of the efficiency of the Paymasters, Col. Larned reported me as not having been on duty in his [Paymaster] Department," he later explained.[56]

Barney closed his books and returned to New York City but did not abandon his ambition to uphold the name of his famous ancestors. Later that year, he wrote Secretary of State William Seward, making an impassioned plea to return to the military: "I feel deeply the disgrace put upon me by the actions of the Senate.... I beg that instead of being thrust out in disgrace, I may be permitted to redeem the tarnished honor of names which brighten the pages of our history from '76 to 1815."[57]

Barney seems to have become especially anxious for a commission as fighting escalated on the Virginia peninsula near Richmond in mid-June 1862. On June 24, 1862, Barney wrote the Secretary of War, requesting authority to raise a "Catholic Brigade" to aid in the war effort, as he had close ties with the Catholic Church, having attended St. Mary's Seminary in Baltimore under Samuel Eccleston, Archbishop of Baltimore. Despite such connections, his proposal to raise a brigade sounds far-fetched, given that he had no resources, no position of authority and limited military experience—excepting two skirmishes at Lewinsville and a day in combat at Bull Run. Assistant Secretary of War C.P. Wolcott gave Barney a polite response, explaining that the organization of volunteer regiments was "under the exclusive control of Governors of States."[58]

Seeing that Congressman Francis P. Blair had been authorized to raise a brigade in Missouri, he wrote Assistant Secretary of War Frederick Seward, asking rhetorically if the rule of the War Department regarding state control was to be "violated in favor of members of Congress only."[59] He urged young Seward to push the Catholic brigade idea with his father, but hearing nothing, wrote Secretary Seward to get reappointed as an additional paymaster. Failing that, it seems he volunteered with either the Sanitary Commission or as a volunteer in the hospital corps of Major General John Pope's newly created Army of Virginia—which was preparing to take on General Robert E. Lee near the old Bull Run battlefield at which Barney had fought the previous year.

Serving in the hospital corps was a task Barney likely regretted, for the Second Battle of Bull Run proved disastrous, not only for Pope, but for his army and medical staff. According to the United States Sanitary Commission, "Forty-three wagon loads of supplies were sent forward by the Surgeon General and relying on the representations of General Pope that he had no intention of retreating they took up a position, which when the army did retreat on the following day, led to their capture by the enemy."⁶⁰ As rebel troops overran the field hospitals, the wounded simply lay on the battlefield for as long as 48 hours, until they finally were carried off or died.

In the aftermath of the defeat, the Sanitary Commission concluded that "the sufferings of the wounded after this battle have probably not been equaled, at least not exceeded, during this war."⁶¹ The shortage of medical personnel and ambulance drivers for Pope's army was so acute, clerks from Washington were organized to help. They found a horrible scene when they arrived. "Attracted by the red bags of Duryee's Zouaves, we proceeded to the field where they lay—nearly a hundred of them—shattered, torn and bloody, in every conceivable form of misery," wrote one volunteer. "As for the wounded, their case was infinitely worse. Away from help, on the bloody ground where they fell dying by inches, recovery was impossible."⁶²

The volunteers did the best they could. The *Alexandria Gazette* reported after the battle that as ambulances and wagons straggled into that city, "the sight was a melancholy one. In one instance a soldier had his shoulder shot off, another had a hand off, many were wounded in the legs, some in the head."⁶³ William Chase Barney, through some influence, was among the few volunteers receiving credit in the Washington press dispatch:

> On Sunday morning [August 31], between eight and nine o'clock, fifteen of the ambulances, being in the advance of the train, were captured. In all, there were two hundred and thirty ambulances and sixty hacks. About twenty-three hundred wounded have, so far, been removed from the field. The movements were facilitated by Major W.C. Barney of New York.⁶⁴

The grim reality of the second defeat at Bull Run undoubtedly colored Barney's view of the war, especially when he received news of the death of his longtime idol, General Philip Kearny, who was killed at the Battle of Chantilly, Virginia, on September 1, 1862.

Barney's frustration with the course of the war was mirrored by Francis G. Young, who on September 10, 1862, wrote a caustic letter to Secretary of State Seward from the Brevoort House Hotel in New York. He warned Seward that "there is organizing in this city a large body of men, Republicans, resolved upon your immediate removal from the Cabinet ... you have not many friends in New York at this time."⁶⁵ Young's attitude towards the administration was mirrored by a British citizen staying at the Brevoort House Hotel that same week, who wrote: "The devil is loose. The Confederates are in Maryland.... The poor bewildered government at Washington, with its imbecile Ministers and Generals, is at a discount, and perhaps before many days are ended, will be among the things that were."[66]

The fashionable Brevoort House may have been where Barney and Young shared similar thoughts earlier that summer, as the French princes stayed there for several days in July 1862, the last opportunity for Barney to see them off, before they returned to Europe.[67] In any case, both soon found a means to restore their tarnished honor with Barney's old commander, Major General George B. McClellan. In the aftermath of the Second Battle of Bull Run, Lincoln had reluctantly reappointed McClellan to command of the Union armies in the East.

Barney's friend and confidant Scoville astutely foresaw the dilemma that now faced the nation as McClellan returned to command. "The President has become for the moment, by accepting M'Clellan as military commander, the abettor of slavery and the protector of the Southern system," he wrote in a letter to his English readers, just days before the Battle of Antietam. "God is pouring out his wrath on both sections for the manner in which we have oppressed our colored brethren … the sun of slavery is setting in blood but setting for ever."[68] Over the next two weeks, President Lincoln would have his own reckoning with God, and agree with Scoville that the solution to the war was the termination of slavery.

9

A Brighter and More Permanent Prosperity

Those who profess to favor freedom and yet deprecate agitation, are men who want crops without plowing the field.[1]
—Frederick Douglass, 1857

The acute shortage of medical supplies and personnel at the Second Battle of Bull Run demonstrated the necessity of the work done by the U.S. Sanitary Commission. In the western theater, the Chicago Sanitary Commission, a branch of the national organization, took on the fundraising and volunteer efforts. On November 1, 1861, they published a circular addressed to "the women of the Northwest," appealing to them "to make full provision for the relief and comfort of our sick and wounded soldiers."[2]

Among the eight commissioners of the Chicago Sanitary Commission was Dr. Otis H. Tiffany, who five years earlier had taught mathematics at Dickinson College in Carlisle, Pennsylvania. Although located north of the Mason-Dixon, it was largely conservative on the issue of slavery. Dickinson alumnus Judge Roger Taney, for example, considered slavery an evil, but ruled with the majority of the Supreme Court in the 1857 Dred Scott case that found African Americans were not and could never be citizens of the United States.[3] Moreover, he believed that slavery must be abolished by the states in which it existed, rather than by the Federal government, and that the solution to the problem was repatriation to Africa, as opposed to abolition.

Dickinson College, however, did have prominent abolitionists among its faculty. Foremost among these was Dr. John McClintock, who had been arrested and tried in 1847 for his suspected participation in what became known as the Carlisle Riot, when free African Americans had attempted to prevent the return of three fugitive runaways to their Maryland slaveholders and in the process, had killed one. Although the court acquitted McCormick, it was clear that his sympathies lay with the runaways, not the slaveholders.[4]

McClintock resigned from teaching at Dickinson in 1848 but had a capable successor in one of his former students, Otis H. Tiffany.[5] A member of the so-called Native American Party or Know-Nothing Party, Tiffany made the mistake of mixing education with politics. He ran unsuccessfully for the U.S. Senate in 1855 while teaching at Dickinson—an action that did not play well with student Democrats and their families. One student's father complained, "I pay Professor Tiffany for teaching my son the mathematics and not for traveling over the State making political speeches."[6]

Democratic newspapers like the *Lancaster Intelligencer* echoed the criticism of Tiffany. "Does this man Professor Tiffany, traverse the State giving his Know-Nothing lecture at the instance or instigation of the faculty at Dickinson College?" they asked rhetorically. "Or does he do it, and thereby neglect his duties in the Chair of Mathematics, by permission of the trustees of that time-honored Institution?"[7] Although Tiffany lost his Senate race, student resentment of his politics lingered.

When Tiffany canceled recitation soon after, Dickinson student Horatio King made a note of it in his diary. "Tiffany unwell—excused us from recitation," he recorded. "He went to his house, equipped himself and went gunning immediately with Dr McClintock and others. Sickness fled from him most surprisingly sudden."[8] Two days later King and three others—Charles Maglaughlin, Charles H. Hepburn and Jennings Hulsey—greased his blackboards with fish oil.

"They smelt and looked very delightful indeed," King recorded sarcastically in his diary, without embellishing on what motivated the prank.[9] The following day, Tiffany had all the students recite on paper, as the blackboard was unusable. "He was awful angry, and we enjoyed the fun," King wrote unsympathetically. "We shall fix him yet."[10] Four days after the fish oil incident, students did "fix" Tiffany by repeating the vandalism with tar. "Went to Tiffs room and found the black boards, table, chairs and benches covered with tar," Horatio King recorded. "Tiff layed papers over all except the boards as made us recite on paper."[11] This time, King did not admit to participating, nor did he when the vandalism was repeated in January 1856, with even more damage.

After Tiffany's classroom was tarred a second time, the offenders were quickly identified and dismissed. They included the three sophomores originally involved in the fish oil prank, as well as Henry H. Lane, a sophomore from Carlisle. The student body, however, had more sympathy for the offenders than for Dr. Tiffany. Almost 100 of them refused to attend class or perform any college duties in protest. In the end, the college reinstated Maglaughlin, Hepburn and Hulsey. Lane was not reinstated, for as Horatio King wrote, most "fear to have him in College."[12]

Although one newspaper account dismissed the tarring of Tiffany's classroom as "mischievous sophomores ... teasing a Professor," the event was more likely an anti-abolition warning, as the incidents had begun with Tiffany canceling class to meet with McClintock.[13] Abolitionist speakers were often threatened with tar and feathering, even in Northern states—where racism still flourished.[14] Beneath the collegiate comradery at Dickinson, serious differences simmered.

Tiffany resigned his teaching position within a year, accepting a position instead with the Associate Reformed Church in Baltimore. "To those who knew him well it was no surprise that he resigned a position that was unsuited to the exercise and fullest development of the peculiar gifts with which he was in so high a degree endowed," said the Dickinson College paper, upon his death in 1891.[15] Despite this rationale, it is hard to imagine that the student revolt didn't affect his decision to pursue a different career.

East College, Dickinson College, Carlisle, Pennsylvania, 1870. (Photograph Collection, Archives and Special Collections, Dickinson College). Thomas Nelson Conrad and Daniel Mountjoy Cloud shared a room here while students, when both were taught mathematics by Professor Otis Tiffany. Five years later they would be on opposite sides of the conflict to perpetuate slavery (C.L. Lochman, *View of East College from N. West Street*, ca. 1870, Carlisle, PA. Photograph. Dickinson College Archives and Special Collections, https://archives.dickinson.edu/).

Four years later, in 1860, Tiffany resigned again, telling the trustees of his Baltimore church that despite the addition of 100 members during his tenure, "he might prove more useful in another field of labor, while the congregation could doubtless get a better man."[16] The trustees accepted his resignation without comment, and hired Baltimore native the Reverend Fielder Israel to replace him. While nothing was said, it is possible that Tiffany's abolition sentiments eventually clashed once again with Baltimore's pro-slavery population.

Contrary to Tiffany's own suggestion that he assume another calling, he returned to the ministry, but this time at the First Methodist Church of Chicago—reportedly the oldest congregation in the city, dating back to 1831. Located at the corner of Clark Street and Washington, it lay in the heart of Chicago's commercial district and utilized a new four-story building constructed in 1858—renting the first floor as retail space, the second floor as offices, and utilizing the third and fourth floors for its sanctuary, whose seats were arranged in rising curved rows, like an amphitheater.[17] His Thanksgiving Day sermon there in 1860 was reportedly "listened to by as large a congregation as has ever gathered within the walls of that edifice."[18]

Tiffany's reputation as a public speaker soon spread across Chicago. "He was a natural orator," one acquaintance later said of him. "His rich voice, and clear enunciation, his fine physique and graceful manner, his genial and attractive face, his elegant and refined style, combined with an exquisite taste as to diction and matter, gave him an influence over his audiences best described perhaps by the word magical."[19]

With the coming of the Civil War, Tiffany put his energies behind the work of the Chicago Sanitary Commission. Shortly after its appeal to women across the Northwest, Tiffany gave a speech for the Soldiers Aid Sociable at Bryan Hall, the largest venue in the city, located on Clark Street opposite the courthouse. After reading letters from soldiers in the field, Tiffany gave an eloquent appeal for contributions. "Remember how your donations are received by the men valiantly fighting your battles," he asked. "You may depend upon it that every article sent into camp takes along with it thoughts of home and sympathy—worth more than medicine for the recovery of the sick and languishing."[20]

In the aftermath of the brutal Battle of Shiloh, Tiffany accompanied an expedition from Cairo, Illinois, to Pittsburg Landing on the Tennessee River, on board the steamer *Champion*. Chartered to remove the wounded from the battlefield, the small steamer carried an entourage of officials, including Illinois governor Yates, several other members of the Chicago Sanitary Commission, many nurses and 15 tons of supplies.[21] Advised by a physician that the river water wasn't potable, Tiffany accepted a flask containing high strength alcohol. "I do not press this upon you Doctor," the physician advised. "You must be the judge of the propriety of drinking it. I have given you my reasons for drinking it."[22]

Without thought, Tiffany took a drink from the flask and for good measure, took a second. According to a later report by the *Chicago Tribune*, the amount was not large, but unaccustomed to alcohol, Tiffany was soon so "deeply intoxicated and crazed by the effects of the liquor," his colleagues had to remove him to a stateroom.[23] Upon sobering up, Tiffany was mortified. Not only was he an officer of the Sanitary Commission and minister of the oldest congregation in Chicago but he had given lectures to the Chicago Temperance Union, having himself been a long-standing advocate of prohibition.[24] He immediately resigned from the commission and returned to Chicago in shame.

Ironically, the one to rally to Tiffany's defense was Democratic editor Wilbur F. Storey of the *Chicago Times*. Despite their political differences, Storey advocated forgiveness. "Many seem to think the punishment is too great for the offense," the *Times* opined. "At any rate, we feel well assured that this is but a cloud that is temporarily obscuring the Doctor's pathway, and that it will pass away ere long, only to give place to a brighter and more permanent prosperity than even that which in times gone by, was apparently promised him."[25] Wilbur F. Storey was never more prophetic and it was an epitaph that might apply equally to the nation, as well as the man.

Freed from the responsibilities of tending to a large congregation and the details of procuring supplies for the Sanitary Commission, Tiffany took a position with the fledgling Methodist Church of Evanston, Illinois, and became an outspoken advocate for both emancipation and war. Upon moving to Evanston, he also came to know John Dempster, president of the Garrett Bible Institute—a man who would encourage Tiffany to pursue his abolitionist leanings.[26] Tiffany credits Dempster, among others, as daring to demand that "the Church should speak in language not to be mistaken, the conviction that slavery was contrary to the law of God and nature and inconsistent with the Golden Rule."[27]

When pro-war advocates held a huge meeting at Bryan Hall in Chicago on July 19, 1862, many stirring speeches were made, but according to one journalist, none was better than that of the former mathematics professor from Dickinson College. "Casting the horoscope of the nation's future, I dare believe when the hour of victory strikes in the hearing of the nations, it will ring out the same old note the first bell of liberty sounded, proclaiming 'liberty throughout the land and to all its inhabitants!'" Tiffany shouted to the enthusiastic crowd. "Our first struggle was for existence, our second is for carrying liberty to all the earth—Southrons, your doom comes swiftly!"[28]

The vehemence of Tiffany's words belied his profession as a minister of the Gospel but reflected years of repressing his beliefs in the company of his students and Baltimore parishioners. "The Southern almanacs predict an eclipse," he told his audience, repressing them no longer. "That eclipse will come soon enough. God has made their sun so dark they can see our stars in the daytime—lay the stripes of our flag about traitors till they revere our stars!"[29]

A former colleague on the Chicago Sanitary Commission, the Rev. William Weston Patton, joined Tiffany at the podium. A native of Massachusetts, Patton had been a long-standing critic of slavery in America and had contributed verses to the popular marching song "John Brown's Body." As early as 1846, Patton had argued the evil of the slaveholding establishment, where "slaveholders, polygamists, concubines, thieves and robbers, become less guilty … as they are enabled to band together and pass laws to justify their evil deeds, and make themselves an essential element of the social state."[30]

The war meeting at Bryan Hall was followed the next week by a massive rally in Courthouse Square, where 5,000 men first heard composer George F. Root's *Battle Cry of Freedom* introduced by vocalists Jules and Frank Lumbard.[31] "The music of this stirring song was capitally rendered," reported the *Chicago Tribune*, "and was received with the utmost enthusiasm and applause."[32] The song became wildly popular, selling 350,000 copies and encouraging more enlistments than any number of speeches combined. Just as important, it gave new life to an abolition movement long dominated by Northern clerics and intellectuals.

As Chicagoans were holding rallies in favor of emancipation, President Lincoln was contemplating how such a revolutionary transformation would work. Towards this end, he met with well-known African American leaders headed by Edward M. Thomas, president of the Anglo-African American Institute, on August 14, 1862. They discussed the possibility of colonization to Central America, as opposed to Liberia, as John H.B. Latrobe had long advocated. "There is an unwillingness on the part of our people, harsh as it may be, for you free colored people, to remain with us," he explained. "At all events, the place I am thinking about having for a colony is Central America. It is nearer to us than Liberia."[33]

The idea of colonization was eventually discarded altogether, but Lincoln's reception of African American leaders at the White House was itself a barrier-breaking event. Frederick Douglass, a harsh critic of the colonization scheme, later described the difference between Lincoln and other political leaders of the day:

> In all my interviews with Mr. Lincoln I was impressed with his entire freedom from popular prejudice against the colored race. He was the first great

man that I talked with in the United States freely, who in no single instance reminded me of the difference between himself and myself, of the difference of color, and I thought that all the more remarkable because he came from a State where there were black laws.[34]

Such openness by Lincoln encouraged Christians of several denominations to adopt a memorial in favor of national emancipation at a meeting held at Bryan Hall in Chicago on September 7, 1862. Drafted by the Rev. William Patton, the memorial espoused ending slavery for moral, political, and military reasons. Among these, Patton's moral argument may have been the most powerful. "The slave oligarchy has organized the most unnatural, perfidious, and formidable rebellion known to history," he wrote simply. "Can we doubt that this is a Divine retribution for national sin, in which our crime has justly shaped our punishment?"[35]

To present the memorial, the delegation chose Patton and the chairman of the committee, the Rev. John Dempster of Evanston, as well as Charles Walker, a "Douglas Democrat"—who was unable to make the journey.[36] Patton and Dempster had some difficulty gaining an audience with the president upon their arrival in Washington. General Robert E. Lee's Army of Northern Virginia had crossed the Potomac River into Maryland only days before and Lincoln had filled his schedule with military matters.[37] Finally, they appealed to Secretary of the Navy Gideon Welles, a known supporter of emancipation, who introduced them to Lincoln at the White House on Saturday, September 13, 1862.

According to Welles, Lincoln "assented cheerfully" when told that Patton and Dempster wished to see him regarding slavery and emancipation and greeted them "in a calm but affable manner."[38] The president invited them to sit in his office, which, according to Illinois congressman Isaac Arnold, featured "a large oak table covered with cloth," around which the cabinet members sat, and another table between the windows, at which the president sat, in "a large arm-chair."[39] One cabinet member had once thought the chair was too shoddy to befit a president. "There are a great many people that want to sit in it," Lincoln replied, "though I'm sure I've often wished some of them had it instead of me."[40]

The Rev. John Dempster, as chairman of the Chicago committee, read the memorial, providing copies to the president in both English and German. "The subject presented in the memorial is not a new one," Lincoln responded. "It has been on my mind for many weeks, I may even say, for many months."[41] On this point, he was sincere. Gideon Welles recorded in his diary that Lincoln had broached the subject with William Seward and himself back on July 13, 1862, in the wake of McClellan's withdrawal from the Virginia Peninsula. Lincoln had thought the action a "military necessity," but thought any such action delicate, and sought their advice.[42]

Three months later, as the Chicago committee presented Lincoln with their memorial, the matter was still delicate. "Those who offer me suggestions do not agree amongst themselves, not even the religious men," Lincoln told Patton and Dempster, frustrated. "I am approached with the most opposite opinions and advice, by those who seem equally certain that they represent the divine will."[43] Dempster and Patton appealed to Lincoln's faith in Providence. "I believe in a divine Providence," Lincoln told them. "Unless I am deceived by myself more than I often am, I wish to know God's will in this matter; and if I can learn it, I will do it."[44]

Lincoln then proceeded to discuss the merits of the case before them, as if the men were clients in his Springfield law office. "What good would a proclamation of emancipation from me do, especially as we are now situated?" Lincoln asked, worried that emancipation might convey weakness, not strength.[45] In a reference to the oft-repeated myth that Pope Callixtus III fruitlessly excommunicated Halley's Comet in 1456 as an "instrument of the devil," he told them bluntly: "I do not want to issue a document that the whole world will see must necessarily be inoperative, like the Pope's bull against the comet! Would my word free the slaves, when I cannot even enforce the Constitution in the rebel States?"[46]

Despite his reservations, the meeting was cordial and lasted over an hour. "Do not misunderstand me, because I have mentioned these objections," the president reassured them, "They indicate the difficulties that have thus far prevented my action in some such way as you desire. I have not decided against a proclamation of liberty to the slaves but hold the matter under advisement. And I can assure you that the subject is on my mind, by day and night, more than any other."[47] At the conclusion of the meeting, Lincoln added a final comment. "Whatever shall appear to be God's will, I will do."[48]

In the hour of the nation's greatest challenge, Lincoln was not the only one seeking God's will. Early in 1862, a New York spiritualist with a gifted ten-year-old daughter thought he had the answer. Sitting down with her in prayer, he claimed she had seen visions of victory—of a great battle "for the purpose of clearing the Potomac River ... in which the Union forces were to be entirely successful."[49] He anxiously wrote General McClellan of the experience, assuring him that the visions came from "God *himself*."[50]

Two weeks later, the girl saw visions with mysterious phrases in Latin that she did not understand. "How are we to understand what we know not?" the father asked, and immediately a phrase in English came from his daughter: "Ye who have been charmed shall force the charmers to submit to authority."[51] The meaning was still not clear, though he thought it referred to the era of the Buchanan administration, when the nation seemed at peace, but was not. At last came a revelation that "a man shall arise for the times."⁵² The spiritualist assumed this must be McClellan—and was thus compelled to write the general a second time, assuring him he was no "common spiritualist, with their abominations" but rather, an "intelligent, educated, religious person" who claimed to have intimately known the wife of Secretary Stanton and resided in "the same position in society."⁵³

Whether or not the Battle of Antietam was the great battle along the Potomac foreseen by the girl, it convinced President Lincoln of God's will. Tactically a draw, it nevertheless forced Robert E. Lee to abort his invasion of Maryland—thus clearing the Potomac, as she had foreseen. It was the closest thing to a victory in the East since the Union abandoned the Peninsula Campaign back in July. In what could be viewed as a sign of divine providence, the battle had been precipitated after an Indiana infantryman chanced upon Lee's Special Orders No. 191, outlining plans for his northern invasion, wrapped around a cigar.⁵⁴

William W. Patton later mused that although Lincoln had contemplated the subject of emancipation for months, "our humble mission was not destitute of some final influence."⁵⁵ Thus, a few days after the battle, on the last day of summer, Lincoln was shuttered in the White House. It was a Sunday, and he declined to see Secretary of the Treasury Salmon P. Chase's personal physician, Dr. S.A. Forsha, who was trying to get the president's endorsement of a balm for wounded soldiers. Lincoln would usually see anyone, but on this day was preoccupied. As he was turned away at the White House, Forsha was told that the president was "busy writing."⁵⁶

Discouraged, the doctor returned to Chase's house and relayed his experience. Lincoln, Chase thought to himself, "must be working on his Proclamation."⁵⁷ Lincoln later told his cabinet members that he had resolved, as he had told Dempster and Patton, to leave the decision with God—that if Union armies prevailed over the Army of Northern Virginia, he would view the result as "an indication of Divine will, and it was his duty to move forward in the cause of emancipation."⁵⁸

The document referred to by Chase was the boldest stoke ever penned by a U.S. president, before or since. It was the Emancipation Proclamation, whereby he would declare all enslaved people in territory under rebellion forever free. It was all the bolder for being issued not from a position of strength, but of relative weakness. Yet, it was a move that journalist Joseph Scoville had recommended almost one year before. "I blame the President for one thing," Scoville had said back in November 1861. "He could have ended this long ago…. When he frees the slaves, whether it is done by act of Congress or by proclamation, the rebellion will be ended, and the only cause of difficulty in this country will be removed. North, east, west, and south will then be united as one nation."⁵⁹

The task of reforming a unified nation would not be as simple as Scoville had predicted. Although Lee had pulled back across the Potomac River, the Confederacy still controlled virtually all territory south of Washington—the same positions both sides held at the start of the rebellion. There was little confidence by Lincoln's cabinet that McClellan could or would finish the job of destroying the rebel army. Secretary of the Treasury Salmon Chase had recorded in his diary weeks earlier that he and Secretary of War Edwin Stanton agreed that McClellan "ought not to be trusted with any army of the Union."[60]

As the administration suspected, destroying Lee's army was the last thing on McClellan's mind. On September 25, he penned a letter to his friend and supporter, New York shipping magnate William H. Aspinwall: "I am very anxious to know how you and men like you regard the Proclamations of the Presdt inaugurating servile war, emancipating the slaves, & at one stroke of the pen changing our free institutions into despotism—for such I regard as the natural effect of the last Proclamation suspending the Habeas Corpus throughout the land."[61]

McClellan was so opposed to emancipation that when he saw the headline in the *Baltimore Sun* that week announcing it, he hurled the paper into the corner, exclaiming: "There! Look at that outrage! I shall resign tomorrow!"[62] By that time, however, McClellan had already taken steps he hoped would prevent emancipation from ever taking place at all—by sending overtures of peace not only to General Robert E. Lee, but to Richmond. Joseph Scoville could never have predicted that on the same day that Lincoln was drafting his proclamation, Scoville's own friend and confidant, William Chase Barney, would be traveling south on a mission to restore what Barney called the "Union as it was."[63]

10

The Curiosity Tour

> *General M'Clellan ... sent an intimate and confidential friend to Jeff. Davis at Richmond to open or to conduct negotiations. The party was William Chase Barney of the City of Baltimore.*[1]
> —Joseph A. Scoville, November 1862

Major General George B. McClellan's ability to stop the rebels along Antietam Creek in Maryland on September 17, 1862, had prevented a catastrophic invasion of the North by Major General Robert E. Lee's Army of Northern Virginia. But the victory had come at a terrible price. As Lincoln penned his proclamation, the casualty lists were still coming in from America's bloodiest day. Despite Union losses, pundits felt the Army of the Potomac could have finished off Lee's army on September 18, had its leaders only been willing to do so.

War correspondent Nathaniel Paige, who had covered the battle for the *New York Tribune*, later reflected over the inaction. "The failure of McClellan to pursue Lee the day after the battle, seemed to me at the time to be monstrous conspiracy to prevent the suppression of the rebellion as long as the ideas of Edwin M. Stanton and the anti-slavery men controlled the Government," Paige told the *Tribune* in an 1880 interview. "If Lee had been caught north of the Potomac with his beaten army his surrender would have been inevitable."[2]

At the time of the Battle of Antietam, Nathaniel Paige had a unique perspective on the mindset of McClellan and his closest subordinates. In the same 1880 interview with the *Tribune*, Paige revealed what he had learned three days before the battle from Colonel Thomas M. Key of McClellan's staff:

> He told me that a plan to countermarch to Washington and intimidate the President had been seriously discussed the night before by the members of McClellan's staff, and his opposition to it had, he thought, caused its abandonment.... I was not greatly surprised at the time, for I knew that the men

McClellan gathered around him were all Copperheads who had no heart for the War.³

Although Key denied that McClellan had direct knowledge of the plot, the conspirators thought they could convince him to do it as a means of changing the administration's policy on emancipation. According to Paige, these officers sought to force Lincoln to abandon "all interference with the institution of slavery. If he could guarantee the perpetuity of slavery, they thought the war could be brought to an end."⁴

Key reportedly told future U.S. senator Augustus O. Bacon of Georgia after the war that a group of McClellan's subordinates renewed their attempt to promote a peace deal with the South immediately after the battle. According to Bacon, he had met Key on the train between Cincinnati and New York in 1868, at which time Key told him that "on the day after the battle of Sharpsburg, a very strong effort was made by a number of prominent officers of the Federal army to induce Gen. McClellan to address to Gen. Lee a proposition to declare a truce prepa[ra]tory to a peace, which they urged the people wanted, and would have if offered an opportunity to secure it."⁵

As McClellan debated what to do, one anonymous New Yorker provided him similar advice sometime that September: "The Union can never be restored by bayonets, will never be restored by politicians, and we have no statesmen.... See that General [Lee] and agree upon an Armistice."⁶ According to Key's account, McClellan sympathized with these objectives, but felt "that if he should declare the truce, it would be repudiated by President Lincoln, who would take advantage of his action to ruin him officially and disgrace him before the people."⁷

Lincoln's private secretary, John Hay, recorded in his diary that powerful men in New York were also urging McClellan to go easy on the rebels. President Lincoln himself told Hay an incredible story in 1864. It was that Vermont governor John Gregory Smith had come to the White House and conveyed that his brother, General W.H.F. "Baldy" Smith, had advised him that immediately after the Battle of Antietam, McClellan had confided that influential Democratic New York mayor Fernando Wood and another New York politician had come to the battlefield and offered "Little Mac" the next Democratic nomination, if only he would conduct the war in a way "so as to conciliate and impress the people of the South with the idea that our armies were intended merely to execute the laws and protect their property, etc."⁸

According to the story conveyed by General Smith, Fernando Wood had made a similar offer on the Peninsula earlier that year, but Smith had convinced McClellan to decline, telling him that it "looks like treason, and ... will ruin you, and all of us."⁹ Despite this warning, McClellan reportedly decided to accept the offer the second time. Rather than declare an outright truce, however, McClellan sought a dialogue with Lee by sending him a letter seeking the return of the horse of Major General Philip Kearny, who had been killed at the battle of Chantilly several weeks earlier. Senator Bacon, always intrigued by vague stories of the truce that never was, learned of this letter by interviewing General Howell Cobb of Georgia on his deathbed.[10] Ironically, General Cobb and other prominent Confederate officers also considered a truce in the wake of the horrific battle.

Cobb had confidently declared on the night of Lincoln's inauguration that "if our wives and daughters cannot whip the Yankees with broomsticks, I want this entire generation discontinued."[11] A U.S. senator from Georgia and Secretary of the Treasury under President Buchannan, Cobb found the task of whipping Yankees somewhat harder than he had predicted. His proud Georgia brigade had been decimated at the Battle of South Mountain on September 14, 1862, while attempting to delay McClellan's advance on Sharpsburg. Among the dead was his brother-in-law, John Basil Lamar, who according to Cobb, "fell in the hottest of the fight, struggling to rally our broken columns."[12]

Cobb had experience negotiating with McClellan. Back on the Peninsula, Cobb had met with Colonel Thomas M. Key on the Mechanicsville Bridge to discuss a prisoner exchange on behalf of General Robert E. Lee, after McClellan had broached the subject in a letter to Lee dated June 13, 1862. That same day, Lee had responded, proposing that "Col. Key shall meet Gen. Cobb at the time you designated, Sunday morning next, 11 o'clock, at the Mechanicsville Bridge."[13]

After Antietam, General Howell Cobb, with the support of his brother, General Thomas R.R. Cobb, "laid their views of the subject of the truce before Gen. Lee and urged their desire as strongly as the circumstances would permit."[14] Lee was sympathetic to the concept of a truce but doubted that President Jefferson Davis would agree to it. In his interview with Bacon, Cobb denied that any communication regarding a truce passed between McClellan and Lee but did recall that, during his visit to Lee's office, "Gen. Lee had in his hand a letter from Gen. McClellan relative to the return of the horse of the Federal Gen. Kearny, who had been killed a few days before at the battle of Chantilly."[15]

A former Confederate soldier, Benjamin J. Keiley, heard a similar story "more than once" after the war from General James Longstreet, who commanded one wing of Lee's Army of Northern Virginia.[16] According to Keiley, Longstreet often visited him in Atlanta after the war, and the two men "often talked of the War and its sequel."[17] Among Longstreet's war stories was one that General Robert E. Lee called on him immediately after the Battle of Antietam to show him a letter from McClellan, "proposing an interview between himself and Gen. Lee."[18] Lee wanted to know what Longstreet made of the odd proposal. According to Keiley, Longstreet's thoughts were unequivocal: "I told Gen. Lee that in my judgment, there was no other construction to be placed on it save one, and that was that Gen. McClellan wished to end the War then and there."[19]

Keiley's credibility was beyond reproach. Although only a teenager during the war, he became the Catholic bishop for Savannah, Georgia, and gave Longstreet's funeral service in 1904. Upon his own death in 1925, newspapers hailed him as "one of the best-loved churchmen the South has ever known."[20] According to Keiley, Lee declined the McClellan interview, telling Longstreet, "President Davis ... is the one to whom such a message must be sent."[21] Unfortunately, no record of McClellan's letter to Lee survives. Lee gave Longstreet a copy, who gave it to Colonel Charles Marshall of Lee's staff. When Keiley asked for it after the war, however, Marshall claimed that "he had mislaid [it] and could never find it."[22]

In February 1886, Longstreet attempted to obtain a copy of the McClellan letter, first from Marshall, and then by appealing to his former aide, Osmun Latrobe: "Just after Sharpsburg.... McClellan wrote General Lee a very remarkable letter, a copy of which General Lee sent me. I am very anxious to recover the letter ... have twice written Col. Marshall for it but have thus far failed."[23] Longstreet wrote Latrobe again a month later, again seeking the missing letter. "The letter from McClellan to Gen Lee that I am particularly anxious to have was written immediately after Lincoln's proclamation freeing the slaves," he instructed Latrobe, "I would judge between the 23rd and 26th of Sept and referred to prisoners of ours that had fallen into McClellan's hands."[24]

The matter of how General Robert E. Lee responded to the letter from McClellan, if at all, remains undocumented. If Lee did respond, it is likely that he conveyed the same message to McClellan that he had to Longstreet: namely, that communications must be conveyed through the opposing governments, not its military commanders. Since McClellan did not trust the Lincoln administration, the logical course would have been for him to attempt to contact the Confederate government directly and stall until negotiations could be arranged. McClellan seems to have done just that— perhaps even before receiving any response from Lee.

On Sunday, September 21, 1862, four days after the battle of Antietam, former Union officer William Chase Barney rode south from Washington with a single companion, to the scene of the latest Federal disaster near Centreville, Virginia. His companion was Francis G. Young, Colonel Edward Baker's former quartermaster, who had been dismissed from the service in February 1862—not long before the United States Senate revoked Barney's commission. Young would report that the two former officers were simply on a "curiosity tour" of the Bull Run battlefield.²⁵ Barney would later admit, however, that they had journeyed to Centreville for the "express purpose of being captured."²⁶

The most complete explanation of their mission came from Joseph Scoville, whose articles Barney had recommended to Secretary of State William H. Seward the month before.²⁷ Scoville would tell his readers, "General M'Clellan ... sent an intimate and confidential friend to Jeff. Davis at Richmond to open or to conduct negotiations. The party was William Chase Barney of the City of Baltimore."²⁸ The mission fulfilled the goal Barney had sought from Frederick Seward seven months earlier, when he had pleaded for a position "in the field or ... diplomacy."²⁹

William Chase Barney had some experience in this role, as he had served as a "special envoy" of the State Department to coordinate the services of the French princes in the Army of the Potomac the previous year.³⁰ In this capacity, he surely knew Colonel Thomas M. Key and other members of McClellan's staff. Philosophically, Barney held the same goals as

Soldiers' graves, Bull Run Battlefield, 1862 (Library of Congress Prints and Photographs Division). A civilian viewing grave markers on the Bull Run battlefield. Former Union officers William Chase Barney and Francis G. Young were on such a "curiosity tour" when they were captured, although Barney later admitted they intended to be, as a means of initiating peace talks with the Confederate government (George N. Barnard, photographer, *Soldiers' graves, Bull Run Battlefield, Va.*, Bull Run, Virginia, 1862 [negative by Brady & Co., Washington. Published by E. & H.T. Anthony & Co., New York]. Photograph. Library of Congress, https://www.loc.gov/item/2015647570/).

McClellan—restoration of the Union and the preservation of slavery. They both naively believed the South would return to the Union if the latter was somehow guaranteed.

A journey to Centreville at that time, however, presented obstacles—the first of which was crossing the Potomac from Washington. "The communication with Virginia from here is still kept up by the chain bridge," the *Evening Star* had reported the month before, "using passes granted by the military authority, and undergoing the ordeal of sentries and guards."[31] As a medical volunteer, Barney likely already had a pass, but Young was another matter, for he was not likely involved in the Second Bull Run debacle at all—having written Secretary Seward from New York as recently as September 10, 1862. The involvement of McClellan and his staff in the pair's mission, however, would guarantee that both had passes into Virginia.

There is little question that McClellan knew both Barney and Young—the former because of his assignment involving the French princes, the latter for his involvement in the Ball's Bluff fiasco and subsequent hearings. Journalist Joseph Scoville described Barney's relationship to McClellan thus:

> W.C. Barney is grandson of William [Samuel] Chase, a signer of the Declaration of Independence, and afterwards a judge of the Supreme Court of the United States. His father was the celebrated Commander Barney of the United States Navy. When Louis Phillippe, the King of France, was in this country in exile, he was the guest of old Judge Chase. In after years, when King, he returned the hospitality to the grandson, the present W.C. Barney. When the French Princes of Orleans were here recently on M'Clellan's staff, they renewed an acquaintance commenced under happier auspices with Mr. Chase. This confidence was approved of by M'Clellan. At the same time, the sister of Mr. Barney ... is a thorough Secessionist, and has the confidence of all the Secession leaders. This led to the sending of Colonel Barney to Jeff. Davis.[32]

Scoville's facts, summarized to the British press, can be independently verified. Louis Philippe did spend more than three years in American exile, from 1796 to 1800, when Judge Chase first joined the Supreme Court. According to his mother, William Chase Barney was virtually raised by Judge Chase's wife, Hannah Kitty Chase, and lived with them as an adult "nearly a year until sometime in 1844 or 1845."[33] This was not long after Barney returned from France, where he met his first wife, Marie Felicite Le Petite—a time during which Louis Philippe was King of France (1830–1848) and could, as Scoville put it, "return the hospitality."[34]

Scoville's characterization of Barney's sister, Catherine Oldfield, as an ardent Secessionist is supported by one of Barney's other sisters, Rosa Postall, who wrote that she "nursed sick Confederate soldiers (prisoners)" and "was one of the ladies Lincoln imprisoned for expressing her sentiments."[35] According to Scoville, it was these Southern connections that led McClellan to send Barney South. General McClellan, however, also knew his companion, Francis G. Young. On December 6, 1861, President Lincoln had written a letter to McClellan on Young's behalf, after having interviewed Young that same day:

> Capt. Francis G. Young, of the California regiment (Col. Baker's) is in some difficulty—I do not precisely understand what.... At length he has brought me the paper which accompanies this, showing I think that he is entitled to respectful consideration.... These things and his late connection with Colonel Baker induce me to ask you if consistently with the public service, the past whatever it is cannot be waived and he placed in service and given another chance?[36]

Lincoln gave the letter to Young personally, so it is reasonable to assume Young delivered it to McClellan himself.[37] Although Little Mac did not find a use for Young at the time, perhaps in September 1862, he found one. As civilians with no direct ties to him or his staff, Barney and Young were the perfect envoys for an undercover mission, for if they failed, McClellan could deny any knowledge of their actions. As an active Republican in New York City, Young had the added benefit of appearing politically neutral.

Although Barney was familiar with the terrain near Centreville, their safety was anything but secure. A Union reconnaissance in force near Centreville the day before "returned without finding any Confederate troops in the district they scoured," but the situation changed daily, as Southern cavalry units were screening Lee's retreat from Maryland.[38] According to Young's later account, the two stopped at a shanty on the plains of Manassas for "rest and refreshment" when they were discovered by rebel troopers of the 13th Virginia Cavalry, a unit he would describe as "handsomely mounted and ... fully equipped."[39]

Invited to the headquarters of Colonel James R. Chambliss, who "pleasantly engaged them in conversation," Barney and Young were informed that to return to Washington, "the shortest route was by way of Richmond."[40] Escorted by a guard, they rode to Culpeper, where they were forced to abandon their horses, and were put on a train for the last leg of the journey to the Confederate capital. The two former Union officers "spent four days pleasantly on the way to Richmond," Young later told Washington correspondents of the Associated Press, and "were treated kindly and hospitably by their captors and all whom they met on the route."[41]

Young's tale of Southern hospitality on their journey to Richmond was a sharp contrast to that told by Lieutenant D.R.B. Nevin, captured by Stonewall Jackson's forces at the Battle of Cedar Mountain six weeks earlier, on August 9, 1862. Nevin claimed that he and fellow Union prisoners were nearly lynched by a mob at the Orange County Courthouse while boarding their train and went hungry on the journey south, save for "Jeff Davis crackers," which according to Nevin, were "harder and more unseemly than our own Federal army crackers."[42] For Nevin, the last five "unpleasant" hours from Gordonsville were accomplished in cattle cars, which arrived in Richmond in the evening, resulting in a night march down "dark, silent streets" under heavy guard.[43]

If Young's account of a four-day journey to Richmond is accurate, they should have arrived on or about September 25, 1862, when according

President Lincoln and General George B. McClellan, 1862 (Library of Congress, Prints and Photographs Division). In early October 1862, President Lincoln still held hope that General McClellan would move his powerful Army of the Potomac southward. McClellan, however, was stalling while the man journalist Joseph Scoville claimed was his personal ambassador, William Chase Barney, languished in Libby Prison (Alexander Gardner, photographer, *Antietam, Md. President Lincoln and Gen. George B. McClellan in the general's tent; another view*, Maryland, October 3, 1862. Photograph. Library of Congress, https://www.loc.gov/item/2018666253/).

to Young, they joined 30 other Union prisoners in Libby Prison—far less than had been incarcerated a few weeks earlier. Upon his arrival in Richmond, Barney undoubtedly expected to obtain a quick audience with General John H. Winder, the superintendent of Confederate prisons. Winder's brother, Charles H. Winder, had represented his brother on child custody matters and Barney likely expected his family connections to gain him an audience.

Barney would be sorely disappointed. "While M'Clellan and his army awaited the results of his mission, Barney had failed in it and was in limbo," Scoville later wrote. While Barney languished in Libby Prison, Abraham Lincoln visited McClellan and the Army of the Potomac in Maryland to urge him to action. On the morning of October 3, Lincoln was surveying the vast camps of the Army of the Potomac with Ozias M. Hatch, the Illinois secretary of state.[44] From a prominent hill, Lincoln placed one hand on Hatch's shoulder and slowly waving the other towards the camp, asked "Mr. Hatch, what is all this before us?"

"Why Mr. President," Hatch answered, "this is General McClellan's army."

"No, Mr. Hatch, no," responded Lincoln, "this is General McClellan's bodyguard."[45]

Lincoln's inference was clear: McClellan considered the great Army of the Potomac his own, not the Union's, and seemed oblivious to the purpose for which it was created or the civilian government to which it answered.

Despite the animosity of McClellan and most of his top generals to the Lincoln administration, there were those who remained loyal to the concept of civilian rule. Major General Ambrose Burnside, for example, had heard talk before about turning the army against Washington among McClellan loyalists. Upon hearing such talk around the campfire at Harrison's Landing on the Peninsula in July, Burnside exploded. "I don't know what you fellows call this talk, but I call it flat Treason, by God!"[46] Whether Burnside discovered the details of Barney's mission is unclear, but someone within the Army of the Potomac seems to have warned the administration that Barney was heading south, as subsequent events bore out.

11

Strange Bedfellows

Mr. Wood is here and refuses to report to me.... Mr. Wood has also brought a clergyman by the name of Conrad.[1]
—Major General John A. Dix, October 1862

Less than a week after William Chase Barney and Francis G. Young rode south from Washington with the sole intent of being captured, William P. Wood, superintendent of the Old Capitol Prison, would receive Special Order 205, authorizing him to travel to Richmond to exchange political prisoners. The Special Order, dated September 28, 1862, was unusual in the extreme. Normally, prisoner exchange went through William H. Ludlow, Commissioner of Prisoner Exchange. In this instance, the order was signed by Brigadier General James A. Wadsworth, commander of the military district of Washington, with no direct authority over prisoner exchange.[2]

The Special Order was also unique for its brevity and for the lack of advance negotiation with the rebels regarding its terms. According to Wood, the mission was approved by Secretary of War Edwin Stanton, who chose to bypass the normal chain of command. By October 3, 1862, Wood was boarding the steamer *John A. Warner* in Washington with 145 political prisoners from the Old Capitol Prison, destined for Virginia.[3]

William P. Wood provided accounts of his trip to Richmond on several occasions—most notably in the *Washington Sunday Gazette* in 1887. During these, he continued to claim the purpose was to secure Union prisoners—especially those involved in espionage, who were in danger of execution. In his last interview, however, he revealed to the press that "at some future time I will state my real business in Richmond."[4] The timing of his departure and return suggests his *real business* was stalking Barney and Young, and that any prisoners he could exchange were a bonus.

William P. Wood was no stranger to espionage, as he used his position as the superintendent of the Old Capitol Prison as a base to track rebel intelligence. "My agents secured charge of the underground mail service between Washington and Richmond," he would later reveal. "I had in my employ the most reliable male and female assistants, and by these means I was enabled to furnish Secretary Stanton with reliable information on the contemplated actions of Confederate authorities and the movements of Confederate troops."[5]

By October 6, 1862, Wood and his entourage were at Aiken's Landing on the James River, where prisoner exchanges were normally conducted. There he met Colonel Robert Ould, the Confederate commissioner for such exchanges. Wood and Ould were immediately at odds. Wood's orders were to proceed to Richmond, while Ould protested that if he did, Wood would likely be "assassinated on the streets," due to his "violent Unionism."[6] Ould finally relented, allowing Wood to go to Richmond, "under guard, as a protection."[7] Wood later asserted that Ould was finally convinced not by any logic, but by a full supply of "Yankee whiskey."[8]

Wood arrived in Richmond on October 7 and spent three days "engaged in learning the condition and whereabouts of state prisoners."[9] On October 9, as he completed his inspection, Francis G. Young was back in Washington, having been released unconditionally earlier in the month. Upon his return, Young provided Northern journalists with his own assessment of Confederate prisons, telling them that he and his fellow prisoners "had no cause to complain" as they "were put in a large and pleasant room and were attended by the guards and servants with marked kindness" with fresh food provided by sutlers and morning papers "served at daylight."[10] Young found the rebels to be "sick of hostilities" but resolved to the reality that the war would not end "until the expiration of Lincoln's term in office."[11] In a further revelation of his purpose, he noted, "All the rebel soldiers denounce Pope but speak in most complimentary terms of McClellan."[12]

Pennsylvania lieutenant D.R.B. Nevin had described his prison experience at Libby just a few weeks earlier in quite different terms. He characterized the "large and pleasant" room referenced by Young as "eighty feet long and forty feet wide" with a floor "covered with a coarse thick matting of tobacco juice and dirt about an inch thick, which could not be eradicated by the combined efforts of soap, water and brush."[13] Nevin agreed with Young that morning papers were generally available—at 25 cents each—but thought the Richmond papers largely propaganda, designed to "exaggerate the outrages of northern soldiery" and "excite public wrath and indignation against us."[14]

Rather than being attended with kindness, Nevin described their treatment as "shameful, and a disgrace to the age."[15] He documented five cases of brutality by prison guards in the month before their arrival,

Libby Prison, 1863 (Library of Congress Prints and Photographs Division). The conditions there were described far differently by Francis G. Young upon his release than by others before him. Fellow prisoner William Chase Barney refused parole until he met with Confederate officials—an act which resulted in him being suspected of espionage. Only his prewar connections with Southern legislators gained him an audience (Charles R. Rees, photographer, *Old "Libby Prison" building, Richmond, Va.*, 1863 [Richmond: Rees, ca. 1882]. Photograph. Library of Congress, https://www.loc.gov/item/2011660492/).

including that of a sutler named Higgins, who was shot and killed by a sentry while reading on his cot on September 5. On September 18, roughly a week before Barney and Young arrived, a prisoner was shot while trying to escape, resulting in an angry and excited mob descending on the prison—armed with shotguns, revolvers, axes, and any other weapons they could find. According to Nevin, "it was with the greatest difficulty this mob was restrained and kept from murdering us in cold blood."[16]

Barney and Young may have received better treatment because they were civilians; or possibly because the rush of prisoners of war after the Battle of Second Bull Run had abated after a series of prisoner exchanges, alleviating the crowded conditions. Alternatively, Young's narrative may have been carefully woven to support a previously determined agenda.

Some historians have argued that Young created precisely such a narrative the year before, when he gave journalist Edmund Stedman of the *New York World* the first reports from the Battle of Ball's Bluff—reports intended to exonerate his commander, Colonel Edmund Baker, and instead place blame for the defeat on General Charles P. Stone.[17]

There is little doubt that Young's statement to the press on October 9 was preplanned, as both he and Barney were acutely aware of the value of an informal news release. Young often engaged Stedman, for example, and in 1863, attempted to use the journalist's influence to get a news article he had written for the *New York Courier* reprinted in the Washington papers. "If you could manage to get it republished by the Republican or any Washington paper, I would be much pleased," he wrote Stedman, "if so, send me a few copies."[18]

Imprisoned in Richmond, Barney did not seek release, but rather, to gain an audience with Confederate officials—an audience they were reluctant to give him. His odd request, however, made his jailors suspicious that he was a Union spy. They may have confused him with Sergeant Thomas O. Harter, who had slipped through their hands two months earlier. Harter was a member of the First Indiana Cavalry when Major General Franz Sigel fitted him with civilian clothing and sent him behind rebel lines on July 21, 1862. Captured at Staunton, Virginia, he was held in irons there for 48 hours by John Avis, who had been John Brown's jailer back in 1859. Convinced that he was a Union operative, Avis sent him to General Winder in Richmond, who held him for eight days before releasing him.

According to Colonel L.C. Turner, it was the "fortunate accidental circumstance that he was recognized & known as a railroad engineer, by a rebel officer, which gave credence to his story that he was a refugee seeking employment, [and] saved him from death as a 'captured spy.'"[19] Upon taking an oath of allegiance to the Confederacy on August 15, 1862, Harter was released from confinement, under the pretense that he would travel to Charlottesville, Virginia, to work on the railroad. Harter arrived just in time to find the Army of Northern Virginia in preparations to attack Pope's exposed position.

Turner later wrote Stanton that "on the 18th of August, he left the Rebels, swam the [Rapidan] river, and instantly reported the position of the rebel army to General Pope, in the presence & hearing of Gens Reno, McDowell & others."[20] Such activities at that time were dangerous in the extreme, for discovery could meet instant death—as General James Longstreet's aide Captain Osmun Latrobe noted when he recorded in his diary that Confederate forces "hung a spy on the road" near Stevensville, Virginia, on August 21.[21] Harter's intervention, however, likely saved Pope's army from total annihilation. General Marcus Reno reportedly told

Harter on the battlefield that if it were not for his warning "we would have been captured and probably Washington might have been taken."[22]

Confederate spy Thomas Nelson Conrad also recognized how vulnerable the capital was to attack at that moment. According to Conrad, when he was ordered to Washington to determine conditions there, he "found the city in the utmost turmoil, frantic with fear and alarmed with fright," and concluded that "at no time during the war had Washington been in such peril."[23] Conrad planned to urge General J.E.B. Stuart to make a rush on Washington and capture Lincoln and his cabinet, but before he could do so, the window of opportunity closed—at least partially due to Harter's warnings.

Unknown to rebel authorities, Harter was released from the ranks on October 9—the same day as Francis G. Young returned to Washington. Levi C. Turner recommended him to Stanton as a "secret detective," as Harter himself thought he could "render good service in Baltimore, in detecting disloyal communications," but it is unclear whether he ever did so.[24] Rebel fears that Barney might be the man that saved Pope's army, however, likely delayed his plans to see Richmond officials in September, as he had undoubtedly planned.

Finally, on October 4, 1862, Barney got a letter through to two Confederate legislators whom he had known before the war—Senator Albert G. Brown of Mississippi and Congressman William Waters Boyce of South Carolina. Barney had likely worked with both legislators to establish a steamship route to New Orleans and may have lobbied Senator Brown after his brother's dismissal from the U.S. Navy. Brown was so close to the Barney family that he sponsored a bill in 1859 to provide Mary Barney a federal pension, on the basis that her grandfather was a signer of the Declaration of Independence.[25]

Barney sent Brown and Boyce the following appeal from Libby Prison, in the hope of making progress on the mission he crossed the lines to accomplish:

> I feel aggrieved at the position I am placed in by the unjust suspicion that I am an enemy to the Southern Confederacy. I state on the word of a gentleman, that I am not in any way connected with the Army of the United States, that I am not the person alluded to in the newspapers at the North as having been at Bull Run battle.... My chief desire is to have my position well defined and that I may possess the full confidence of my friends here and of the officers of the Confederate States. In this desire, I respectfully solicit your good offices with General Winder to procure for me the treatment due to a true friend.[26]

Ironically, the man who sought to raise a brigade of Catholics to defeat the rebels two months earlier now swore "never to take arms against the Confederate States."[27] Nevertheless, Brown and Boyce found Barney's note credible and forwarded it on to General Winder. "If Mr. Barney is really our friend, it is a great wrong to throw him into prison," they added. "We knew him in Washington City and from our knowledge of him we do not think he would write such a letter as we now enclose you, if his heart was against the South."[28]

In Senator Brown and Congressman Boyce, Barney may have had a sympathetic audience, for both were frequent critics of Confederate war policy and sponsored peace initiatives later in the conflict.[29] Despite his fiery rhetoric on the eve of Lincoln's election, William Waters Boyce may himself have reconsidered the wisdom of secession, for back in 1851, he had argued vociferously against such a move, writing that "if secession should take place—of which I have no idea, for I cannot believe in the existence of such a stupendous madness—I shall consider the institution of slavery as doomed, and that the Great God in our blindness has made us the instruments of its destruction."[30]

With the intervention of Brown and Boyce, General Winder was apparently satisfied that Barney was not a Union spy but still hesitated to give him free rein of Richmond. "The prisoners have gone, and I remain alone," Barney wrote him on October 6, 1862. "I respectfully request that you will allow me to visit my friends in the city, all of whom are office holders in the Confederate States."[31] Winder seems to have granted this last request, but the timing was awkward, for just as Barney was freed from Libby Prison, Colonel Wood was touring Richmond's prisons, checking the status of every Northern prisoner.

This added mission seems to have been conjured by Wood as a more efficient method to track Barney's activities. To add more drama to Wood's covert mission, he brought an unusual associate with him. Union major general John A. Dix, stationed at Fortress Monroe at the mouth of the James River, had choice words about both upon their return from Richmond. "Mr. Wood is here and refuses to report to me though ordered to do so," Dix wrote Stanton on October 31. "If he was a military officer, I would put him in the guard house.... Mr. Wood has also brought a clergyman by the name of Conrad, a case which I think should be looked into at Washington, where he has been confined."[32]

War Department records show that William P. Wood paid Thomas Nelson Conrad $175 over the course of the war for unspecified duties, expenditures for which he sought reimbursement from the Federal government at the close of hostilities.[33] In return, Conrad paid Wood the highest of compliments in his postwar autobiography. "As a friend he never wavered," Conrad would say of him, "as an enemy he never ... called for quarter."[34] Conrad was imprisoned under Wood's care at various times during the War and the two seemed to have developed a grudging respect for each other, despite Conrad's role as a Confederate chaplain and Wood's Unionist atheism. Conrad would later say that Wood "treated me like a father would treat a misguided son."³⁵

In his postwar autobiography, *A Confederate Spy*, Conrad notes that Wood "owed his life to the generosity of Confederate foes," for he was recognized on the streets of Richmond no less than three times by former inmates of the Old Capitol, but never turned in.³⁶ Although Conrad prefaced this story by saying that Wood told him this, the reader is left with the belief that Conrad witnessed at least one of these events personally. Wood likely sought to use Conrad to obtain details of Barney's mission from Confederate officials—a task he could only accomplish with someone they trusted.

Although Conrad had been arrested for treason, it is unlikely that Wood knew the full extent of his espionage activities, just as Conrad was unaware of Wood's. Conrad later admitted that "Colonel Wood, while cognizant of my being a one-time 'rebel spy' had likewise been a spy himself in the Union service, although this fact I was not aware of ... until months after Lee's surrender."³⁷

Southern sympathizer D.A. Mahoney of Iowa, confined in the Old Capitol Prison in 1862, would

Left: **Chaplain Thomas Nelson Conrad, 1864 (Library of Congress Prints and Photographs Division).** A note on the back indicates Conrad gave this photograph to "Mr. Ball & family," undoubtedly a reference to Confederate cavalryman Reverend Dabney Ball, the former minister of the Columbia Methodist Episcopal Church in Baltimore. Columbia may have been the home church of Conrad's parents before they moved to the Potomac River coast during the war, as they lived but a few blocks away on Baltimore's west side (Alexander Gardner, photographer, *Chaplain Thomas Nelson Conrad of 3rd Virginia Cavalry Regiment,* 1864 [Washington, D.C.: Gardner, 1864]. Photograph. Library of Congress, https://www.loc.gov/item/2020635979/).

later allege that Wood's mission to Richmond was "in reality, to make propositions of peace to the Confederates."[38] According to Mahoney, Wood was authorized to make the following peace propositions:

> 1st. That the Slave States should have a Congress of their own to regulate their domestic institutions.
> 2nd. That the fugitive slave law should be enforced or failing to do so the State to which a fugitive escaped should pay his value and the costs made in an effort to reclaim him.
> 3rd. That the representation in the Federal Congress should be based on white population only.
> 4th. That the debts of the Confederacy incurred to carry on the war should be assumed and paid by the United States as restored to the Union.
> 5th. That slavery should be under the control of the respective States exclusively but that no laws should be passed by Territories to exclude or permit the introduction of slaves.[39]

Wood biographer Curtis Carroll Davis would later contemplate whether such a peace mission was the "real business" in Richmond of which Wood alluded to in 1887.[40] However, the idea that Secretary of War Stanton would have authorized such a mission in the wake of the Emancipation Proclamation is preposterous and unsupported by other facts. Mahoney never provided his source, but it was likely fellow prisoner Tom Conrad, who was not exchanged during the Richmond mission, but returned to the Old Capitol Prison. Conrad had his own motives for spreading this rumor—for it gave more credence to the fallacy that the Union could be resurrected, if only slavery was preserved.

Although Conrad readily admitted to plotting to assassinate General Winfield Scott, kidnapping Lincoln and even some role with the Booth conspirators, he was forever silent on Wood's mission to Richmond and the peace rumors which followed. Instead, his two wartime autobiographies leave a large gap between the Battle of Antietam and the Battle of Fredericksburg in December 1862. His silence guaranteed that Wood's curious mission to secure a prisoner exchange and the events which followed would remain one of the war's best kept secrets.

Wood left Richmond on October 10, 1862, for Salisbury, North Carolina, to inspect prisoners there, but may have left Conrad to watch Barney, who was still meeting with Confederate officials. "I am informed that the flag of truce boat will not leave Aiken's Landing before 1 p m tomorrow, Tuesday," Barney wrote General Winder on October 13, "and as I did not come to Richmond voluntarily to be detained in prison, but for the purposes I have heretofore stated to you, I respectfully request that you will permit me to return to the North by this present boat and allow me to visit Governor Brown, Senator and Mr. Boyce, Member of Congress, before I leave."[41]

By October 25, 1862, William Chase Barney had returned to Fortress Monroe. "Mr. Wood, keeper of [Old] Capitol Prison remains at Richmond," Lieutenant Colonel William H. Ludlow informed Secretary Stanton that day. "Major Barney, who just came from there, proceeds to Washington to report to you facts in reference to him, which you ought to know."[42] The following day, Ludlow wrote the Adjutant General, obviously much agitated: "Mr. Wood is doing most absurd things at Richmond, where he now is and Major Barney, paymaster US Army, just released from there has gone to Washington to report his misconduct to the Secretary of War."[43]

Assuming Stanton directed General Wadsworth to issue Special Order 205 to track William Chase Barney's movements in Richmond, it is highly ironic that Dix would send Barney back to Stanton to report the alleged misdeeds of Wood. According to press reports, Barney arrived back in Washington on October 27, 1862.[44] That same day, Secretary Stanton abruptly disavowed Wood's prisoner exchange and instructed Lieutenant Colonel William H. Ludlow to "adopt what measures may be necessary for the return of Mr. Wood to this city."[45] Stanton's action the day of Barney's return is more evidence that Wood's primary mission had been to watch Barney, and that the prisoner exchange was merely a ruse.

Despite Ludlow's promise, there is no evidence that Barney ever saw Secretary Stanton about Wood's conduct. A correspondent of the *New York Tribune*, however, would later write that Barney "had an interview with Secretary Seward and President Lincoln as soon as he returned to Washington, but they declined to consider the matter in the shape in which he presented it to them."[46] The *Tribune* quickly issued a correction, saying that contrary to their original report, Barney actually "had no personal communication with the President."[47] He may have met with Assistant Secretary of State Frederick Seward, who had helped him gain his appointment as an additional paymaster the previous year, but if so, there is no corroborating evidence of such a meeting.

As Barney attempted to sell his peace plan to the administration, officials at Fortress Monroe were still fuming about Wood. A correspondent of the *New York Herald* at Fortress Monroe noted wryly that Wood "made himself obnoxious, not only to the rebel authorities, but also to the War Department in Washington."[48] On October 31, Major General John A. Dix wrote Stanton in a rage. "Mr. Wood is here and refuses to report to me, though ordered to do so. If he were a military officer, I would put him in the guard house."[49] The Secretary of War replied quickly, in a manner designed to protect Wood's cover. "You should have sent Wood to the guard house. When you think any man deserves it, 'shoot him on the spot.'"[50]

There seems to be no record of when Wood returned to Washington with his paroled prisoners. However, if he left Fortress Monroe the following day and took three days to move from Fortress Monroe up Chesapeake Bay and the Potomac River, as he had on the journey down, he would have arrived in Washington sometime on Monday, November 3, 1862, and upon his arrival, have immediately reported to Stanton. Lincoln met with his cabinet the day following Wood's probable return—on Tuesday, November 4, 1862.

Secretary of the Navy Gideon Welles made a point to record that day that Stanton's "dislike for McC increases."[51] Given that Stanton had petitioned the president to immediately remove McClellan from "the command of any army of the United States" back on August 30, Welles' observation suggests new information had come to light recently, far beyond Lincoln's observation that McClellan had a case of "the slows."[52] Much of the meeting, in fact, revolved around finally removing McClellan for good. As justification, Lincoln simply produced a copy of a letter he had written McClellan on October 13, ordering him to move against Lee, which he hadn't.

Stanton and Lincoln already had substantial evidence of McClellan's duplicity. A week after the battle of Antietam, Major Levi C. Turner of the Judge Advocates office asked Major John J. Key, brother of McClellan staff officer Colonel Thomas Key, why McClellan hadn't "bagged" Lee while he had the chance. "That's not the game," Key replied. "The object is that neither army shall get much advantage of the other; that both shall be kept in the field till they are exhausted, when we will make a compromise and save slavery."[53]

Turner reported the conversation and on the morning of September 24, 1862, Lincoln called both men to the White House. Key did not detract his statement, but sought to demonstrate his loyalty, to no avail. "Your views upon the slavery question may be what you please," Lincoln reportedly replied, "but I will not knowingly harbor any officer in my armies who does not desire to crush the enemy."[54] He dismissed Key from the service on the spot.

The day after the cabinet meeting on November 4, the president formally relieved General George B. McClellan of command of the Army of the Potomac as well.[55] There is no record of whether William Chase Barney ever saw McClellan or his staff after his return to Washington. In a letter to the *New York Herald* dated January 1, 1863, however, Barney maintained his belief that a negotiated peace would have been possible, "any time after the Battle of Antietam up to the removal of General McClellan."[56] Despite never admitting outright that McClellan had sent him to Richmond, his statement spoke for itself.

12

A Fraudulent Peace

If the proclamation of Mr. Lincoln was not suspended or revoked, it would only be a stimulus to an interminable and ruinous war.[1]

—John Wesley Greene, December 9, 1862

The week following the dismissal of General McClellan, a letter, dated November 11, 1862, arrived at the White House which read, in part:

> An entire stranger to fame, and almost unknown beyond the mere business and social circles in which I move; but at the same time an ardent lover of the country which for nearly fifty years has encompassed me with its protection, I presume to introduce myself to your notice in reference to the all-absorbing interest of the times—the termination of the Rebellion and the restoration of the Union.[2]

The author claimed to have just met with Confederate president Jefferson Davis and found him "anxious for an end of hostilities and a return to the Union."[3] Signed by J. Wesley Greene of Pittsburgh, the letter was likely hand delivered, for there is no accompanying envelope within the records of the Library of Congress. Witnesses saw him at Willard's Hotel the previous weekend "in company with several ladies," noting that while there, "he lived rather fast."[4]

After delivering the letter, Greene returned to Pittsburgh, but soon received a telegram from Secretary of War Edwin M. Stanton on November 16, urging him back to Washington. Upon his arrival there the following day, he once again took a room at Willard's Hotel, this time in the company of a man known as "Cullison."[5] Upon gaining an audience with Secretary Stanton on the morning of Tuesday, November 18, 1862, Greene presented a letter of introduction, supposedly from Thomas Bakewell, an influential friend of Stanton's from Pittsburgh. He also provided as references his employer, John Dunlap, and the Rev. A.J. Endsley, a well-known Pittsburgh minister.

In the hallway of the War Department, Greene brushed past Stanton's

12. A Fraudulent Peace

chief of detectives, Allan Pinkerton—who recognized him at once, but could not recall his name. Concerned that Greene was "engaged in some swindle or fraud," Pinkerton alerted Assistant Secretary of War Peter H. Watson, who made a note of it.[6] Neither was aware that Greene was, in fact, meeting with Stanton himself. Pinkerton undoubtedly remembered Greene from his brief incarceration in September 1861, while a chaplain for the Tenth Pennsylvania Reserves. Although he was acquitted of any crime after members of his regiment refused to testify against him, insiders knew different.

Greene had never returned to West Middlesex, Pennsylvania, but instead relocated to Pittsburgh, where the regiment had originally mustered. In a testament to the generous ladies of the Liberty Methodist Episcopal Church, who had donated 500 pies to the new recruits, Greene and his wife joined their congregation shortly after his removal from the service.[7] In the Tenth Pennsylvania Reserves, Greene was replaced by veteran pastor Latshaw McGuire and his memory was essentially washed from the record books—so much so, that the otherwise thorough *History of the Pennsylvania Reserve Corps*, written at the close of the war, does not even list him as a member of the regiment.[8]

Ignorant of Pinkerton's warning about Greene, Secretary of War Edwin Stanton wrote a brief note to President Lincoln the next day, advising him of the presence in Washington of "Wesley Greene, the man you wished me to telegraph."[9] Greene was ushered into Lincoln's office, to present the peace offer to the president in all its detail. It was a room Greene described as the "executive chamber," most likely Lincoln's office on the second story of the White House, where Lincoln had met with the Rev. W.W. Patton and the Rev. John Dempster about emancipation just two months before.[10]

According to Greene's later affidavit, Lincoln greeted him "in an easy, affable manner," virtually the same words used by Gideon Welles to describe his greeting of Chicago abolitionists two months earlier. Lincoln handed him Greene's own letter: "'Did you write that letter?'"[11] Receiving an affirmative response, the president asked that he recount the peace proposal of Jefferson Davis which Greene alluded to, but had not fully described, having written that the terms were "of a nature which forbids me to commit them to writing from this distance."[12]

Greene told Lincoln that he had been approached in Pittsburgh on October 22, 1862, by a former Baltimore policeman living in Richmond, Horace N. Wilson, who requested that he act as a peace envoy to Washington, for the purpose of restoring the old Union. Greene claimed to have done a personal favor for Jefferson Davis during the Mexican War, while serving in the Third Artillery at the Battle of Buena Vista, which Davis never forgot. By

Greene's reckoning, Davis thought him to be both trustworthy and neutral—the perfect go-between with Lincoln, with no political agenda of his own.[13]

It was a plausible story. Greene was just about the right age to have served in the conflict that had made Davis famous, when his Mississippi Rifles had beaten back a massive Mexican assault with the help of the Third Artillery. Greene claimed to have accompanied Wilson to Richmond, where he met Davis personally on Sunday, October 26—the same day William Chase Barney was released and sent north after his meeting with Confederate officials. According to Greene's affidavit, the Confederate president laid out the following three conditions for restoration of the Union:

> First—A general and unconditional amnesty of all political offenders against the Federal Government, such as would place them in the position they occupied before the commencement of hostilities, as it respected their immunities, rights and privileges.
>
> Secondly—The restoration of all fugitive slaves within the control of the Federal Government; and a guarantee that the General Government will give the entire weight of its influence and authority in carrying out the provisions of the Fugitive Slave law, in the recovery of those fugitive slaves who may have passed beyond the immediate control of the Government.
>
> Thirdly—That each of the contending parties shall be held responsible only for the debt incurred by it, in the same manner as if they had been recognized and independent Powers.[14]

Greene cited the Emancipation Proclamation as the motivating force behind the South's purported peace proposal—warning that abolishing slavery would produce Armageddon. The proclamation, said Greene, was the equivalent of a call for "general servile insurrection" which would result in "acts of barbarism having no parallel in the history of the civilized world."[15] Further, he claimed, it would likely result in "the extermination of the colored population in the Confederate States, unless the European Powers interposed to prevent it." In this case, Davis supposedly warned, intervention would "involve so many interests, he believed, as to produce a general warfare throughout the world."[16]

According to Greene, Lincoln saw nothing objectionable in the conditions for peace. In fact, he thought the president receptive to the point that "if left to the impulses and convictions of his own heart, and at liberty to do so, he would inaugurate a peace on the basis of these proposals."[17] Lincoln, however, called in Edwin Stanton, and repeated the story himself, asking for Greene's input only to verify its accuracy. Later that day, at five in the afternoon, Greene met again, this time with Lincoln and several cabinet members, including Secretary of State William Seward, Secretary of the Navy Gideon Welles and Stanton, who conducted most of the remaining interview.

Greene found the Secretary of War skeptical. "A most searching inquiry then commenced," Greene remembered of Stanton's questions. "My birthplace; my relatives; my occupation ... and every other conceivable question designed to arrive at as full a knowledge of my history and character as far as could be obtained by questioning."[18] Davis' thoughts and motives were also questioned, as were Greene's own thoughts on the Emancipation Proclamation.

The meeting supposedly lasted until eleven that night. Mary Lincoln was in New York City that week, and thus unencumbered by family obligations, Lincoln and Stanton took the time necessary to vet the matter in its entirety.[19] Although Greene's affidavit is the only known record of the interview, his claim of it lasting most of the day is supported by other sources, which record little else on Lincoln's calendar.[20] According to Greene, the two met again the following morning, and again over the next several days, but these additional meetings cannot be corroborated by other sources, and Greene himself described them as "trifling."[21]

By the time they were done with him, Greene concluded that the administration was not interested in his offer, although they did provide him $100 for his expenses back to Pittsburgh. Yet, Greene was not going to let his visit to the capital pass without a memento of his meeting with the president. According to the *Washington Evening Star*, Greene had visited the hat and fur shop of B.H. Steinmetz, a block down Pennsylvania Avenue from Willard's, on several occasions that week to look at a fur cape, at least once with a "friend"—likely the man named Cullison.[22]

On Saturday, November 22, 1862, Greene stopped again at the furrier and agreed to a price of $175, claiming that the bill would be paid by the War Department. Skeptical that the government would want to purchase furs, Steinmetz had his young clerk, Walter Ker, accompany Greene to the War Department offices to receive payment. There, on War Department letterhead, Greene boldly wrote the following requisition to the Secretary of the Treasury: "Pay B.H. Stinemetz one hundred and seventy-five dollars, and charge to the account of J.W. Green."[23]

When the clerk expressed concern that the Treasury office was closed, Greene "offered to go to the Treasury and see him get the money."[24] They never made it. Upon passing the White House, Greene "told the man to walk on, and he would overtake him—that he had some business with the President—and he bolted in the front door."[25] W.B. Webb of the metropolitan police verified that "Green called with the clerk at the President's House" that day.[26] Greene did not likely see Lincoln personally, as the president was known to be holding a conference at Secretary Seward's house, possibly about the Greene interviews earlier that week.[27]

To the dismay of poor Steinmetz, the requisition was worthless when he tried to cash it the following Monday.[28] By that time, Greene was gone, having left Washington on Saturday from the Baltimore and Ohio depot near the Capitol. Perhaps to distract Federal authorities, Greene sent Lincoln a note before leaving Washington: "Horace M. Wilson is now at Baltimore. I believe him to be in treasonable correspondence with parties there. What shall be done with him? I can put him in the hands of authorities soon after reaching the city. I await your excellency's reply."[29]

Greene left the capital under the watchful eyes of two detectives under Colonel Lafayette Baker. Detective William S. Radle described the surveillance of Greene from Willard's Hotel that Saturday, November 22, 1862:

> The first I saw of him (Greene) he came down stairs and walked up to the Office and called for his bill ... then he went up stairs I thought for his Baggage but he did not return. Then I was bound to track Cullison ... we followed him to the Depot, about the time we all got fairly seated, in came Mr. Green. He seemed to be very uneasy and when he got to the Relay House he got up and put on his Over coat and went out of the cars and went down the steps and took a look around and then he came back.[30]

Sergeant John Lee would telegraph Colonel Lafayette Baker from Baltimore that evening, noting that Greene "ran away from Willard's Hotel without paying his bill" and would identify the man Cullison as a "hay contractor."[31] This last clue would confirm that the man previously known only by his last name was, in fact, Greene's brother-in-law, 44-year-old Jesse Marling Cullison, a resident of Baltimore.[32] Greene himself would reveal his connection to the family when he admitted using another brother-in-law's name as an alias later in the war.[33]

The two detectives followed Greene and Cullison on the train north from Washington. Using the military telegraph at Major General John E. Wool's Baltimore headquarters at the Western District police station, they kept a running dialogue with Colonel Lafayette Baker back in Washington. "We have traced both men Cullison & Green to Biddle & Penn Ave to Cullison's own house," Lee telegraphed at 8:30 Saturday evening. "I will stay by the house all night."[34] Colonel Baker sent this response: "Don't let the parties out of your sight. Talk to no one about your business, not even the Balto. Police."[35]

Unfortunately for Baker's detectives, Greene knew he'd been followed and slipped out the back door. Sergeant Lee had been watching the front of the house, while Radle watched the street leading to the Susquehanna Depot. Detective Lee rushed another telegram to Baker at midnight: "Mr. Riddle (Radle) has gone after Green. He got out of the back fence. I don't know whether he will be successful or not. Green is running as fast as he can.... If I was to arrest Collison I think he would tell us where Green has gone to.... Answer what I should do."[36]

"You have no orders to arrest either party but only to follow them & report their movements to me," Lafayette Baker instructed Lee. "If they come this way or any other way follow them up. If you see Radle tell him the same thing. Don't give them any reason to suspect your movements."[37]

With the aid of a Baltimore policeman, who "saw a man going out the back way with a paper bundle," detective William Radle tracked a man meeting Greene's description to the train depot. The paper bundle was undoubtedly his fur from Steinmetz, although Radle said "it looked like a coat."[38] The detective followed him south on the Baltimore and Ohio line towards Washington but lost him where the track branched west at the Relay House. "I started in pursuit of him, I heard of him or a man that answered the description of him precisely … going up toward the Relay House," Radle recorded in his report. "I got a conveyance and thought to head him off by going to Ellicot's Mills, but he did not come that way for I watched the road and went through every train till Monday noon."[39]

Relay House on the Baltimore and Ohio Railroad, 1861–1865 (Library of Congress Prints and Photographs Division). This junction is where John Wesley Greene lost Federal detectives, who trailed him after his meeting with President Lincoln. Although a detective suspected Greene took the western branch back to Pittsburgh, he likely took refuge at Reverend William G. Jackson's home in nearby Elkridge instead (E. & H.T. Anthony, publisher, *The famous Relay House on the Baltimore & Ohio R.R.*, Maryland [New York: E. & H.T. Anthony, between 1861 and 1865]. Photograph. Library of Congress, https://www.loc.gov/item/2022631305/).

Exhausted by that time, Radle gave up the stakeout and returned to Baltimore, where Sergeant Lee had been fruitlessly watching Cullison. On the afternoon of November 24, Lee telegraphed Baker: "Mr. Collison is at work at his hay presses near his residence & I think there is no danger of his going away. I have him in sight all the time."[40] John Wesley Greene, however, would not return to Baltimore, nor to his job in Pittsburgh, leaving the two detectives empty-handed.

Greene, suspicious of being followed, would later admit that he traveled west by a "zig zag route."[41] He wrote an associate in Pittsburgh, asking him to send his wife to Cleveland, where he would meet her at the Weddell House Hotel. Greene gave explicit instructions for her not to acknowledge him on the street if she saw him.[42] From Cleveland, they journeyed to Chicago, where they reportedly checked in at the City Hotel in late November or early December.[43] Greene would take his story to the *Chicago Times*, the leading Copperhead paper in the country, edited by Wilbur F. Storey—the man who had advocated forgiveness for the Rev. Otis Tiffany's inadvertent night of drunkenness.

Storey had come to Chicago from the *Detroit Free Press* in 1861 and turned the struggling *Times* into one of the most popular periodicals in the country. His formula for success involved extensive battlefield coverage combined masterfully with tales of corruption and incompetency by Federal officials. He was an advocate of peace with the Confederacy and naively espoused the theory that Southern states would return to the Union if only allowed to do so. To Wilbur Storey, abolitionists were the real enemy, not the Confederacy. He claimed in March 1862, that "the worst traitors were not at the south.... It is the abolitionists and fanatical Republicans at the North, and chiefly those in Congress ... who prevent the return of the Southern states to their allegiance."[44]

Thus, when Greene came to him with his story that the Confederacy had offered peace, Storey was receptive to the message and reportedly paid him $500 to disclose it.[45] Since by his own admission he had been paid by in gold by Horace Wilson, and the Lincoln administration had paid him for expenses to Pittsburgh, he was now paid a third time. Greene had more than just his own word to support his claims—the *Chicago Times* would report that they had total confidence in him, not only based on many interviews with him, but "by numerous testimonials as to his character."[46] Who provided such testimonials and how Greene obtained them was a measure of how well organized the rebel underground was in Maryland and how extensive the plot to stop emancipation.

13

Mission to Maryland

> *He [Jefferson Davis] was thus always hasty to send peace messengers to Washington ... but in convenient disguise, so they might not convey any confession of weakness.*[1]
> —Edward A. Pollard, 1869

Since William Chase Barney's true mission to Richmond had not been made public when Greene met Lincoln, it seems likely that either the same source in the North sent them both or Greene was sent by rebel operatives in the wake of Barney's meetings in Richmond. Available evidence suggests the latter. According to Edward A. Pollard of the *Richmond Examiner*, Confederate president Jefferson Davis prepared a peace mission to Washington before the Battle of Antietam, not with the intent of negotiating a true peace, but to "furnish capital to the Democratic party in the North, widen divisions there, and excite a political diversion in favor of the South."[2]

Davis was not the only Southerner with such a peace plan, for on September 20 the *Richmond Enquirer* published a proposed resolution from Confederate congressman Henry S. Foote, recommending that the Confederacy send peace ambassadors to Washington.[3] In Foote's case, the proposal was genuine, for Union forces controlled much of his district. Pollard thought Davis and Foote colluded to float the peace proposals, a charge Foote vigorously denied, noting that the two had hardly spoken since their "painful contest" for the post of Mississippi governor in 1851.[4]

Despite Foote's bad relations with Davis, he had sought a meeting with the Confederate president about the idea on September 10, 1862, a meeting Davis declined, citing that he was too busy.[5] After the war, Foote took all responsibility upon himself. "The truth is, that I brought forward peace resolutions, or counseled others to bring them forward repeatedly," he wrote, "and always simply because I preferred peace to war and thought it better to strike for peace while an honorable one could be obtained."[6]

Foote not only got the cold shoulder from Davis; his proposal was actively opposed by many Southern legislators, such as Mississippi congressman Ethelbert Barksdale, who argued that the best and only way to secure peace was by "vigorous fighting."[7] Nevertheless, it seems likely that the Davis administration had their own peace plan, if only to impress the Europeans and further their own war plans. According to Pollard, a peace ambassador was being groomed to go north amid Lee's invasion, but "while the Commissioner for Washington was being prepared ... news came that Lee's army had fallen back across the Potomac, having fought the unhappy Battle of Sharpsburg."[8]

Unknown to Pollard, William Chase Barney's clumsy peace mission and the issuance of Lincoln's Emancipation Proclamation seems to have reinvigorated the Davis administration's fraudulent peace plan after all. With the prospect of emancipation at hand, the goals of the mission undoubtedly changed: it was now not sufficient simply to excite a political diversion—rather, it was imperative that Lincoln be forced to withdraw his proclamation before it went into effect on January 1, 1863.

To convey their message, the so-called "peace ambassador" must appear neutral, but still convey the consequences of emancipation in apocalyptic terms, as Representative Charles W. Russell did before the Confederate Congress on October 1, 1862, when he proclaimed that the proclamation was designed specifically to invite "servile insurrection."[9] John Wesley Greene, a resident of Pittsburgh, met these requirements. A native of New York, he was, nevertheless, thoroughly versed in the doctrine of the South's biblical defense of slavery. He had selected the Rev. Nathan Rice to officiate his 1859 wedding in Cincinnati—a man best known for defending slavery in a debate with abolitionist Jonathon Blanchard on October 1, 1845.[10]

Although Murat Halstead of the *Cincinnati Commercial* would later conclude that the wedding was performed by "Rev. Rice of the Disciples [of the Presbyterian] Church," Halstead likely confused Rice, a Presbyterian, with Alexander Campbell, founder of the Disciples Church, whom Rice had famously debated on the subject of baptism in 1843.[11] Greene's choice of Rice to officiate his wedding was likely no accident, for neither Greene nor his bride was Presbyterian—suggesting Rice's fame in defense of slavery was the reason for his selection.

Superficially, Greene seemed the perfect choice to present the peace proposal to Lincoln. One earlier acquaintance described him as "silver tongued, voluble, plausible in speech, of a highly imaginative turn of mind, and in his ecclesiastical exercises, very emotional," while another thought him "talented and fascinating."[12] He was just the right age to have served with Jefferson Davis in Mexico, his cover story for why the Confederate president chose him for the delicate mission in the first place.

The degree to which Confederate president Jefferson Davis was involved in Greene's plot is debatable, but in the wake of Lincoln's Emancipation Proclamation, Davis might well have agreed to a covert plan to undo it, for it threatened the entire fabric of Southern society they were fighting to maintain. Besides halting emancipation, however, Davis had other strategic objectives. Foremost among these was obtaining intelligence on the Baltimore and Ohio Railroad, which by the fall of 1862 had become critical to the Union war effort. It not only served as a means of resupply to military operations in the lower Shenandoah Valley and trans-Allegheny region, but it also brought coal from the western coalfields to the East Coast.

On September 15, 1862, Virginia governor John Letcher warned the Virginia legislature that something must be done about the troublesome railroad line:

> The Baltimore & Ohio rail road has been a positive nuisance to this state from the opening of this war to the present time; and unless its management shall herafter be in friendly hands, and the government under which it exists be part of our confederacy, it must be abated. If it should be permanently destroyed, we must assure our people of some other communication with the seaboard.[13]

Lee's army did their best to permanently destroy the Baltimore and Ohio during the Antietam campaign, demolishing bridges, track, crossties and virtually all infrastructure in Martinsburg, including engine houses, machine shops, offices, blacksmith shop and pumping station. Fortuitously for the Union, however, the railroad had stockpiled track supplies between the Relay House and Washington with the intent of laying a second track on that busy section, which they quickly diverted to repair the destroyed sections to the west.[14]

At least as critical as the destruction of the Baltimore and Ohio was the need to resupply Lee's army with horses, for by the end of 1862, the Confederacy was in dire need of fresh mounts. The great horse-breeding regions of Kentucky and west Tennessee were in Union hands, and their loss severely hampered the Confederate army's ability to sustain itself.[15] By November, Confederate secretary of war George W. Randolph wrote General Robert E. Lee, suggesting that he was "sending an officer to Texas to purchase 1,000 horses, if possible, intending to resell them at cost to the cavalry of your army."[16] This plan never seems to have worked. Instead, Lee seems to have relied heavily on smuggling them out of Maryland—but such an effort required forethought and an organized network of Southern sympathizers behind Union lines.

Because of the complexity of a mission to accomplish all three objectives, Jefferson Davis likely relied upon on a small cadre of trusted associates led by Thomas Nelson Conrad, whom William P. Wood had conveniently brought to Richmond from his captivity in Washington.

By the fall of 1862, Conrad had already gained the trust of Davis, recalling that earlier that year, he had spent "a most delightful evening" with the Confederate president, during which time Davis introduced him to others as his "confidential scout."[17] After Conrad's death in 1905, the *Washington Evening Star* went so far as to deem Conrad "one of Jefferson Davis's closest aides."[18]

Aside from Conrad, the mission was undoubtedly authorized at the highest level, probably by Secretary of State Judah P. Benjamin, with whom William Chase Barney claimed to have had "frequent interviews" about a so-called "peace Congress" while in Richmond.[19] Although Benjamin had no real interest in such an idea, he undoubtedly saw an opportunity to divide the North and force the rescission of Lincoln's proclamation. To do so, he likely consulted his college friend from Yale, Baltimore attorney William H. Norris—who already had a vast network of friends and family in northern Virginia and Maryland.[20]

Largely forgotten by history, William Henry Norris was highly influential among Baltimore secessionists. On July 5, 1862, Norris had returned to Benjamin bonds entrusted to Henry Steuart to arm Captain Henry B. Latrobe's Third Maryland Artillery. Benjamin subsequently made the following accounting to Confederate treasury secretary Christopher Memminger:

> This morning I received from my friend William H Norris Esq of Baltimore the accompanying bundle containing 28,000 in bonds, which bundle was placed by Major Rhett in the hands of Mrs. Norris for safe keeping. Major Rhett received the bundle from [Harry Steuart]. These 28,000 are therefore returned to the Treasury to be placed to the credit of Stewart, from whom no account of the disposal of the remaining 2,000 has been received.[21]

The major referenced by Benjamin was undoubtedly Thomas Smith Rhett, who graduated from West Point in 1848 in the same class as George H. "Maryland" Steuart—the lieutenant colonel of the First Maryland Infantry, to whom Henry Steuart was related. From 1855 to 1861, Rhett was a clerk in the Union Bank of Baltimore, a bank whose board of directors included Captain Latrobe's father—John H.B. Latrobe.[22]

It seems likely that Captain Henry B. Latrobe used his father's influence with Rhett and the Union Bank to help purchase military supplies for the formation of the Third Maryland Artillery in Richmond. Rhett was appointed a captain in the Confederate Artillery on November 19, 1861, with an effective date of November 15, 1861—the same date as Steuart left Richmond for Baltimore. According to former Baltimore architect Richard Snowden Andrews, commander of the Maryland "Flying Artillery," he personally notified Rhett of his commission. Rhett, however, responded that "he could not leave Baltimore for several months."[23] Rhett's delay was probably related to his commitment to purchase military supplies on behalf of Henry Steuart, but when Steuart was captured in December, Rhett transferred the bonds to Norris—who by then was likely working in northern Virginia, for he fled Baltimore in November 1861, while "orders were in the hands of the police for [his] arrest."[24]

During this time, Norris and his wife, Mary, were likely working from "Clifton," the country estate of her brother-in-law, Algernon S. Allen, just east of Winchester, where she appears to have acted as a supply agent for rebel forces.[25] Records of the Confederate War Department show a trail of payments to "Mrs. Mary Norris" at Winchester for flour, corn and a team to haul them totaling $573.50, the last of such invoices being issued on October 2, 1862.[26] It was not a coincidence that one of her sons, James William Lyon, was given a commission as major of commissary under fellow Emmanuel Church member General Isaac Trimble, effective February 13, 1862.[27]

From Clifton, the Norrises could have coordinated the flow of both military supplies and intelligence out of Baltimore, where they still maintained their home. Clifton gained a reputation for such clandestine activities, for it was reportedly used later to shelter the family of Colonel John S. Moseby.[28] The home was largely vacant, as her sister, Anne Boyd Owen Allen, had died before the war and the three Allen sons had joined the Confederate army at the outbreak of hostilities.[29]

During the winter of 1862, Federal authorities realized to their chagrin that Mary Norris had been receiving messages in cipher from Richard Thomas Zarvona, who was incarcerated with her son, Samuel Lyon, in Fort Lafayette. She was quickly arrested at her house by four policemen and confined in the Old Capitol Prison, where, according to her son, she was "not allowed visitors, not even relatives, on the grounds she was considered 'dangerous.'"[30]

Despite the concerns of Federal officials, Mary Norris was released on March 18, 1862, under what was called a "parole of honor."[31] As an intermediate step, she was removed from the prison and allowed to stay at what Lyon called the "jailers house"—the residence of William P. Wood.[32] Whether Wood was testing her allegiance or surreptitiously attempting to learn of Confederate plans by housing her at his home is a matter of conjecture, for as one biographer noted, Wood was the "craftiest of men."[33] In any case, her association with Colonel Wood may have borne fruit later that year, when Wood was in Richmond on the heels of William Chase Barney.

It appears that Norris lobbied Benjamin to make the release of Zarvona and Lyon a priority when Wood was there discussing a prisoner exchange. On November 2, 1862, Confederate congressman William Porcher Miles

Clifton Estate, Berryville, Virginia, 1933 (Library of Congress Prints and Photographs Division). This was the Shenandoah Valley home of Mary Norris' sister, Ann Boyd Owen Allen. Confederate records suggest Mary Norris supplied the Confederate army from it in 1861 and 1862. A Confederate government loan for $8,800, upon which she made payments starting in November 1862, may have funded Mountjoy Cloud's secret mission to Baltimore (Historic American Buildings Survey, creator, *Clifton, State Route 610 vicinity, Berryville, Clarke County, VA*, [1933]. Photograph. Library of Congress, https://www.loc.gov/item/va0323/).

wrote General P.G.T. Beauregard, advising him of the attempts to free Zarvona:

> A proposition has been recently made by our Government to Mr Wood, the Yankee commissioner of exchanges who has been in Richmond, to the effect that if the Yankees would give up Mr Soulé and Colonel Thomas Zarvona, we would give up two Yankee spies whom we have here under sentence of death. Mr Wood was quite favorable to the proposition but had no authority to act.[34]

Although attempts to release Zarvona failed, Lyon was exchanged for a Union officer by Stanton's order on November 26, 1862, after Wood's return to Washington.[35] It may have been the one solid concession that Confederate officials obtained from Wood, in exchange for evidence that Barney was in Richmond on McClellan's behalf.

According to his correspondence with General John H. Winder, who held him in Libby Prison, Barney met with Confederate officials sometime between October 7 and October 14, 1862. It is apparent that Judah P. Benjamin and William H. Norris were in close contact during this same time, as Benjamin wrote the following recommendation to President Davis on October 16:

> I beg respectfully to recommend Wm H Norris Esq of Maryland for appointment as a member of one the military commissions for Gen Lee's army—I have known Mr Norris from boyhood.... Mrs Norris is an indefatigable laborer in the good work done in Baltimore for our wounded and suffering soldiers and has been incarcerated in Ft McHenry for her active kindness and aid to our prisoners. I feel Mr. Norris would be an excellent appointment.[36]

The effective date of Norris' commission was not until December 16, 1862, giving him adequate time to help organize a clandestine mission to Washington and Baltimore from Clifton, near where Lee's Army of Northern Virginia was deployed.

After his release, Norris' son Samuel Lyon seemed acutely aware that his exchange was the result of high-level subterfuge. Apparently concerned that Federal authorities would think he was involved in such activities, he fled to France at the end of the war and requested a pardon from President Andrew Johnson via an attorney in August 1865. Although he admitted serving in the Confederate army as a private soldier, he felt obliged to claim "no connection with any Rebel agents or schemes."[37]

The fraudulent peace initiative was likely foremost among the schemes Lyon was referring to, and his stepfather was likely central to its planning. Such a mission, however, was not without cost. It may be for this reason that Mary Norris began making large subscription payments on a Confederate loan totaling $8,800, starting on November 8, 1862, and ending July 1, 1863.[38] Such a slush fund would be adequate to pay off operatives in Virginia and Maryland and pay for the services of someone like John Wesley Greene, who claimed to be paid for his traveling expenses in "American gold."[39]

Mary Norris likely had a direct contact in the Confederate Treasury Department in the person of Charles Howard, Jr., who had sought a position in that department as early as November 28, 1861. He wrote Secretary Christopher Memminger that day, citing his "large experience as clerk, having had charge of the books of a large Mercantile House for six years."[40] The extent of Howard's influence over the course of the war is unclear, but in March 1865, as the South was collapsing, he seems to have convinced his parents back in Baltimore to deposit $14,000 in silver and $6,000 in gold in the Bank of Virginia on behalf of the Confederacy.[41]

The large donation to a truly lost cause in 1865 shows how easily Mary Norris might have obtained donations to repay her $8,800 loan in 1862. She also had the resources to organize a network to smuggle horses south and wreck the railroad network heading west. Not only did her husband know every influential secessionist in Baltimore but he was closely associated with many former officers of the Baltimore and Ohio, such as James Carroll, John H.B. Latrobe, and Benjamin H. Latrobe II—who as the railroad's chief civil engineer had designed many of its bridges. Benjamin Latrobe had offered his services to the Confederacy back on April 25, 1861, but apparently had never gone South.[42] If anyone had the knowledge to permanently disable the line, it was he, the man who helped build it.

Despite his influence, William H. Norris likely left the details of such a clandestine mission to experienced operatives like Tom Conrad. A plan involving John Wesley Greene as a peace envoy bears Conrad's signature, for the plan not only utilized a clergyman, as Conrad was fond of doing, but also sowed disinformation—a tactic at which he was a master. An incident in 1873, when he was editor of the *Montgomery (VA) Messenger*, demonstrates how clever he was at such trickery. Former Confederate president Jefferson Davis had delivered a fiery speech before the Southern Historical Association at White Sulfur Springs that year, and Conrad saw an opportunity to embarrass his liberal political rivals at the *Lynchburg Republican*.

Conrad concocted a bogus interview with Davis, complete with embarrassing details, and offered it to the *Republican*, on the condition they print it at once or he would withdraw the offer and print it himself. They took the bait and printed it without vetting the story. When Davis denied the interview ever took place, the *Republican* stubbornly stuck by their source. Only intervention by the *Alexandria Gazette* saved them from humiliation, by challenging Conrad to substantiate the interview or confess to "making the *Republican* his victim."[43] Forced to backpedal, Conrad sheepishly admitted being the source of the story, but claimed the interview came from "notes of a third person, whose address he does not know."[44]

Although Conrad was the probable mastermind behind the fraudulent peace plan, his obligation to return to Washington with Colonel William P. Wood likely caused him to nominate his old roommate from Dickinson College, Daniel Mountjoy Cloud, to carry it out. Conrad himself alluded to this after the war, when he recalled that "a college mate ... and myself were perhaps among the few who not only scouted within our line, but were frequently sent by President Davis and our general officers into Washington and sometimes into Canada."[45]

Thomas Conrad and the man called "Mountjoy" by his friends had considerable experience working in secrecy. Five years earlier, at Dickinson College, both were members of Phi Kappa Sigma, a secret campus fraternity. Started at the University of Pennsylvania in 1850, Phi Kappa Sigma quickly spread to other schools, including Dickinson, whose Epsilon Chapter was formed in 1854. The fraternity was so hush-hush, its existence was unknown to anyone outside its members—including parents and faculty. Members recognized one another with "signs of recognition" and secret handshakes. "Phi Kappa Siga is a glorious institution," Dickinson student Horatio King confided in his personal diary, after being initiated in 1856, "being connected therewith is one of the luckiest and happiest circumstances of one's life."[46] In 1856, the Epsilon Chapter contained almost 20 members—what King called "a choice crowd: the best in College."[47]

Despite precautions, the existence of Phi Kappa Sigma was somehow disclosed to Dickinson faculty in 1857—a potentially catastrophic event for the members, as secret societies were expressly forbidden. The faculty left the affected students in suspense for two weeks, then brought them in for what King called a "long winded speech," and had the members sign a paper promising to discontinue the fraternity.[48] The punishment was short-lived, for according to King, many members "deemed the Φ.K. oath more binding than the promise."[49] Tom Conrad and Mountjoy Cloud were among those who immediately re-formed. "So we still flourish," King noted, "but the most profound secrecy is required, and the least suspicion would almost be our College death warrant."[50]

The stealth Conrad and Cloud learned at Dickinson would serve them well in the Confederate underground. Unlike Tom Conrad, however, Cloud started his service with the South conventionally, enlisting with the Warren County Cavalry in 1861, together with his older brother William and several cousins. Commanded by Captain Walter Bowen, a graduate of the Virginia Military Institute, the company became part of Turner Ashby's Seventh Virginia Cavalry, where Cloud became fourth sergeant.[51]

By the end of 1862, the company was led by Cloud's cousin, Captain Thomas Horace Buck—whose unusual middle name may have been the inspiration for the alias "Horace N. Wilson," adopted for John Wesley Greene's mysterious visitor from Richmond.[52] Buck often went simply by the name "Horace" as noted by Chaplain James B. Averitt in his biography of Turner Ashby.[53] The surname "Wilson" may have been the brainchild of rebel spy Thomas Henry Harbin, who was known to use it as an alias and regularly ran dispatches between Baltimore and Richmond, reporting directly to Jefferson Davis.⁵⁴

Harbin was clearly active during this time, for a resident of Harbin's hometown of Piscataway, Maryland, alerted the authorities to his return on November 29, 1862, telling them: "That fellow Thos H. Harbin who has given us so much trouble here has just returned from dixie whither he has been engaged in running our young men over & various other acts against the government."⁵⁵ Harbin's brother, George F. Harbin, was arrested in September 1861 for writing letters denouncing the federal government and was held at the Old Capitol Prison for five months, where he may have gained familiarity with the spy network of Tom Conrad.⁵⁶ Like Mountjoy Cloud, Thomas Harbin would become a member of Ridgely Brown's First Maryland Cavalry but continue his activities in espionage regardless.⁵⁷

Cloud would accompany Baltimore native Harry Gilmor and four others on a dangerous escapade near Luray in the Shenandoah Valley in 1862—an event which demonstrated that Cloud was eminently qualified for the Confederate Secret Service. Caught between a large body of Federal cavalry and pickets blocking the road, Gilmor attributed their escape to the "cool, deliberate courage of Cloud," who sufficiently distracted the pickets to allow the others to escape.⁵⁸ "He was dressed in dark clothes and wore [a] hat ... with the initials of the 6th Ohio Cavalry and crossed sabers on the front,

Daniel Mountjoy Cloud, 1858 (Dickinson College, Archives and Special Collections). Credited for his "cool deliberate courage," Cloud was the perfect operative to find John Wesley Greene. Adopting the middle name of his company commander and cousin, Captain Thomas Horace Buck, as an alias, Cloud was likely the man Greene called "Horace N. Wilson." He first learned subterfuge as a fraternity member at Dickinson College, where Thomas Nelson Conrad was his roommate (*Daniel Mountjoy Cloud, Class of 1858*, Dickinson College, Carlisle, Pennsylvania. Sketch. House Divided: The Civil War Research Engine at Dickinson College, https://hd.housedivided.dickinson.edu/node/5422).

making Cloud look, at a short distance, not unlike a Federal," Gilmor later recalled. "He came upon a whole company drawn up in single rank, with carbines resting on their hips, ready to fire on anything coming along the road. Cloud still rode on, coolly looking on them."[59] Thinking he was one of them, the bluecoats never fired.

Handsome and affable, Cloud was so popular with his fraternity brothers that he was elected Orator on the first ballot at the anniversary exercises of the Epsilon Chapter in 1858, despite being junior to students like Horatio King. Although aspiring to the position himself, King grudgingly admitted that Cloud's anniversary oration that year "was quite well written ... and rather exceeded the anticipations of the most of us."[60] Cloud's college success was an indication of his natural skill and popularity among his peers—traits which undoubtedly led Conrad to recruit him later into the ranks of the Confederate secret service.

Conveniently, Cloud was posted in the Shenandoah Valley near Winchester in October 1862. His cousin, Lucy Rebecca Buck of Front Royal, recorded in her diary that when she visited his mother's house on November 3, 1862, she "found Mr. Daniel Cloud there."[61] His visit coincided neatly with the short break between Horace N. Wilson's visit to Pittsburgh in October and John Wesley Greene's interview with President Lincoln, after which he warned Lincoln that Wilson was then "at Baltimore ... in treasonable correspondence with parties there."[62]

Cloud was no stranger to the Buck family. "Cousin Mount at Cousin Sam's sick," Lucy Buck wrote that spring from Bel Air, the family estate. "Fear the Feds. will get him."[63] They never did, despite close encounters like that he experienced with Harry Gilmor. Although Lucy's father, wealthy merchant William Mason Buck, was too old to serve, numerous other relatives enlisted in the Warren County Cavalry with Cloud, including her uncle, John Nelson Buck, who was assigned "special duty" from the time he joined the regiment in August 1861.[64]

The extent of Buck's duties is unclear, but likely involved securing provisions, as notes in his war records in 1864 cite assignments with the brigade quartermaster. In any case, Cloud's connections in the valley further bolstered his resume for a special mission into Maryland. Conrad and Cloud seem to have used Bel Air as a safe house later in the war, when hiding from Union patrols, a location that Conrad would later refer to as "Dr. Buck's, near Front Royal."[65]

From nearby Clifton, the estate of his sister-in-law, William H. Norris could have easily organized an expedition across the Potomac—using the same Loudoun County fords with which Turner Ashby's men were so familiar. Cloud's young cousin, William A. Buck, was "on detached service as orderly" at this time, an assignment which provided Cloud direct communication with the Confederate chain of command. According to subsequent court documents, Cloud's mother "frequently stayed" at Buck's house. Although no more than 18 years old in 1862, he and Mountjoy Cloud had collaborated on financial matters involving his mother earlier that year, evidence that they had developed a trust relationship already.[66]

Despite his young age, Turner Ashby had trusted William Buck with the dangerous task of being an orderly, an assignment which led to his horse being shot from under him at Buckton Station earlier that year. According to Buck, Ashby found him lugging his equipment from the field, but was himself oblivious to danger. As a rifle ball passed through the ear of Ashby's mount, the Colonel merely talked to the steed and quieted him, seemingly unconcerned for his own safety. "That was only a stray ball," Ashby said calmly, "but you'd better see to yourself. Go to your company and have one of the boys take you behind him."[67]

Buck later relayed the story to Ashby's chaplain, James B. Averitt. It's likely that Averitt also aided Cloud on his mission to Baltimore, rallying support among members of the Episcopal Church in northern Virginia and Maryland anxious to stop emancipation. The same network that had successfully smuggled men and material south from Maryland could be used in reverse to smuggle Cloud safely north. Once across the border, he would have been in familiar surroundings, for despite his connections to northern Virginia, fraternity brother Horatio King referred to him in 1858 as "D.M. Cloud from Baltimore."[68]

14

The Church Militant

> *When ... a clergyman along the border shows a disposition to aid and abet secession and rebellion, he must be muzzled at once, or great harm to the Union will follow.*[1]
> —Colonel William P. Wood

Mountjoy Cloud's son, Major D. Mountjoy Cloud, shed light on his father's wartime adventures at a dedication in Richmond in 1937. According to his son, Cloud was involved in "a secret mission in Baltimore" during which time he "stayed in the home of a Mr. Jackson, an Episcopal clergyman, who was a friend and Southern sympathizer."[2] The clergyman was undoubtedly the Rev. William G. Jackson, rector of Grace Episcopal Church in Howard County.[3] Jackson lived at Elkridge Landing, across the Patapsco River from the Relay House on the Baltimore and Ohio line, not far from "Lawyer's Hill," the country residence of John H.B. Latrobe. Grace Episcopal was so close to the tracks, the building later burnt down from embers thrown by passing locomotives.[4]

Jackson was the son of the Rev. Thomas Jackson, who had been rector of Sherburne Parrish in Leesburg, Virginia, during the 1820s, home of many of Elijah White's troopers who rode with Cloud.[5] Young Jackson had started his ministerial career as a deacon in Staunton, Virginia—only 37 miles from Conrad's Store, where Mountjoy Cloud had enlisted in 1861.[6] If Cloud did not know Jackson personally, fellow members of Turner Ashby's command undoubtedly did, including Episcopalian chaplain James Battle Averitt.

Like many Southern Episcopalians, the Rev. William G. Jackson had only disdain for the Lincoln administration. Back in 1861, a member of his congregation protested to Bishop Whittingham after Jackson refused to recognize a day of fasting and prayer declared by President Lincoln. "Could you not appoint some one to officiate for the congregation on the occasion?" S.E. Horgewerff asked the bishop. "Apart from being deprived of the services, it may have the effect of giving a political character to the congregation which would be unpleasant to the majority of its members."[7] The bishop appealed to Jackson to accommodate the request, but refused to intervene directly, thus allowing Jackson the freedom to act as he chose.

Jackson's home at Elkridge Landing was strategically located for coordinating the secret mission, as it lay at the railroad junction between Washington, Baltimore, and Pittsburgh. John Wesley Greene may have planned to meet Mountjoy Cloud at the Relay House on his way north from Washington after his interview with President Lincoln, but suspecting he was under surveillance, waved off the rendezvous when he left the cars.

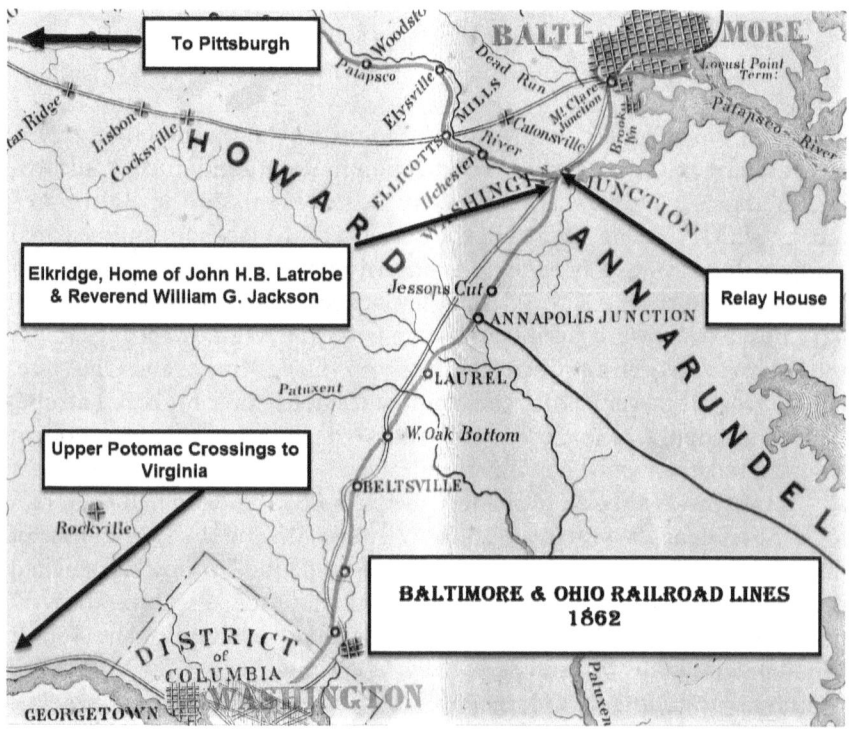

Baltimore and Ohio Lines, 1862 (Library of Congress Geography and Map Division). The map shows the strategic location of Elkridge, south of the Relay House junction to Pittsburgh. Working from the house of Reverend William G. Jackson, Mountjoy Cloud could easily travel between Pittsburgh, Baltimore, and Washington. The assistance of attorney John H. B. Latrobe, Jackson's former trustee at Grace Episcopal Church in Elkridge, would have helped further, for Latrobe was a regular commuter to Baltimore (L. Jacobi and Baltimore and Ohio Railroad Company, *Map and profiles showing the Baltimore and Ohio Railroad with its branches and immediately tributary lines,* Baltimore, 1858. Map. Library of Congress, https://www.loc.gov/item/98688592/).

When Greene later disappeared at the Relay House while being tracked south from Baltimore, all he would need to do was cross the Patapsco River to be safe at Jackson's house in Elkridge Landing. Radle would lose Greene's trail at the Relay House and efforts to track him down the line toward Pittsburgh proved fruitless.[8]

Greene's disappearance at the Relay House near the home of the Rev. William G. Jackson provides further evidence that Mountjoy Cloud was the mysterious Horace N. Wilson, identified by John Wesley Greene as his contact from Richmond.

Besides a safe house, the sponsorship of Jackson would have provided Mountjoy Cloud with access to the Rev. Noah Schenck at Emmanuel Episcopal in Baltimore. If accompanied by someone such as John H.B. Latrobe—Jackson's former trustee at Grace Episcopal—Cloud could have traveled without suspicion. A member of both congregations, Latrobe lived near the Relay House, but worked in Baltimore and had commuted for years between the two. Although he claimed to be a "Union man," this may have been a position of practical convenience, as the location of his country estate behind Union lines left him open to suspicion and possible arrest—especially since his wife hailed from Natchez, Mississippi, and all three of his sons fought for the Confederacy.[9]

Like the members of the YMCA peace committee that had met with Lincoln in the early days of the war, Latrobe was all for the Union, provided slaveholders could free their captives voluntarily. Universal emancipation was another matter entirely. Latrobe had written Secretary of State William Seward in December 1861 to address just such a prospect, urging the administration to recognize the independence of Liberia, as a first step towards the mass emigration of free African Americans, given what he cited as "the impossibility of two free races, which cannot amalgamate by intermarriage, living in the same land on terms of social and political equality."[9]

The theory that Latrobe surreptitiously aided Mountjoy Cloud in the fall of 1862 is buoyed by the fact that Latrobe had extensive business dealings with Cloud's cousins, William Mason Buck and John Nelson Buck, dating to the early 1850s, when he and fellow attorney George W. Dobbin became co-investors with them in the elegant Mountain House Hotel in Capon Springs, Virginia. Located at a popular mineral spring on a spur of the Baltimore and Ohio Railroad 23 miles west of Winchester, the five-story hotel could accommodate up to 600 guests and be reached by rail in a day from Baltimore and Washington.[10] William M. Buck was close enough to Latrobe that when his youngest son was born, at the outbreak of the Civil War, he was christened Frank Latrobe Buck and nicknamed "Dixie."[11]

Cloud may have also received support from their neighbor on Lawyer's Hill, George W. Dobbin, who also attended Grace Episcopal in Elkridge and saw his daughter married there by the Reverend Jackson in November 1860.[12] Himself a former director of the Baltimore and Ohio, Dobbin had, like Latrobe, invested in the Mountain House Hotel with Cloud's cousins and socialized with William Henry Norris in a group called the "Friday Club" before the war.[13] Union troops encamped at his estate, "The Lawn," caused his daughter to complain bitterly about the "thieving, rude, and unsanitary troops" living there.[14] According to one biographer, the Dobbin family "were known supporters of the southern cause throughout the war," an attitude likely worsened by having troops posted there.[15]

Camp Life near the Viaduct, 1861–1865 (Library of Congress Prints and Photographs Division). Union troops camped near the Baltimore and Ohio viaduct caused George W. Dobbin's daughter to complain bitterly after the war about *thieving, unsanitary* troops. The presence of such forces at their idyllic country home on Lawyer's Hill in Elkridge likely caused the Dobbins to seek a quick end to the conflict, by war or peace. Dobbin's son, Robert A. Dobbin, had sought a position with the Confederate Signal Corps in September 1862—from which he could have materially aided Mountjoy Cloud in this effort (E. & H.T. Anthony, publisher, *Camp Life, Army of the Potomac, Taking it Easy*, Maryland, 1861–1865 [New York: E. & H.T. Anthony, between 1861 and 1865]. Photograph. Library of Congress, https://www.loc.gov/item/2022631057/).

The assistance of Latrobe and Dobbin in Elkridge would have allowed Cloud to get safely in and out of Baltimore and provided direct access to the influential members of the Emmanuel Episcopal Church in Baltimore, where Latrobe maintained a pew. The most likely scenario is that Mountjoy Cloud was aided in his mission by Latrobe's teenage son, Richard Steuart Latrobe, and George W. Dobbin's son, Robert Archibald Dobbin. Like Latrobe, young Dobbin had an intimate connection to the Monument Street neighborhood, for in 1870, he married Elizabeth Key Howard's niece, Elizabeth Swan Key.[16]

Dobbin had applied to Confederate Secretary of War G. . Randolph for a position in the newly created Confederate Signal Corps on September 26, 1862, and aiding Cloud would be the perfect assignment to test his mettle.[17] Thomas Nelson Conrad relied heavily on the men of the Signal Corps later in the war, especially for negotiating the Potomac River crossings.[18] Although there is no direct evidence he was formally employed as a spy, young Latrobe was arrested by Federal authorities toward the end of 1862 and incarcerated in Fort McHenry.[19]

After growing up together on Lawyer's Hill, Steuart Latrobe and George Dobbin remained close. Latrobe seems to have lived with Dobbin in Richmond in the winter of 1863 after being paroled and awaiting exchange, for a letter to his mother in March instructed her to write him via Dobbin, by then employed with the Confederate Nitre and Mining Bureau.[20] His mother may have encouraged him to return to Maryland, for by June 1863, he was attending classes at St. James College near Hagerstown. Young Latrobe's mind, however, was more focused on war than books.

When Lee's army invaded Maryland in June 1863, Latrobe and classmate Henry P. Hayward abandoned their classes and went to Hagerstown to enlist in the First Maryland Cavalry, as Confederate troops marched north in the invasion that would culminate in the Battle of Gettysburg.[21] The two were connected by family ties, as Henry Hayward's grandfather had been a partner in Hayward and Company, which manufactured the so-called Latrobe stove in Baltimore using the design John H.B. Latrobe had conceived, reportedly as a "comforting surprise" to Mrs. Latrobe when she returned to Baltimore from her family home in Natchez, Mississippi.[22]

Wounded in the retreat from Gettysburg, Steuart Latrobe was recognized among a group of rebel prisoners taken to Baltimore the following week.[23] He had barely arrived in the city when orders were issued by Secretary of War Stanton to "retain R. Stuart Latrobe, a prisoner of war lately captured ... until further orders."[24] Stanton was apparently convinced that young Latrobe was engaged in undercover espionage, for three months later, in mid–October, he was still confined in Fort McHenry. He had been granted liberty within the grounds, but only on his oath that he would neither attempt to escape nor engage in "conversation or correspondence with any person or persons within the garrison."[25]

Steuart Latrobe and young Dobbin would have been particularly useful in coordinating communications with influential members of the Emmanuel Episcopal Church in Baltimore. The Rev. Noah Schenck had a congregation there "equally divided between Unionists and Southern sympathizers" and was likely happy to do anything to promote peace.[26] One of its most influential members was former congressman James Carroll, whose son-in-law was the Rev. Thomas B. Sargent—the former minister of Strawbridge Methodist Episcopal Church.

Sargent had married Monument Street girl Sophia Gough Carroll, and the two lived at Carroll's home at 105 West Monument, where the battle song "My Maryland" had been created the year before at the suggestion of Mary Norris. Their son, Henry Dorsey Gough Carroll Sargent, served in Richard Snowden Andrew's Maryland Flying Artillery and was virtually an "orphan," with no way to return home if the conflict persisted.

Cloud likely recruited John Wesley Greene on Tom Conrad's recommendation, but finding him in Pittsburgh may have been difficult, if it were not for the close association between Cloud and Sargent. He was not only the former minister of Strawbridge, but a long-serving trustee of Dickinson College—so well respected there that one of Cloud's classmates, Thomas Sargent Reese, had been named in his honor. In order to find Cullison and Greene, Cloud simply needed to contact Sargent or the minister of Strawbridge at the time, the Rev. John H. Dashiell, another Dickinson graduate.[27]

Dashiell, like Schenck, was as eager for peace as anyone, for his congregation was literally torn apart by divergent views on the war and emancipation—causing the church's historian to later write that "the Secession movement rent the church in twain."[28] Seven of the nine trustees and six of the nine stewards eventually left the church in a body, taking everything with them, and formed the Trinity Methodist Episcopal Church South, at the corner of Preston and Madison Avenue.[29] Among them was John W. Selby, the former president of the Strawbridge YMCA, who became a "class leader" at Trinity after the war.[30]

Dashiell did his best to prevent the division—to the point where he was jailed for it. Before establishing Trinity, members of the congregation with Southern sympathies held separate church services in the Northwestern Young Men's Christian Association Hall at the corner of Biddle and Ross.[31] Neighborhood Unionists resented the secessionists, and one of them, on a Saturday night, secured a large Union flag in the second story window, and nailed the window from the outside, so it could not be easily removed. The Reverend Dashiell, when he arrived for morning services, was dismayed to find members leaving, rather than enter the building under the stars and stripes. So, he went upstairs, broke the window, and removed the flag.

Union Lieutenant J. Emory Gault, who responded to the event, noted that neighbors with Southern sympathies "rejoiced over the affair," while Union people felt "that such an outrage committed in open daylight, upon the flag that affords protection to the monster that committed the outrage should be met with the severest punishment."[32] The Reverend Dashiell was arrested that afternoon. The following day, he explained his actions this way in a letter to the *Baltimore American*:

> I did not know by what hand or at what hour it had been done. Lest it should, by the oddness of the thing, attract around the door a crowd & produce a difficulty, because it had not been done by a constituted authority but surreptitiously in the night.... I removed it. Who put it there & what were the motives—or where was the policeman when it was done—I shall not now inquire.[33]

Anxious to avoid a furor over the arrest of a clergyman, authorities released him upon his issuance of an apology letter. The incident, however, was indicative of the bad blood between members of the same congregation and of the extent to which Dashiell would go to secure peace. Referring Cloud to Jesse Cullison, Greene's brother-in-law, was a simple matter—as he lived just down the street, on West Biddle.

Cullison, of course, knew exactly where to find Greene—in Pittsburgh, working for John Dunlap, and attending the Liberty Street Methodist Episcopal Church. Thus, a witness in Pittsburgh would later recall that at the end of October, "a stranger visited Greene at Mr. Dunlap's store and had a long conversation with him," while another revealed that the stranger "was closeted with him for several hours at Mrs. Littles, Liberty Street, where he boarded."[34] Traveling to Pittsburgh simply involved taking the Baltimore and Ohio line west from the Relay House, a journey that would not only take him to Greene, but allow a survey of vulnerable bridges along the line heading west—bridges Cloud would attempt to destroy the following year.

There is evidence that the Cullison family did far more than simply provide access to John Wesley Greene, but that they materially engaged in the secret mission's other probable objectives: gathering intelligence on the Baltimore and Ohio and establishing a network to smuggle horses out of Maryland. With property in both Baltimore and Carroll County west of the city, they were in a perfect position to do the latter. Twenty-six-year-old James M. Cullison, a probable cousin who lived next to Jessie Cullison on West Biddle, was finally caught at this enterprise in 1864.[35]

A butcher named Maximillian Plitt filed a complaint that in July 1864, Cullison came to him, purporting to have an order to impound his horse for the government. Plitt refused to relinquish the horse but took it to the government stable himself. When Cullison offered to sell it back, Plitt accepted, but thought it "very strange that you can take a horse for the Gov't and then give it back again."[36] Arrested by Union authorities, Cullison claimed to be a loyal Union man, "falsely imprisoned," and that the real culprit was Plitt, whom he called a "rank rebel."[37] As John Wesley Greene had done in 1861, he pled for mercy based on his being "a poor man with a large and helpless family."[38] He was eventually released, but Plitt's testimony had the ring of truth. James Cullison may have been falsely impounding horses for months, before Plitt finally reported him to authorities.

Greene's brother-in-law, Micajah M. Cullison, may have provided intelligence on Union troop dispositions along the Baltimore and Ohio Railroad directly to Cloud in 1862. He had joined the Union's First Maryland Potomac Home Brigade in Carroll County on October 24, 1861, but was far from a model soldier.[39] His official troubles began in April 1862, when he was court-martialed for an unspecified offense and lost a quarter of his pay for the month. Four months later, on August 10, 1862, he deserted at Monocacy Junction near Frederick, Maryland.

Micajah Cullison was not seen by his regiment until he suspiciously rejoined them on October 22 at Marriottsville, Maryland—the same day Horace N. Wilson supposedly met John Wesley Greene in Pittsburgh. He deserted again, ten days later, on November 2, 1862.[40] Cullison's regiment had been used extensively to guard bridges along the Baltimore and Ohio Railroad that year. It is altogether possible that the prospect of emancipation caused him to literally switch sides and gather intelligence for the South, at the bequest of his family.

Such a case of treason was not unknown. One of the most famous cases was that of Sergeant Alexander G. Babcock of William Chase Barney's 71st New York State Militia, who scored six runs in the American Guard's 42–13 victory over the National Baseball Club on July 2, 1861, while the regiment was stationed at the Washington Navy Yard. Formerly a member of the Brooklyn Atlantic Baseball Club, the New Jersey native switched sides during the war and became one of Colonel John S. Moseby's most trusted partisan rangers.[41] According to one account, he cast his fortunes with the Confederacy after concluding that "the rights of the southern people were being invaded" and their country "wasted by fire and sword, without warrant of law."[42]

Whatever his own motivation was for deserting, Micajah Cullison was eventually arrested on April 18, 1863, and confined in Fort McHenry.

Although allowed to rejoin the regiment in June, he deserted a third time in February 1864, telling the Eighth Corps provost marshal that he "was a week in Loudoun Co. (Va) opposite Point of Rocks & went home to Carroll Co. MD."[43] That Cullison chose to hide from Federal authorities in Loudoun County, Virginia, suggests he had connections in the same area where Elijah White, Turner Ashby and Mountjoy Cloud had operated so effectively earlier in the war.

Any intelligence on the Baltimore and Ohio gathered by Mountjoy Cloud in the fall of 1862 would subsequently be used in the so-called Jones-Imboden raid in April 1863, when Southern cavalry under General John Imboden and General W.E. "Grumble" Jones set out to destroy the railroad bridges west of the Alleghenies and replenish mounts for the Confederacy.[44] Jones' command contained the First Maryland Cavalry, Elijah White's 35th Virginia Battalion and Ashby's Seventh Virginia Cavalry—the so-called "Laurel Brigade."

The raid was not without losses. Mountjoy Cloud had a horse killed at Greenland Gap, Virginia, on April 25, 1863, in the same action in which Mary Norris' nephew, Kennedy Grogan, was killed.[45] A month earlier, Baltimore native Joseph G.W. Marriott had met an ignominious death near New Creek, Virginia, as he and three others were attempting to steal horses from local Unionist J.H. Carskadon.[46] Marriott, a former lieutenant in the First Maryland Regiment, had been an active member of the Southern Volunteer Association in Baltimore and served with William H. Norris on the committee to elect John Breckinridge in 1860. When his company was disbanded in the summer of 1862, he joined Ridgely Brown's First Maryland Cavalry.[47]

Despite the loss of men like Grogan and Marriott, the raid destroyed several railroad bridges and netted a considerable number of mounts. General Grumble Jones' command took some 1,200 to 1,500 of them, while Imboden claimed to have reaped $100,000 worth—probably several hundred.[48] Many of these were likely smuggled to the raiders by Southern sympathizers across Maryland. Union brigadier general Benjamin S. Roberts later described the problem of rebel partisans along the Upper Potomac:

> This class is very much more numerous than I had expected.... They harbor and shelter the guerrillas and the rebel soldiers who in disguise pass into our lines bringing information and returning with intelligence for our enemies and carrying off horses and other property they steal from Union citizens or that are supplied to them by the class who conceal them.[49]

The dirty work of smuggling horses to the Confederacy largely fell on those like the Cullisons. Nevertheless, there is evidence that the well-heeled families of the Mount Vernon neighborhood participated actively in the smuggling activity. The magnificent new home of Augustus

J. Albert on Monument Street, for example, is rumored to have "housed horses" during the war—likely to be staged until they could be transferred to rural areas, like the Cullison's property in Carroll County.[50] Not surprisingly, Albert's son, Augustus J. Albert, Jr., was a member of Richard Snowden Andrew's "Flying Artillery" that relied on such horses to earn their nickname.[51]

Federal authorities had long known the Mount Vernon neighborhood of Baltimore to be a hotbed of secession sentiment. For this reason, Colonel Lafayette Baker attempted to plant an undercover agent there as early as 1861, choosing a Canadian by the name of Joseph T. Kerby (or Kirby).[52] According to one account, he arrived in Baltimore that winter, where "his fine personal address and earnest Southern expressions … ensured his introduction to the very exclusive clubs and coteries of the Southern gentleman of Mount Vernon Place."[53] By December 1861, he was at General Beauregard's headquarters at Manassas, where he was "intimate with the officers and members of the First Maryland Regiment," having smuggled letters from their families and friends through the Union lines.[54]

Kerby's knowledge of Baltimore society made him the perfect choice to sniff out the mission to Baltimore in October 1862, when he was conveniently within Lee's camp near Winchester. Reportedly, while there, he "had the run of the town and the camps, and a seat at the officers mess and card tables, when he desired it."[55] Whether he learned anything of the mission while there is impossible to say, but in early November 1862, Lee's aide-de-camp, Major Charles Marshall, received a letter from an intimate friend and fellow attorney he called "a gentleman of large property and high standing in Baltimore."[56]

The letter contained a stern warning. "Kirby [Kerby] the Canadian or Englishman who is in your lines should be arrested at once," the man advised Marshall. "He knows and tells too much."[57] The timing of the letter suggests that the operative named Horace N. Wilson, whether he be Mountjoy Cloud or someone else, revealed Kerby's presence in Lee's camp upon reaching Baltimore. If so, the warning to Marshall prevented vital information from reaching Lafayette Baker, for Kerby was immediately arrested as a spy and confined in Castle Thunder.[58]

Although Kerby was exchanged in May 1863, it was too late for any intelligence he may have gained to be of use. Nevertheless, upon his release, Major General John Dix at Fortress Monroe telegraphed Secretary of War Stanton: "Mr. Kirby who has been in prison six months in Richmond is here. If it is your wish to see him, please apprise me."[59] That Dix telegraphed Stanton directly is an indication of how tightly the Secretary of War controlled military intelligence. Federal operatives often did not know their colleagues. Such was the case when Pinkerton agent Enoch

H. Stein reported Kerby for suspicious activities in September 1862, citing, among other evidence, that Kerby kept a photo of Harry Gilmor and claimed the rebel partisan was a "particular friend" of his.[60]

By the fall of 1862, Kerby had convinced everyone that he was "secesh" except the rebel underground in Baltimore, who were careful about whom they trusted. Thus, they smuggled a letter to one of their own, Major Charles Marshall—who had lived with Richard Snowden Andrews in the Mount Vernon neighborhood before the war.[61] If Marshall was unaware of the fraudulent peace scheme at the time it happened, he surely learned of it after the war, when he returned to Baltimore. His complicity in the conspiracy of silence about the matter may be why he claimed in 1886 to have mislaid McClellan's letter to Lee after Antietam, as any revelations about trading peace for slavery might easily lead back to Baltimore.

A close examination of the anonymous letter to Marshall reveals it was likely written by John H.B. Latrobe, likely to protect his son Steuart from prosecution based on intelligence Kerby may have garnered in Baltimore. If so, the plan worked—until Kerby was released from Castle Thunder and briefed Stanton. Thus, when young Latrobe was captured in the retreat from Gettysburg a month later, Stanton personally intervened to prevent Latrobe's exchange or parole.

15

Attack of the Copperheads

My voice today is for conciliation; my voice is for compromise.... Gentlemen, let the seceding States depart in peace.[1]
—Ohio senator George H. Pendleton, 1861

The week John Wesley Greene visited President Lincoln with his purported peace initiative from Jefferson Davis, William Chase Barney attempted to contact Assistant Secretary of State Frederick Seward regarding the same subject. According to his later correspondence, he wrote Seward on November 17, 1862, stating that from his observations in Richmond, "a general amnesty," coupled with the meeting of the next Congress in March 1863, would be "readily accepted by the South."[2] According to Barney, however, he was never "honored with a notice of the reception of my letter."[3]

Why Barney waited until mid-November to attempt to contact the Lincoln administration when he arrived back in Washington on October 27 is a mystery, especially since Lieutenant Colonel William H. Ludlow at Fortress Monroe had promised that Barney was going to report William P. Wood to Secretary Stanton for his "misdeeds" immediately upon his return. It is possible that Barney instead reported directly to General McClellan or his staff—the ones that likely sent him to Richmond in the first place. By late October, however, McClellan may have reconsidered his ill-advised attempts to negotiate with the Confederacy.

After McClellan requested advice from his friend and supporter William H. Aspinwall, the latter took the extraordinary step of rushing to Sharpsburg to counsel him personally. Aspinwall arrived the first week of October, awkwardly meeting McClellan and President Lincoln on the road to South Mountain, as they toured the scenes of recent battles. Aspinwall seems to have had a moderating influence on McClellan. The general wrote his wife on October 5, 1862, that Aspinwall had convinced him that it was "my duty to submit to the Presdt's proclamation & quietly continue doing my duty as a soldier."[4] By the end of the month, after Barney was back in Washington, McClellan wrote his wife again, telling her, "It will not do for me to visit Washington now.... The tone of the telegrams I receive from the authorities is such [that] ... I should at once be accused of purposely delaying the movement."⁵

Likely rebuffed by both McClellan and Seward, Barney returned to New York City, taking up residence at the Irving House Hotel, where Francis G. Young had moved in mid–October 1862, after returning from Richmond.⁶ Located at 825 Broadway, it was conveniently located just blocks from the William H. Aspinwall's Manhattan home. From the Irving House, Barney wrote a letter to one or more influential Democrats on November 23, 1862, outlining his mission to the South and urging them to initiate peace negotiations:

> I was a prisoner in Richmond from the 24th September to the 26th October. Between those dates, I had several conversations with former acquaintances, ex. U.S. Senators and Representatives, now holding similar positions in the so-called Confederate States Government. I had also a long conversation with them of their Administration. It is not necessary at this time to state all of their remarks, or to name these persons. I was authorized to say—that if the abolition party should be defeated in the elections of Representatives in the next Congress, so that if the Southern States were represented there could be a decided anti-abolition majority, then the Southern States would send their Representatives. No guarantees or favors are asked for other than that a full and general amnesty should put it in their power to elect and send their Senators and Representatives to Washington, and that the Congress shall be convened as soon after the 4th March next as possible.⁷

Among those Barney later claimed to have contacted were New York mayor Fernando Wood, Maryland senator Reverdy Johnson, Delaware senator James A. Bayard, Congressman John J. Crittenden of Kentucky and former New York attorney general John Van Buren, the son of former president Martin Van Buren—a leading advocate for peace.⁸

Barney surely must have shared the information with John Van Buren well before drafting the letter, for on November 17, at a Democratic meeting in New York, Van Buren proposed a similar plan. According to one newspaper, Van Buren suggested that "President Lincoln grant an armistice, so the rebel soldiers could go home and vote ... elect members to Congress ... [then] call a Convention to have the United States Constitution altered to suit the circumstances."⁹

It may not have been coincidence that during Barney's stay at the Irving House, detective Allan Pinkerton arrived in New York City on a mysterious mission. The *New York Herald* jumped to the conclusion that Pinkerton was following McClellan, who had recently moved to New York City. "General McClellan has been dogged all through his campaigns by government spies, and at this moment, the head spy, calling himself Allen,

Irving House Hotel, New York City, 1852 (New York Public Library Digital Collections). The residence of William Chase Barney and Francis G. Young in November 1862, Barney used it as his base to lobby prominent Democrats to negotiate peace with the Confederate government. Barney and Young's choice of this hotel, located close to William H. Aspinwall's Manhattan residence, suggests they may have communicated with George B. McClellan through Aspinwall after returning from Richmond (Doolittle & Burroughs, *Daily Menu, Irving House, New York, NY*, 1852 Rare Book Division, New York Public Library Digital Collections. https://digitalcollections.nypl.org/items/510d47 db-19f6-a3d9-e040-e00a18064a99).

is on his track in this city," the *Herald* wrote. "Those who know McClellan best know it is impossible to impeach his loyalty and truth. But ... it is notorious that innocence is no protection from the machinations of detective adventurers, who desire to distinguish themselves, and are not very scrupulous about what they say, do, or swear."[10]

Outraged, Pinkerton wrote McClellan that same day, disavowing the article. "I enclose a slip from this morning's *Herald*, charging me with being a spy upon your movements, both in the Army and in this City. You can imagine what I feel about such a groundless accusation. I cannot, in justice to you or myself, allow this gross slander to pass without contradiction."[11] Pinkerton had been McClellan's chief intelligence officer throughout his campaigns with the Army of the Potomac and the inference that he had been watching McClellan as closely as he watched the rebels was offensive. Yet, others besides the *Herald* thought McClellan was secretly being watched.

G.H. Eldridge, who visited McClellan at the Fifth Avenue Hotel at this time, wrote to McClellan's father in Philadelphia on the same day as the *Herald*'s accusations, expressing much the same concern:

> I am convinced that a constant surveillance is kept of all the General's movements, who he associates with, what he does, where he goes ... carefully

observed & recorded by his enemies.... The General went to the opera one evening, intending no doubt to be incog. But soon it was whispered around that he was in the house. The orchestra played National airs, the audience cheered lustily, and he was brought forward to bow an acknowledgement from John Van Buren—he was in Duncan's box—with Belmont and Sam Barlow.... They are known to be ultra democrats. I almost said rabid, for they lean to the cause of the rebels and are as near to being secessionists as they dare to be.[12]

The men with Van Buren at the opera were likely banker August Belmont, the national chair of the Democratic Party, and Samuel Barlow, who had bought a controlling interest in the *New York World* earlier that year at the urging of Belmont, converting it from a pro-war periodical to a solidly Democratic paper opposed to emancipation. Upon his death, the *New York Times* called him "an apologist for slavery."[13]

Barlow was far from being a stranger to George B. McClellan. Barlow helped McClellan get his first job as an executive of the Illinois Central Railroad upon leaving the army in 1856, and two years later, the former general sought Barlow's help in getting back into the army.[14] In November 1861, McClellan had expressed concern to Barlow that the war to save the Union might become a war for abolition. "Help me to dodge the n_____— we want nothing to do with him. I am fighting to preserve the integrity of the Union.... To gain that end we cannot afford to mix up the negro question."[15] McClellan again confided in Barlow at the end of the Peninsula Campaign in July 1862: "I have lost all regard and respect for the majority of the Administration & doubt the propriety of my brave men's blood being spilled to further the designs of such a set of heartless villains.... Well, burn this up when you have read it."[16]

Assuming Pinkerton was truthful when he denied tracking McClellan to New York, there was another reason he might have been there at that time: namely, to track the whereabouts of William Chase Barney and his connections with New York Copperheads—taking up where William P. Wood left off. Such a step was prudent, for Barney's testimony regarding the prospects for peace, vague as they were, had the potential to seriously undermine the war effort. The *Brooklyn Daily Eagle*, for example, reported that New York mayor Fernando Wood delivered the following news in a speech given on November 30, 1862:

> Mr. Wood said he had received information, and communicated it to [the] government, that under certain circumstances the South were ready to return, ay from leading statesmen of the South. Men of position and influence in the Southern Confederacy had expressed a desire to return, under a Democratic rule, the past to be forgotten, the public debt on both sides to be provided for; and they were willing to let by-gones be by-gones, if the North would and the Union once again be restored.[17]

Wood apparently also made a reference to some validation from the Virginia governor, although such reference is not well documented.

Barney wrote another letter that day to one or more Democrats, warning them that another battle would present "serious obstacles" to peace, and that "should 1st January [1863] with its Emancipation Proclamation come before the offer of an amnesty ... it would be too late to entertain the hope to save the Union."[18] Barney's concern over the possibility of a battle disrupting the chances for peace coincide closely with McClellan's own inaction after Antietam.

The basis for the Fernando Wood speech on reconciliation of the nation was revealed on December 5, when the *New York Daily Tribune* published a letter from its Washington correspondent, reporting that a Dr. Barney of Baltimore intentionally crossed the lines at Centreville, Virginia, on September 21 and was taken to Richmond, where he had "frequent interviews with members of the Confederate cabinet" regarding peace.[19] The reference to "Dr. Barney" was undoubtedly based on his brief coordination of Pope's ambulance train during the Second Battle of Bull Run.

Virginia governor John Letcher, in a letter to the *Richmond Whig* on December 8, vehemently denied any communication with Mayor Wood, or any other intermediary. Referencing a previous statement on such matters, he declared, "From the time Virginia seceded, I have always been opposed to reconstruction.... I have no personal acquaintance with Fernando Wood, do not know that I have ever met him.... I state further, that I have no communication, verbal or written, with any Northern man, upon this subject, since Virginia seceded."[20]

Any inference to meetings with the governor of Virginia likely referred to former Virginia governor Henry A. Wise, who had collaborated with Fernando Wood before the war, and after whom Wood later named his son, Henry A. Wise Wood. Back in 1857, Samuel Chase Barney had used Wise's son, O. Jennings Wise, to assist with his hearing before the Naval Retirement Board.[21] Although the brilliant young attorney had been killed in action earlier in the year, the former governor of Virginia may have welcomed Barney as someone who remembered his son from happier times.

Although Lincoln administration sources dismissed the peace overtures referenced by Fernando Wood, their credibility was temporarily buoyed by the appearance of what appeared to be a corroborating story in the *Chicago Times* on December 4, 1862:

> It may be stated positively that the administration at Washington have before them propositions from Richmond for peace and restoration of the Union—informal propositions, but none the less authoritative, and none the less of extraordinary interest to the people of the North, and indeed, to the civilized

world. We do not make this announcement on the strength of the speech of Fernando Wood on Saturday last—though Mr. Wood spoke positively and distinctly of such propositions having been made. We make it on the strength of information direct, explicit, and which we ourselves know to be perfectly reliable.[22]

The statement from the *Times,* however, was too vague—even for solidly Democratic journals. The *Brooklyn Eagle,* for example, opined that "if the *Chicago Times* has any information on this subject, it should be placed before the people."[23] It quickly became plain that the source for the *Chicago Times* was John Wesley Greene.

Apparently in response to editorials like that of the *Brooklyn Eagle,* Greene provided a detailed affidavit to Philip A. Hoyne, a prominent Chicago attorney and United States commissioner, on December 9, 1862. Hoyne was a sympathetic witness. He had created a stir in 1860, when his deputy marshals refused to arrest a 20-year-old African American, Eliza Grayson, under the fugitive slave law of 1850. Not to be frustrated, he quickly deputized a local Democrat named Jake Newsome to seize her anyway.[24] When authorities attempted to move Grayson to the jail, however, she was rescued by a crowd and whisked away—reportedly on a boat to Canada.[25] It was an act of heroism that resulted in indictments against nine of the rescuers and a rebuke from President James Buchanan, who wrote an angry letter to the U.S. attorney in Chicago, urging severe penalties for those involved in Grayson's escape.[26]

A portion of Greene's affidavit appeared in the *Chicago Times* on December 10, 1862. In it, Greene gave this explanation of his purported journey to Richmond:

> I was called on by a gentleman from Baltimore on October 22, who informed me that Jeff. Davis greatly desired me to go to Richmond. After two or three interviews with this gentleman, I consented to go. I was at Richmond on the 26th of October, and on calling on Mr. Davis I was informed that he desired a termination of the war. and an amicable adjustment of the difficulties between the North and the South.[27]

According to Greene, Davis had remembered him from the Mexican War, where Greene claimed to have served in the Third Artillery, where he claimed to have rendered Davis "a personal service, which he deemed of sufficient importance to extend to me his grateful friendship."[28]

Upon his departure from Richmond, Greene once again claims to have been escorted by the ubiquitous Horace Wilson to within four miles of Harpers Ferry:

> On parting with Mr. WILSON, he handed me an amount of American gold sufficient to cover my expenses homeward. At Harper's Ferry I took the cars

for Baltimore; but, though I fancied myself sharply looked at, no man ever asked me who I was, where I came from, or whither I was bound. On the morning of the 29th of October, I left Harper's Ferry, and in the afternoon reached Baltimore. The next morning, I went to my father-in-law's residence, in Carroll County. Maryland, about twenty-six miles from Baltimore; and, after spending a couple of days there, returned to my home in Pittsburgh.[29]

Greene gave references which included his employer, John Dunlap; the Rev. A.J. Endslett, a "well-known clergyman" of Pittsburgh; and Thomas Bakewell of Pittsburgh, a personal friend of Secretary of War Stanton.[30]

The same day as the affidavit appeared, the Lincoln administration released a terse statement to the Associated Press: "J. WESLEY GREENE who furnished the Chicago TIMES some reported peace propositions from JEFFERSON DAVIS to President LINCOLN, is an imposter. He came to Washington to see President LINCOLN, who soon ascertained that there was no ground for his nonsensical statements."[31]

Several hours later, the administration released another, more complete explanation:

> On inquiry, it is ascertained that a man, calling himself WESLEY GREEN, and professing to reside at Pittsburgh, Penn., called on the President some time in November, and stated to him that he had had two interviews with JEFF. DAVIS, at Richmond, on the last day in October, and also related certain statements, which he said DAVIS had made to him upon the occasion. The President, however, became satisfied that GREEN had not seen DAVIS at all, and that the entire story was a very shallow attempt at "humbuggery."[32]

In rejoinder, the *Chicago Times* posed numerous questions to the administration in print, as an attorney might cross-examine a witness, and concluded by stating confidently that "we have no more doubt than we have in our own existence that Mr. Greene came from Mr. Davis at Richmond to Mr. Lincoln at Washington.... We reserve further comment on the extraordinary attitude of the administration and perhaps the public will hear from Mr. Greene again in our next issue."[33]

Greene, however, did not appear in the *Times* again. On December 11, 1862, a telegraphic dispatch came into Chicago Police headquarters from W. B Webb, superintendent of police in Washington: "Arrest and hold, subject to our order, J. Wesley Greene for swindling. Will send warrant."[34] A Chicago Police detective quietly arrested Greene at the City Hotel the following day. The man claimed he wasn't Greene, but documents on him at the time, showing that he was a licensed exhorter at a Methodist church in Pittsburgh, proved otherwise.[35]

Arresting Greene had been easy; holding him would be more difficult. Oddly enough, the warrant was not for trying to defraud the government, but rather, for obtaining goods under false pretenses—the fur cape worth $175 that he had swindled from Steinmetz while in Washington. He quickly retained attorney Barnard G. Caulfield, who kept offices in the McCormick building adjacent to the office of the *Times*. Caulfield, a Virginia native, had been at the bedside of Senator Stephen Douglas when he died in 1861 and would post bond for *Times* editor Wilbur Storey in 1864, when he was arrested for libel.[36]

Caulfield quickly got Greene released, arguing that a telegraphic dispatch was not sufficient evidence of a crime, and that "no bail or bond is needed to hold him here."[37] Bolstering Caulfield's argument was the fact that obtaining goods under false pretenses was not a felony in Illinois. Greene was released and promptly disappeared. In a postwar interview, he would say he was "released through the interference of friends" and escaped to Canada, where he "became acquainted with many Southern sympathizers like myself."[38] Mountjoy Cloud followed him there in 1863, supposedly to "arouse sympathy and gain assistance for the Confederacy," but likely to debrief Greene on his Lincoln interview as well—since the opportunity to do this earlier evaporated when Lafayette Baker's detectives followed Greene from Washington.[39]

It remains for historians to speculate on who provided Wilbur Storey testimonials to Greene's character, but they were likely influential voices from

Reverend Noah Hunt Schenck, 1860–1870 (National Portrait Gallery, Smithsonian Institution; Frederick Hill Meserve Collection). Schenck led the Baltimore congregation the *Chicago Tribune* called the "church militant." His wife, Anna, was the sister of Congressman "Gentleman" George Hunt Pendleton of Cincinnati, General McClellan's running mate in the presidential election of 1864. Anna likely knew John Wesley Greene's second wife, Martha Borland, in Cincinnati as her father's law office was across the street from her parent's boardinghouse. Whether Schenck lived at Borland's with Greene in 1849 remains a mystery (Mathew Brady Studio, *Noah Hunt Schenck*, c. 1860–70. Photograph. National Portrait Gallery, Smithsonian Institution; Frederick Hill Meserve Collection, https://npg.si.edu/object/npg_NPG.81.M1388).

Baltimore, such as John H.B. Latrobe, the Rev. John H. Dashiell, the Rev. Thomas B. Sargent and the Rev. Noah Schenck of the Emmanuel Episcopal Church—the congregation the *Chicago Tribune* once accused of being the "church militant."[40] Of these, Schenck, the former Chicagoan, may have been the most influential. His wife, the former Anna Pendleton of Cincinnati, was a member of the prominent Key and Howard families of Baltimore, and her brother, Congressman George H. Pendleton of Ohio, had married Mary Alicia Key, the sister of Mrs. Charles Howard.[41] Had Schenck obtained testimonials for Greene from Congressman Pendleton and other key Democrats in the legislature, the effect would be even more powerful.

Schenck's brother-in-law, "Gentleman George" Pendleton, would be General George B. McClellan's running mate against President Lincoln in the election of 1864. Although not as vocal as Fernando Wood and Clement Vallandigham, Pendleton voted consistently with the Copperheads. According to Virginia Clay, wife of Alabama senator Clement Clay, Pendleton frequented their home often before the war, and was one of several Northern politicians who "were friendly to our people and believed in our right to defend the principles we had maintained since the administration of the first President of the United States."[42]

Pendleton's thoughts on the war could be summarized by a speech he gave on January 18, 1861, after four states had seceded from the Union:

> My voice today is for conciliation; my voice is for compromise; and it is but the echo of the voice of my constituents.... If your differences are so that you cannot or will not reconcile them, then gentlemen let the seceding States depart in peace; let them establish their government and empire and work out their destiny according to the wisdom which God has given them.[43]

Pendleton's voting record consistently opposed any attempt to coerce the South back into the Union, either militarily or economically.[44] When Democrats considered whom to nominate as McClellan's running mate in 1864, the *Chicago Tribune* observed that Pendleton was "well supported by the northwestern democracy, while peace men everywhere find him acceptable."[45] Given the support Greene received in Chicago from Storey, Hoyne, and Caulfield, there is, at least, circumstantial evidence that Northern Copperheads supported and defended Greene—even when it was apparent that his peace offer was a sham.

Insiders in Baltimore knew that Greene was not alone in his attempt to defraud Lincoln and stop emancipation. After the war, the Rev. William Harden of the Emory Methodist Episcopal Church in Baltimore claimed Greene was simply a "scapegoat."[46] Harden would know, as Frances Cullison Greene was among the members of his congregation at the time.

Harden had married the Rev. Henry Slicer's daughter, Elizabeth Selby Slicer, in 1853, and although she passed away a year later, Harden undoubtedly stayed close to his father-in-law.[47]

If a peace plan was afoot in Baltimore to stop emancipation, the Rev. Henry Slicer would know of it. Slicer was a probable cousin of John W. Selby, for his mother was a Selby and both hailed from Annapolis.[48] A close colleague of Reverends Thomas Sargent and John Dashiell, he was also among the best-known Methodist clergyman of the 1850s. Especially popular within the Democratic Party, he served as chaplain to the United States Senate multiple times and was well known for his aggressive defense of slavery.

In 1856, when the Methodist Episcopal Church sought to make non-slaveholding a condition of membership, Slicer gave a vigorous speech against the proposal, arguing that there were numerous examples of slaveholding in the Old Testament, and that all slaveholders wanted was "peace and quiet, and to be let alone."[49] This pro-slavery oration would not be his last. In 1858, when the Baltimore Conference of the Methodist Episcopal Church proposed establishing a church newspaper to clarify its stance on slavery to its members, Slicer strenuously objected. "It would be better that there were no newspapers," he argued, "than that they should carry on controversy on the slavery question."[50] At least one critical editor, after reading the speech, was horrified at the implications of Slicer's position— that he was "the advocate or apologist of something so rotten, that it cannot bear the light of what a Free Press throws upon it."[51]

Because of Slicer's credentials, he was often a speaker at political events across the East Coast, and by one estimate "probably made more public addresses in the course of his long and active life than any other man in the country."[52] Nevertheless, in March 1862, Slicer was the center of controversy at the annual meeting of the East Baltimore Conference when a member mounted the platform and charged him with "being disloyal to the government of the United States."[53] Although Slicer vehemently denied the accusation, he was subsequently demoted from a Presiding Eldership to charge of the Seamen's Bethel, a post paying only $400 per year—far less than a regimental chaplain.[54] One Republican daily saw the move as "a sign that a reaction of that body in favor of the black man's liberty has finally settled in."[55]

On October 23, 1862, the day after the mysterious Horace Wilson called on Greene in Pittsburgh, Slicer was visiting a grievously wounded Confederate officer.[56] He was Captain Wesley Fletcher Jones, one of six brothers to join the so-called "Fireside Defenders" that became company G, 22nd Georgia Infantry. He had been severely wounded at Antietam Creek, captured, and brought to a Baltimore hospital to die—accompanied by his brother, who, like Slicer, was a Methodist minister.[57] Thus, if Mountjoy Cloud had subsequently sought testimonials for John Wesley Greene to promote peace, Slicer may have been in the mood to willingly provide it—despite having little knowledge of Greene's past.

16

A Shallow Attempt at Humbuggery

> *Praise be unto the press, the free press ... which will not lie for tyrants, but make tyrants speak the truth.*[1]
> —Herman Melville, *The Confidence Man*

Aside from the *Chicago Times*, the rest of the national media did not know what to make of Greene's affidavit. At the *New York Tribune*, editor Horace Greeley was intrigued, noting that Greene's assertions were "identical to those of the Barney letter."[2] Like the *New York Tribune*, other news journals were drawn to the story, but skeptical. "The narrative, though incredible, is ingeniously and rather ably written," admitted the *Pittsburg Post-Gazette*.[3] Finally, Southern and Northern journals had something upon which to agree. The *Memphis Appeal* had almost an identical reaction. "The account is circumstantial and prepared with care," the editors of that paper wrote upon obtaining a copy of the December 10 edition of the *Chicago Times*, "yet we cannot but regard it as a fabrication, and express the opinion that Mr. Greene is a myth."[4]

Despite the dismissive response by the administration, portions of Greene's story were corroborated by witnesses in Pittsburgh. The Rev. A.J. Endsley of the Liberty Street Methodist Episcopal Church vouched for Greene's membership in his congregation, and several members there testified to his "ability and intelligence."[5] Other aspects of Greene's story, however, quickly unraveled.

Thomas Bakewell declared Greene's letter of introduction to Secretary of War Stanton "an unmitigated falsehood" and denied ever seeing or hearing of him until the publication of his affidavit.[6] Greene's employer in Pittsburgh, John Dunlap, testified that he had never "heard of his adventures in Mexico, either through himself or any other person in my employment," thus casting doubt on Greene's claims of a prior acquaintance with Jefferson Davis during the Mexican War.[7] Dunlap also undermined Greene's timeline for supposedly meeting President Davis in Richmond, indicating Greene had seldom been absent from work, except around October 17, when he was gone for some five days—claiming that he had gone on a visit to Buffalo. Other witnesses thought it might have been seven or eight days, but all of them doubted he was gone long enough to visit Richmond and return.[8]

More damning testimony came from the Rev. J.D. Herr, the pastor of the First Methodist Church in Pittsburgh, with whom Greene sought membership in October 1861, indicating he aspired to the ministry.[9] In support of his application, Greene had submitted credentials from Grace Methodist Episcopal Church in Buffalo and the First Methodist Episcopal Church of Cincinnati, apparently thinking they would never be checked. Herr, however, did check, by writing each of the congregations for their recommendations.

The Rev. A.D. Wilbur in Buffalo responded quickly to Herr's request. "I have to say that J.W. Greene received no 'credentials,' no 'certificate' from me whatsoever," he replied. "He left Buffalo very quietly or I should have arraigned him for serious crimes.... In a word, I would trust him for nothing."[10] The Rev. Joseph J. White of the First Methodist Episcopal Church of Cincinnati, too new to remember Greene's past, chose to interview his ex-wife, who still lived at her mother's boardinghouse. White wrote Herr back the same day. "This morning, through the rain—leaving all personal, domestic and pastoral interests—I went forth through the pitiless storm, threading my way from street to street, till at last I found the residence of Mrs. Greene and her mother."[11]

Although the *Pittsburgh Gazette* didn't reveal their names, a cross reference of city directories and census records reveals Greene's ex-wife to be the former Martha Borland.[12] Her parents, Phoebe and William Borland, had operated a successful boardinghouse on Third Street in downtown Cincinnati since the early 1830s, with as many as 20 boarders in 1836.[13] After her husband died sometime in the 1840s, Phoebe Borland successfully continued the business, at least until John Wesley Greene arrived in 1847.

The Reverend White interviewed Martha Borland about his arrival in Cincinnati, the year she turned 17. "Mr. Greene came to board with her mother, representing himself as a young man from New York," she told him. "He united with Morris Chapel of the ME Church and was by them licensed to preach. Talented and fascinating, he was held in great esteem."[14] Greene's "fascinating" preaching at Morris Chapel may have substantially increased their fundraising, for in 1848, the Missionary Society of the Ohio Conference of the Methodist Episcopal Church, reported that of the eight Methodist congregations in Cincinnati, Morris Chapel was second among them in funds raised.¹⁵

On the strength of his eloquence, the Reverend White reported that Greene "won the affections of this lady [Martha Borland], to whom he was united in marriage."¹⁶ Unfortunately, young Martha and her mother soon learned that Greene's piety was an illusion. "His mother-in-law was possessed of some property on Third St.—the site of the Daily Times office, we believe—which John Wesley persuaded her to sell," recalled journalist Murat Halstead of the *Cincinnati Commercial*. "He got the notes in his possession, had them discounted—and with the proceeds—some three or four thousand dollars—set up shop in opposition to his employer."¹⁷ The property to which Halstead referred was the Borland boarding house itself, located on the north side of Third Street, west of Walnut, in the same block as the post office—a prime location in downtown Cincinnati.¹⁸

Halstead also squashed the notion that Greene could have possibly met Jefferson Davis at the Battle of Buena Vista in February 1847, for according to Halstead, Greene came to Cincinnati that month, where he "found secular employment in the shop of George D. Winchell and improved his Sundays as a class-leader and exhorter."¹⁹ With the money he had leveraged from the Borland Boarding House, he set up shop on the southwest corner of Walnut and Pearl, across the street from Winchell's, under the impressive name of the "Great Western Japanned Tin Ware Manufactory" and boldly advertised that dealers should "examine his store and prices before purchasing elsewhere."²⁰ Winchell had nothing to fear. Greene ran through his assets in four months and disappeared, leaving various bills unpaid. Among these was his debt to a local jeweler named Joseph Draper on Fourth Street, who had sold him a watch on credit, after Greene claimed he was Winchell's partner.²¹

With the aid of Halstead and journalists like him, the American public knew the criminal history of John Wesley Greene within days. As with his post office fraud in Philadelphia, he failed to anticipate that his past would come out—and even failed to use an alias, as he had done with limited success in New York City in 1856. Nevertheless, some journalists were fascinated by the extent of the fraud, one of them commenting that "the lie was so stupendous, the romance so dazzling, that ... the whole thing evinces genius and talent that is hard to excel."²²

What the public never learned was who supported Greene in his effort to defraud America into thinking peace was imminent, if only emancipation was withdrawn before New Year's. That answer likely lay in Cincinnati—from the days Greene lived in the boardinghouse on Third Street and was, according to Murat Halstead, considered an "industrious, exemplary man," for his neighbors in the Queen City would, ten years later, yield significant influence.[23]

One of Greene's influential neighbors was attorney Nathaniel G. Pendleton, who maintained his law office across the street from Borland's, opposite the post office. Pendleton had moved to Cincinnati in 1818, where he became a prominent lawyer, city attorney, city councilman, state senator and a United States congressman. Among his several children were "Gentleman" George Pendleton, also an attorney, and Anna Pierce Pendleton. Born in 1830, Anna Pendleton was the same age as Martha Borland, whose father, William Borland, was a trustee of Cincinnati Township in 1834, when a land swap was consummated with the city—a deal likely negotiated while George Pendleton was president of the city council.[24]

Martha Borland was likely already married to John Wesley Greene when young attorney Noah Hunt Schenck moved to Cincinnati from New Jersey in 1848. There is no record of where Schenck resided his first year there, but he set up his law office at the *Cincinnati Gazette* Building on Main Street between Third and Fourth, less than two blocks from Borland's. It would have been the perfect spot for him to room during his first year in Cincinnati. Roughly at the same time as Phoebe Borland moved to Center Street, Schenck moved into the luxurious Burnet House, described by the *Illustrated London News* at the time as "the finest hotel in the world," which opened in May 1850 at Third and Vine.[25]

Schenck, while in Cincinnati, met and married Anna Pierce Pendleton, whose father was for decades a lay officer at the Christ Protestant Episcopal Church on Fourth Street, not far from Borland's.[26] It is altogether likely that he met John Wesley Greene there, who may have switched denominations at the bequest of his new wife. Years later, speaking of this time, Greene would say that he "severed my connection to the mother [Methodist Episcopal] church and united with the Methodist Protestants."[27] There is no hard evidence that the Schencks socialized with the Greenes during those years, but it may not have been a coincidence that the Greenes named their third child "Anna," when she was born to them shortly before his arrest in Baltimore in 1852.[28]

Schenck left Cincinnati in 1851, when he gave up his law practice and entered the seminary in Gambier, Ohio—finally becoming an Episcopal minister in 1854.[29] Therefore, he likely never heard of the scandalous deal that cost the Borlands their home, for it was a well-kept secret for years. Upon Greene's release from prison, Martha convinced him to leave town only by threat of exposure. Thus, if Greene's name had been raised as a peace representative, Schenck would have been happy to endorse him and convince his brother-in-law, Congressman George H. Pendleton, to do the same, remembering their happier times in Cincinnati.

16. A Shallow Attempt at Humbuggery

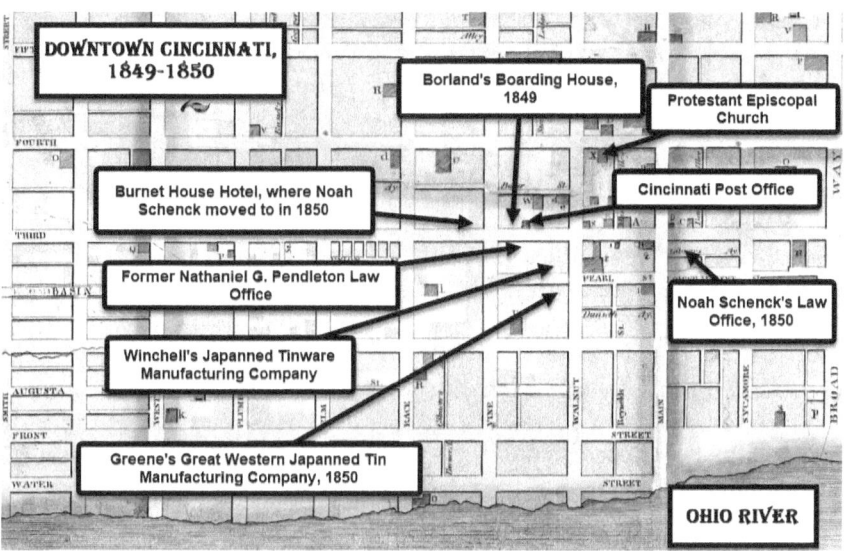

Map of Downtown Cincinnati, 1849–1850 (Base Map from Library of Congress Geography and Map Division). Borland's Boarding House on Third Street, where Greene lived with Martha Borland, would have been an ideal residence for Schenck when he first moved to the city. Nathaniel G. Pendleton, father of future congressman George H. Pendleton, had maintained his law office across the street and was an officer at the Protestant Episcopal Church. Schenck married his daughter, Anna Pendleton (Doolittle & Munson, *Topographical map of the city of Cincinnati, from actual survey*, [1841]. Map. Library of Congress, https://www.loc.gov/item/2006626028/).

Greene may have found endorsements from prominent Baltimore Methodists to be even easier. The Rev. John H. Dashiell, anxious to end the divisions that had split his congregation, would have likely supported him based on Jesse Cullison's recommendation alone and may have gained an additional testimonial from his friend the Rev. Henry Slicer, the former chaplain of the United States Senate. The possibility that Greene obtained endorsements from prominent legislators and clergymen explains why Wilbur Storey proclaimed in the *Chicago Times* that he had total confidence in him, based on "numerous testimonials as to his character."[30]

Unfortunately for Confederate attempts to derail emancipation before years end, they had not vetted him as closely as Northern journalists. Murat Halstead, for example, was not only familiar with Greene's time in Cincinnati, but also with his history with the Pennsylvania Reserves the previous year, writing that:

> During the Fall of 1861, the writer of this article was at Tennallytown, D.C. where the Penn. Reserve, then under the command of Gen. McCall, was

stationed. There was a great scandal in camp circulation, to the effect that the chaplain of one of the regiments, the Rev. J. Wesley Greene, to whom had been assigned the regimental post office, had been guilty of opening the letters of soldiers and purloining whatever money they contained.[31]

Like Halstead, the editor of *National Police Gazette*, George W. Matsell, knew Greene well—for he was not only a newspaper editor, but commissioner of the New York Police Department, with which he served from 1845 until 1857.[32] Matsell had not only covered Greene's arrest in Tennallytown in 1861, but was intimately familiar with his various frauds in New York City.

Thinking Greene was reformed after his lengthy stint in Sing Sing, the *Police Gazette* took him on as an employee upon his release, knowing him to be of "fine education and fair talents."[33] Despite giving him "plain talk" before he started, the editors would later admit that Greene soon "undertook to play the confidence lay on us," and they were forced to release him.[34] In 1862, apparently short on cash, Greene offered the *Police Gazette* the rights to his autobiography—an offer they rejected, knowing him to be "an unmitigated scamp and liar."[35]

After his affidavit was published by the *Chicago Times* in December, the *Police Gazette* quickly declared Greene to be "one of the most plausible and arrant imposters now outside of state prison," and based on his record of various frauds both bold and slick, declared him "the king of the confidence men."[36] His offer to sell them his autobiography, however, revealed how easily the Confederate underground could have obtained his cooperation with gold as an incentive later that year.

All in all, the evidence against Greene was overwhelming, leading to a rash of scathing headlines across the nation. Those of the *Pittsburgh Gazette* screamed "The Knave Unmasked! A Career of Crime and Hypocrisy!!"[37] The nemesis of Wilbur Storey, the *Chicago Tribune*, quickly picked up the news from Pittsburgh and elsewhere. The *Tribune* headline for December 13, 1862, asked the rhetorical question: "Who is J. Wesley Greene?" and then proceeded to answer the question, with the subheading: "A Bigamist, Forger, Convict and Swindler Exposed,"[38] and they spent the next week blasting both Greene and the *Times*.

In Washington, the *National Republican* announced its conclusions on December 15. "It appears that Rev. J. Wesley Greene, the 'confidence man' who attempted to practice some of his games on President Lincoln, is a consummate villain," the paper declared. "He has already spent some twelve months in the Eastern Penitentiary. He has several aliases."[39] An Iowa paper may have summed it up best. "The man who took in and 'did' the Chicago Times—J. Wesley Greene, we mean—seems to have had more acquaintances than any man we ever heard of," the *Burlington Weekly*

Hawk-Eye announced to its readers. "He has doubtless married more women, galled more credulous men and gone through more infamous adventures than any man in America … !"[40]

Aside from his famous cons, Greene seems to have had an unquenchable passion for young women. By the Civil War, he had been married no fewer than four times.[41] Of his first wife, little is known except that he abandoned her in Elizabethtown, New Jersey, in 1847 with up to four children. He would later identify her as the former Rachel Smeltzer, "the daughter of a wealthy farmer in Seneca, N.Y.," and say she divorced him because he had "become entangled in an improper alliance" with a member of his congregation—an event which led to his dismissal, despite his being so popular, he was "little less than an idol."[42]

He initially fled to Philadelphia, where he found employment lettering gas meters, but finding that he earned only a "pittance" at this trade, he moved west to Cincinnati.[43] Business failures there eventually caused him to wander the country, using Methodist churches as his base. Early in 1851, he was found at the North Fifth Street Methodist Episcopal Church in New York City, out of which he lectured on "the Great West—Its Political Position and its Resources" on Valentine's Day.[44] Greene also appeared in Newport, Rhode Island, where locals reported "his eloquence, his zeal, his apparent sincerity, charmed his unsuspecting brethren" to the point where one of them donated a corner lot in the village of Jamestown to him, an asset which he "realized at the earliest opportunity."[45]

A "respectable gentleman" in Chicago, claiming to have known Greene for 11 years, later told the *Chicago Tribune* that Greene also came to Monroe, Michigan, in 1851 as a revivalist, who was "superabundant in zeal, unctuous in prayer, and especially occupied with a tender concern for the female members of the flock."[46] According to the source, he was about to marry a teacher at the Monroe Female Seminary, when "a dead stand still was put to the proceeding by a telegram from Mrs. J. Wesley Greene of Cincinnati."[47]

Although eyewitness accounts of John Wesley Greene's exploits in New York City, Newport, and Monroe in 1851 are not corroborated by other evidence, his frauds in Philadelphia the following year are better documented. "The Rev. John W. Greene gave himself out as a Methodist preacher," one journalist recalled in 1862, "and was as cute in extracting tears from the eyes of audiences as he subsequently proved himself in extracting money from the pockets of street passengers."[48] The *Philadelphia Press* recalled the details: "Early in the year 1852, he made his appearance in this city and preached in a number of Methodist churches. Great crowds flocked to hear him. He was eloquent.… He gave out that he was the confidential agent of the Postmaster General of the United States and had a large number of offices to give out."[49]

Up to this time, most of Greene's scams were trifling, but here he developed his first large-scale confidence game. He concocted a scheme whereby he claimed to be a government official of the postal service, responsible for establishing a new postal route between New York and New Orleans. Advertising for route clerks, he promised them an excellent salary of $1,500 a year if they were willing to pay a modest enlistment fee of $25. Five young men happily traveled to Washington to start their job, only to find it didn't exist, one having sold his house and furniture to start his new career.[50]

When Greene's disgruntled clients took their complaints to the police, he fled, and was traced to Baltimore, where he was found at the luxurious Barnum's Hotel with his wife, Martha, who had just delivered their daughter Anna three weeks before. Greene hid beneath her bed to elude police, but to no avail.[51] On March 22, 1852, the *New York Times* reported from Baltimore that "Rev. J.W. Green, the Philadelphia imposter, was arrested at Barnum's Hotel.... Several watches, and a number of other valuable articles were found upon him. He has confessed his guilt."[52] Left at Barnum's Hotel penniless were Martha and his three children. The proprietors of Barnum's, "owing to the very delicate and destitute condition in which she was left," had little choice but to supply her with accommodations until they could be sent home to Cincinnati.[53]

Ironically, in the weeks preceding his arrest, Greene had preached sermons at Woodbury Chapel and the Light Street Methodist Episcopal Church in Baltimore.[54] Nevertheless, on May 6, 1852, Greene was convicted of two counts of obtaining money under false pretenses and sentenced to 21 months in prison, despite an "eloquent appeal" for leniency.[55] He was reportedly sent to the infamous Eastern Penitentiary, where he impersonated his younger brother by writing "a series of articles about his travels all round the world," and where he "laid claim to the name of Herman Melville, the fascinating romanticist of Omoo and Typee."[56]

John Wesley Greene would spend at least 15 months of his sentence behind bars. Upon his release, he returned to Cincinnati, but his long-suffering wife had finally divorced him. His repeated attempts to reconcile were rebuffed until, according to Halstead's *Cincinnati Commercial*, Greene "was warned to quit the city by her friends, under pain of exposure."[57] To earn his relocation expenses, he wrote a "pathetic letter" to a Cincinnati newspaper, that "he had been unfortunate, a victim of circumstances."[58] According to the witnesses who reported the story, he "made so plausible a statement that he was referred to a benevolent gentleman as an unfortunate, and received $100 as an evidence of the sympathy felt for one whom disaster had so persistently followed."[59]

Greene did not move far—just across the Ohio River to Louisville,

Kentucky, where he obtained a position as a clerk at Hagan, Estcott and Moore, an engraving and printing house on Main Street.[60] According to the *Louisville Times* he took "a very active part in prayer meetings and Sabbath schools," but somehow scammed two young students out of $160 late in 1854.[61] There is no record of whether he was prosecuted, but he seems to have quickly fled Louisville for Sandusky, Ohio, to join his younger brother, Richard "Toby" Greene.

An obscure telegraph operator on the Lake Erie Line in 1854, Toby had taken a position with the *Sandusky Mirror* and together with his wife, Mary Jane, dabbled with the Cosmopolitan Art Association, an enterprise of her brother-in-law, Chauncey Derby, who kept offices in both New York and Sandusky.[62] According to one account in the *Chicago Tribune*, he met his third wife, likely Mary Jane's sister Elizabeth Flower, at this time:

> After staying in Sandusky—most of his time being spent in gambling and bawd houses, and in seducing young and giddy girls—as long as circumstances would permit, he went to Elyria, in the same State, and there again played preacher. While there, he contrived to win the affections of a most estimable young lady, connected with one of the best families in town, and married her.[63]

It was not long after his marriage that he brought his new wife to New York City, where he was arrested and imprisoned in 1856. According to one source, Greene ran into George Winchell in New York upon his release, and was able to return to work in Cincinnati, at his old trade.[64] Free from prison and freshly married for a fourth time to Frances Cullison in 1859, Greene wrote a poem titled "The World's Not Shrouded," which read, in part:

> There is a song of sorrow—
> The death dirge of the gay—
> That tells, ere dawn of morrow;
> Those charms may melt away.[65]

The verse was prophetic—not only of Greene's own fortunes, but those of the Old South.

In the wake of the revelations against him in December 1862 came the disastrous Union defeat at Fredericksburg, Virginia—where Union columns attacking Lee's fortified position were decimated by rebel artillery fire. Surveying the field afterward, Confederate staff officer Osmun Latrobe, son of John H.B. Latrobe, savored the carnage his artillery had wrought. "I rode over the battlefield, and en[j]oyed the sight of hundred[s] of dead Yankees," he recorded in his diary. "Saw much of the work I had done in the way of severed limbs, decapitated bodies, and mutilated remains of all kinds. Doing my soul good. Would that the whole Northern army were as such, and I had had my hand in it."[66]

Burial of the Union dead at Fredericksburg (Library of Congress Prints and Photographs Division). Major Osmun Latrobe delighted in the carnage wrought on Union troops by rebel artillery at the Battle of Fredericksburg, a victory which caused Confederate president Jefferson Davis to repudiate any notion of peace to restore the old Union (John C. Taylor, copyright claimant, *Burial of the Union dead at Fredericksburg,* Fredericksburg, Virginia, 1864. [Hartford: John C. Taylor, 1864]. Photograph. Library of Congress, https://www.loc.gov/item/2011649991/).

Latrobe's glee at the Fredericksburg bloodbath recalled Greene's poetic *death dirge of the gay.* Emboldened by the lopsided rebel victory, Jefferson Davis dropped the subterfuge of peace and issued a retaliatory proclamation to that of Lincoln, declaring that all slaves captured under arms, together with their officers, be treated as if they were in insurrection—a crime typically punishable by death. Davis reportedly announced that the Southern people would rather "unite with a nation of hyenas than with the detestable Yankee nation."[67]

Reluctantly, most Northern Democrats came to agree that prosecution of the war was the only viable option to restore the Union. Even prominent peace advocate John Van Buren abandoned hope of a negotiated settlement. In a speech to fellow Democrats in February 1863, he professed that he always knew that Jefferson Davis and other Rebel leaders were opposed to reunion, and that until those leaders were put down, "the war must go on."[68]

16. A Shallow Attempt at Humbuggery

Lincoln himself could not have conceived of a better way to discredit Northern Copperheads at the close of 1862 than Greene's arrival at the White House. The sign of divine will that Lincoln had long sought on emancipation shouted to the American public with each successive headline. Despite the *Chicago Times'* promise that the public would hear from Greene again, they did not, and no new peace claims emerged, except one sarcastic tale from Lincoln's favorite humorist, Orpheus C. Kerr. "Hostilities shall at once cease, and the two armies shall be consolidated under the title of the Confederate states forces," went the joke. "The war debts of the North and South shall be united that the North may be able to pay them without confusion."[69]

The dire warnings of a race war never materialized, and as Greene once wrote, fortunes could change *ere dawn of morrow*. And they did. Union victories at Gettysburg and Vicksburg in 1863, together with African American regiments raised by the Union, eventually helped turn the tide against the Confederacy. With the passage of the Thirteenth Amendment to the Constitution in 1865 went any chance of returning to the nation of 1860—that tenuous, unstable balance of free and slave states that William Chase Barney had wistfully called "the Union as it was."[70]

Instead, the nation would eventually become what many thought it always should be—the home of the free, everywhere. Even former Copperheads had to agree that Lincoln had been right all along. *Chicago Times* editor Wilbur Storey reportedly regretted his harsh criticism of the Federal government and remarked that "after this, the *Times* will support all wars the country may undertake."[71] John Wesley Greene had a similar reaction. "So then, slavery could be abolished, and the nation preserved," he mused reflectively after the war. "Glory, Hallelujah!"[72]

Postscript

William Chase Barney, under intense criticism in the wake of the John Wesley Greene scandal, fled to Europe in 1863. Barney maintained until his death that peace was possible in 1862, if only McClellan had not been removed from command. However, his nephew, Samuel Chase Barney, Jr., would convince Congress to legally change his name from Barney to DeKraft, on the basis "that his father and uncle had disgraced the name."[1]

Daniel Mountjoy Cloud journeyed to Canada in 1863 on the heels of John Wesley Greene. He returned in 1864 and according to his son, he became an officer in the First Maryland Cavalry, the same regiment that attracted Richard Steuart Latrobe, Samuel H. Lyon, Frank Hume, and Thomas H. Harbin. Despite surviving numerous campaigns during the Civil War, he succumbed to an early death in Vicksburg, Mississippi, in 1871, preventing him from providing a firsthand account of his role in the secret mission to Baltimore.[2]

Thomas Nelson Conrad continued his undercover exploits for the duration of the war. In 1864, he and Cloud devised a plan to abduct President Lincoln but canceled it when security proved too heavy. When the war was over, he returned to teaching until he finally rose to become president of the Virginia Agricultural and Mechanical College in Blacksburg, Virginia—now known as Virginia Tech. Despite two biographies of his Civil War exploits, he avoided all mention of his journey to Richmond with William P. Wood or the secret mission to Baltimore.[3]

Jesse Marling Cullison continued his profession as a hay dealer in Baltimore after the war. His son, Jesse Marling Cullison, Jr., inexplicably left the successful business in 1897 and joined the U.S. Army as a private, eventually rising to become a Lieutenant Colonel in the 28th Infantry, First Division, U.S. Expeditionary Force. He was awarded the Distinguished Service Cross for extraordinary heroism at Laversines, France, on July 18, 1918, and is buried in Arlington National Cemetery. Whether he joined the United States Army to atone for his father's treasonous activity 35 years before is a matter of speculation.[4]

Private Micajah M. Cullison, Greene's brother-in-law, returned to his regiment on June 15, 1863, after spending two months confined in Fort McHenry for desertion. Whether he was present when they won distinction at Gettysburg for blunting the assault of Maryland Confederates at Culp's Hill, reportedly including Mountjoy Cloud, is not known. He deserted again in 1864.[5]

John Wesley Greene, tired of his exile in Canada, took the name of his brother-in-law, M.M. Cullison, and moved to Connecticut. Just as he had been before the war, he was always one step ahead of the police—leapfrogging from Connecticut to Indiana to New York to Chicago. His former regiment, the Tenth Pennsylvania Reserves (39th Pennsylvania Infantry) who sought to maintain their honor in 1861 by refusing to testify against their chaplain, won glory at Gettysburg for holding Cemetery Ridge against Confederate assault on the third day.[6]

Murat Halstead, who helped break the story of John Wesley Greene's career as a confidence man while news editor of the *Cincinnati Commercial*, became one of the most famous editors of the 19th century. From the execution of John Brown in 1859 to the war in the Philippines, it was said that Halstead "had written more 'copy'... than any man of his generation."[7]

Rev. Noah Hunt Schenck left his congregation in Baltimore and moved to Brooklyn in 1869. His brother-in-law, Senator George H. Pendleton, became Major General George McClellan's running mate on the Democratic ticket in the presidential election of 1864. On the strength of Union victories, they were soundly defeated by incumbent Abraham Lincoln.[8]

John W. Selby returned to the dry goods business in Baltimore after the war. However, the lifelong Methodist who may have introduced John Wesley Greene to Tom Conrad in August 1861 took a page from Greene's book in 1872 when he unexpectedly left his wife and family and eloped with a Sunday school teacher. He moved to Georgia, changed careers, and became a Presbyterian.[9]

Ignatius Smallwood returned to Washington after his fortuitous escape from rebel forces at Manassas in July 1861. He lived on Washington's southwest side for 40 years, working odd jobs and serving as sexton of the Epiphany Chapel, in the basement of which he died of a heart attack in 1902. According to the *Evening Star*, "his death was a shock to his many relatives and friends." The man who intended to enslave him, Major John B. Prados, was reassigned in late 1862 to the task of rounding up deserters on Lake Pontchartrain, Louisiana, where he was brutally knifed to death in January 1863 aboard a schooner, ironically named *Virtue*.[10]

William P. Wood became the first director of the U.S. Secret Service. Despite writing several articles for the *Washington Sunday Gazette* and the *National Free Press*, he never revealed the true purpose of his mission to Richmond in the fall of 1862 on behalf of Secretary of War Edwin Stanton, nor publicly revealed that he had journeyed there with Confederate spymaster Thomas Nelson Conrad.[11]

Francis G. Young continued unsuccessfully to lobby the Lincoln administration for a military commission. Despite his bitterness towards the president in 1862, he later defended Mrs. Lincoln from charges she wore a lilac dress at Senator Baker's funeral, remembering wistfully the day he had ridden in a carriage with the Lincolns on that sad day, 25 years before.[12]

Chapter Notes

Preface

1. "About the Historical Forensics Project," https://www.historicalforensics.com/, accessed July 30, 2023.

Introduction

1. "Lincoln, Nixon, Forrest and Hackett—the Great Theatrical Men of the Day," *New York Daily Herald*, September 24, 1862, https://chroniclingamerica.loc.gov/lccn/sn83030313/1862-09-24/ed-1/seq-4/.
2. "The President's Proclamation," *Chicago Daily Tribune*, September 23, 1862, https://chroniclingamerica.loc.gov/lccn/sn84031490/1862-09-23/ed-1/seq-1/.
3. "Emancipation," *The Potter Journal* (Coudersport, PA), October 1, 1862, https://chroniclingamerica.loc.gov/lccn/sn86081096/1862-10-01/ed-1/seq-3/.
4. Manhattan [Joseph Alfred Scoville], "North and South," *Standard* (London), October 31, 1862, https://newscomwc.newspapers.com/image/401691119/.
5. Manhattan [Joseph Alfred Scoville], "North and South," *Standard* (London), October 25, 1862, https://newscomwc.newspapers.com/image/401687945/.
6. William Roscoe Thayer, *John Hay*, Vol. 1 (Boston: Riverside, 1915), 130–133.
7. William B. Styple, *McClellan's Other Story* (Kearny, NJ: Belle Grove, 2012).
8. "The News," *Chicago Daily Tribune*, June 26, 1864, https://chroniclingamerica.loc.gov/lccn/sn84031490/1864-06-26/ed-1/seq-1/.
9. "Obituary," *Gentleman's Magazine and Historical Review* 217 (August 1864), 258.

Chapter 1

1. *National Police Gazette*, December 13, 1862, Rpt. in "J. Wesley Greene," *New York Daily Herald*, December 19, 1862, https://newscomwc.newspapers.com/image/329344744/.
2. Herman Melville, *The Confidence-Man: His Masquerade* (London: Longman Brown Green Longmans & Roberts, 1857), 3–4.
3. Ibid.
4. Ibid.
5. "The Confidence Man: His Masquerade," *New York Dispatch*, April 5, 1857, https://chroniclingamerica.loc.gov/lccn/sn83030364/1857-04-05/ed-1/seq-4/.
6. John J. Gross, "Melville's "The Confidence-Man": The Problem of Source and Meaning," *Modern Language Society* 60, no. 3 (1959), https://www.jstor.org/stable/43341981.
7. John Pistelli, "Herman Melville, The Confidence-Man: His Masquerade," August 18, 2019, https://johnpistelli.com/2019/08/18/herman-melville-the-confidence-man-his-masquerade/.
8. Michael S. Reynolds, "The Protype for Melville's Confidence Man," *PMLA* 86 (October 1971), 1009–1013.
9. "Incident of the 'Confidence Man,'" *New York Daily Herald*, July 14, 1849, https://newscomwc.newspapers.com/image/466604923/.
10. "The Confidence Man Caged," *New York Tribune*, April 30, 1855, https://newscomwc.newspapers.com/image/50602700/.
11. Ibid.
12. Watson Branch, Hershel Parker, and Harrison Hayford, eds. "Historical

Note," *The Confidence-Man: His Masquerade* (Evanston: Northwestern University Press, 1984), 277.

13. "Arrest of a Shrewd Confidence Man," *New York Herald*, January 18, 1856, https://chroniclingamerica.loc.gov/lccn/sn83030313/1856-01-18/ed-1/seq-1/.

14. "The King of the Confidence Men," *New York Dispatch*, January 20, 1856, https://www.loc.gov/item/sn83030364/1856-01-20/ed-1/.

15. "Police Intelligence," *New York Times*, January 17, 1856, https://nytimes.com/1856/01/17/archives.

16. "Arrest of a Shrewd Confidence Man."

17. H. Wilson, *Trow's New York City Directory, 1855/56* (New York: Trow, 1855), 732.

18. "A Strange Man and A Strange Story," *New York Times*, January 19, 1856, https://nytimes.com/1856/01/19/archives.

19. Ibid.

20. Ibid.

21. "Police Intelligence"; "Arrest of a Shrewd Confidence Man."

22. "Greer, the 'Respectable' Confidence-Man," *New York Times*, March 13, 1856, https://nytimes.com/1856/03/13/archives.

23. "The Great Confidence Man," *New York Daily Herald*, January 19, 1856, https://chroniclingamerica.loc.gov/lccn/sn83030313/1856-01-19/ed-1/seq-1/.

24. "Caution," *New York Times*, December 6, 1855.

25. "J. Wesley Greene," *New York Daily Herald*, December 19, 1862.

26. "The 'Confidence Man Tired of Prison," *New York Dispatch*, February 03, 1856, https://www.loc.gov/item/sn83030364/1856-02-03/ed-1/.

27. "A Visit to the Tombs," *New York Dispatch*, March 2, 1856, https://www.loc.gov/item/sn83030364/1856-03-02/ed-1/.

28. Ibid.

29. "Arrest of a Shrewd Confidence Man."

30. "A Strange Man."

31. "The Confidence Man: His Masquerade," *New York Dispatch*, April 05, 1857, https://www.loc.gov/item/sn83030364/1857-04-05/ed-1/.

32. "Arrest of a Shrewd Confidence Man."

33. "J. Wesley Greene."

34. 1860 U.S. Census, Cook County, Illinois, Population Schedule, Chicago 2nd Ward, p. 8, line 38, Elizabeth Flower in household of Richard Green, NARA Publication M653, sheet 8, p. 302, https://records.myheritagelibraryedition.com/research/collection-10127/1860-united-states-federal-census.

35. Ibid.

36. Elizabeth Ann Anema, *Family Tree of Elizabeth Ada Flower (1835–?)*, https://records.myheritagelibraryedition.com/site-545244791/hackett.

37. Wilson Heflin, Mary K. Bercaw Edwards, and Thomas Farel Heffernan, *Herman Melville's Whaling Years* (Nashville: Vanderbilt University Press, 2004), 217.

38. Gary Dexter, *Why Not Catch-21? The Stories Behind the Titles* (London: Francis Franklin Limited, 2007), 88.

39. Herman Melville, *The Writings of Herman Melville: Correspondence*, ed. Lynn Horth (Evanston: Northwestern University Press, 1993), 646.

40. 1860 U.S. Census, Cook County, Illinois, Chicago 2nd Ward, Elizabeth Flower.

41. "Wesley Greene, Tinker," *Chicago Daily Tribune*, December 15, 1862, https://chroniclingamerica.loc.gov/lccn/sn84031490/1862-12-15/ed-1/seq-2/.

42. *Cincinnati Daily Commercial*, December 12, 1862. Rpt. in "Toby of Typee," *Chicago Daily Tribune*, December 16, 1862, https://chroniclingamerica.loc.gov/lccn/sn84031490/1862-12-16/ed-1/seq-3/.

43. "After a Reverend Bigamist," *Chicago Inter Ocean*, September 6, 1888, https://newscomwc-newspapers-com.eu1.proxy.openathens.net/image/33425806/.

44. Ibid.

45. "Crime of a Clergyman," *Indianapolis Journal*, September 7, 1888, https://chroniclingamerica.loc.gov/lccn/sn82015679/1888-09-07/ed-1/seq-2/.

46. "Greer, the Confidence Man at the Court of Sessions," *New York Herald*, March 13, 1856, https://newscomwc.newspapers.com/image/329311173/.

47. Ibid.

48. Horth Melville, ed. *Writings of Herman Melville*, 645–646.

49. Melville, *The Confidence-Man*, 354.

Chapter 2

1. "'The Confidence Man' on a Grand Scale," *New York Herald*, July 11, 1849, https://newscomwc.newspapers./image/466604782/.
2. Ibid.
3. "The Latest News," *New York Herald*, January 29, 1857, https://newscomwc.newspapers.com/image/466601779/.
4. "Racy News from Washington," *New York Herald*, January 30, 1857, https://newscomwc.newspapers.com/image/466601899/.
5. Josh S. Cutler, *Mobtown Massacre: Alexander Hanson and the Baltimore Newspaper War of 1812* (Charleston: History Press, 2019), 82; Mary Barney, *A Biographical Memoir of the late Commodore Barney* (Boston: Gray and Bowen, 1832), 193.
6. "William Chase Barney," *Baltimore Sun*, January 23, 1892, https://baltimoresun.newspapers.com/image/371349717/.
7. Blaine Barney, *Family Tree of William Chase Barney (1814–1892)*, https://records.myheritagelibraryedition.com/site-245203301/barney.
8. "Obituary," *Savannah Daily Republican*, April 1, 1843, https://www.newspaperarchive.com/us/georgia/savannah/savannah-daily-republican/1843/04-01/page-4/.
9. "William Chase Barney."
10. "Foreign Intelligence," *Washington Sentinel*, August 7, 1855, https://www.newspaperarchive.com/us/washington-dc/washington/washington-sentinel/1855/08-07/page-3/.
11. "The Naval Board," *Washington Daily Union*, August 19, 1855, https://chroniclingamerica.loc.gov/lccn/sn82003410/1855-08-19/ed-1/seq-2/; *Brooklyn Evening Star*, September 17, 1855, p. 2.
12. Kennard R. Wiggins Jr., *America's Anchor* (Jefferson, NC: McFarland, 2019), 102.
13. "Obituary," *Washington National Republican*, February 13, 1861, https://chroniclingamerica.loc.gov/lccn/sn82014760/1861-02-13/ed-1/seq-3/.
14. Senator A.G. Brown and Hon. W.W. Boyce to Gen. Winder, October 4, 1862, *The War of the Rebellion: A Compilation of the Official Records of the Union and Confederate Armies* (hereafter *Official Records*), III, Vol. II (Washington: GPO, 1899), 178.
15. Michael W. Cluskey, *Speeches Messages and Other Writings of The Hon. Albert Gallatin Brown* (Philadelphia: James B. Smith & Co, 1859), 403.
16. "The Barney Case Before the Orphan's Court," *Washington Evening Star*, October 4, 1861, https://chroniclingamerica.loc.gov/lccn/sn83045462/1861-10-04/ed-1/seq-3/.
17. Ibid.
18. "Case for Court," *American Republican and Baltimore Daily Clipper*, June 16, 1845, https://chroniclingamerica.loc.gov/lccn/sn83009567/1845-06-16/ed-1/seq-2/.
19. *Journal of the Senate of the United States of America* (Washington: A.O.P. Nicholson, 1856–57), 167; William C. Barney, "Ocean Steamers from New Orleans to France," *DeBow's Review* 22 (1857), 318–320.
20. William C. Barney, "Steamships at the South," *De Bow's Review* 22 (1857), 410–414.
21. Winthrop L Marvin, *The American Merchant Marine Its History and Romance from 1620 to 1902* (New York: Charles Scribner, 1916), 275.
22. Robert Royal Russel, *Economic Aspects of Southern Sectionalism, 1841–1860* (New York: Noble, 1924), 164.
23. *Reports of Committees of the House of Representatives of the Thirty-Fifth Congress* (Washington: James B. Steedman, 1858), 21.
24. Testimony of William H. Davidge, May 25, 1860, *The Covode Investigation* (Washington: USPO, 1860), 791.
25. "Baltimore," *New York Daily Herald*, July 10, 1845, https://newscomwc.newspapers.com/image/329341712/.
26. "County Court," *Baltimore Daily Commercial*, June 16, 1845, https://newscomwc.newspapers.com/image/3255819 78/.
27. John Barney to Lewis Cass, March 1843, Lewis Cass Papers, 1774–1924, William L. Clements Library, University of Michigan.
28. Donal Shaw, *London in the Sixties: One of the Old Brigade* (London: Everett & Co, 1908).

29. John Barney to Lewis Cass, March 1843, Cass Papers.
30. "William Chase Barney."
31. John Barney to Lewis Cass, April 29, 1843, Cass Papers.
32. Oliver Miller, *Maryland Reports*, Vol. XI (Annapolis: Robert F. Bonsall, 1858), 204.
33. Ibid.
34. Ibid., 205.
35. Ibid., 203.
36. "Baltimore."
37. Ibid.
38. "Another Statement," *Baltimore Daily Commercial*, July 10, 1845, https://newscomwc.newspapers.com/image/325585372/; "Case for Court."
39. Ibid.
40. "Fine Weather—Closing Scene of the Barney Marriage Case," *New York Herald*, January 30, 1846, https://chroniclingamerica.loc.gov/lccn/sn83030313/1846-01-30/ed-1/seq-4/.
41. *Fayetteville North Carolinian*, November 27, 1847, https://newscomwc.newspapers.com/image/66021154/.
42. *Milwaukee Sentinel and Gazette*, December 18, 1847, https://www.newspaperarchive.com/us/wisconsin/milwaukee/sentinel-and-gazette/1847/12-18.
43. J. Thomas Scharf, *The Chronicles of Baltimore* (Baltimore: Turnbull Brothers, 1874), 93.
44. Thomas Prentice Kettel, *The United States Magazine and Democratic Review* 22 (1848), 379.
45. *United States Catholic Magazine and Monthly Review* 7 (January 1848), 224.
46. Ibid.
47. Jan Simmons Johnson, *The House of Franciscus, 1710–2000 A.D.* (Madison: University of Wisconsin Press, 1989), 1529.
48. Faculty of Eastern High School, *Through the Years at Eastern High* (Baltimore: H.G. Roebuck & Son, 1944), 2, 5.
49. "Prospectus, The Court Journal," *Washington Daily National Whig*, January 27, 1849, https://newscomwc.newspapers.com/image/320635517/.
50. "The 'Court Journal,'" *Philadelphia Public Ledger*, February 27, 1849, https://newscomwc.newspapers.com/image/40229826/.
51. *Boston Post*, January 18, 1849, https://www.newspaperarchive.com/us/massachusetts/boston/boston-post/1849/-01-18/page-2/; "Ridiculous Absurdity," *New Orleans Crescent*, February 6, 1849, https://www.newspaperarchive.com/us/louisiana/new-orleans/new-orleans-daily-crescent/1849/02-06/page-2/.
52. 1850 U.S. Census, Bergen County, New Jersey, Population Schedule, Hackensack Township, William Chase Barney in household of George Lester, NARA Publication M432page 252, https://records.myheritagelibraryedition.com/research/-collection-10126/1850-united-states-federal-census.
53. "Official," *New York Tribune*, June 25, 1850, https://newscomwc.newspapers.com/image/467620144/.
54. "Editor's Correspondence," *Washington Union*, July 7, 1850, https://chroniclingamerica.loc.gov/lccn/sn82003410/1850-07-07/ed-1/seq-3/.
55. "Passports—Alleged Frauds—W. Chase Barney," *New York Tribune*, June 26, 1850, https://newscomwc.newspapers.com/image/467620274/.
56. "Private Enterprise," *Buffalo Daily Republic*, July 10, 1851, https://newscomwc.newspapers.com/image/255007025/.
57. *Bangor Daily Whig and Courier*, October 3, 1851, https://newscomwc.newspapers.com/image/662983449/; "California Tickets," *New York Daily Herald*, April 12, 1852, https://newscomwc.newspapers.com/image/329311698/.
58. *Bangor Daily Whig and Courier*, July 20, 1852, https://newscomwc.newspapers.com/image/663050014/.
59. "Suit for Damages," *New Orleans Times-Picayune*, July 20, 1852, https://newscomwc.newspapers.com/image/25544325/.
60. "Second Act in the California Swindle Tragedy," *New York Sunday Dispatch*, April 4, 1852, https://newscomwc.newspapers.com/image/593807497/.
61. "California Tickets."
62. Ibid.
63. "The California Ticket Swindle Case." *New York Tribune*, April 6, 1852, https://newscomwc.newspapers.com/image/88210571/.
64. "Our New York Correspondence," *Portsmouth* [OH] *Inquirer*, April 16, 1852, https://newscomwc.newspapers.com/image/171661985/.

65. "Dissolution of Co-Partnership," *New York Daily Herald*, May 2, 1852, https://newscomwc.newspapers.com/image/329315861/.
66. "European Express by Every Steamer," *New York Daily Herald*, July 31, 1853, https://newscomwc.newspapers.com/image/843814502/.
67. U.S. Congress, House Select Committee on Alleged Corruptions in Government, *The Covode Investigation* (Washington: USPO, 1860), 823–828.
68. "The Covode Investigation," 810–811.
69. "Letter from Baltimore," *Cincinnati Daily Gazette*, December 12, 1862, https://www.newspaperarchive.com/us/ohio/cincinnati/cincinnati-daily-gazette/1862/12-12/.

Chapter 3

1. Henry Elliott Shepard, *History of Baltimore, MD* (Baltimore: S.B. Nelson, 1893), 133.
2. "Mass Meeting of the friends of Breckinridge and Lane," *Baltimore Daily Exchange*, October 23, 1860, https://chroniclingamerica.loc.gov/lccn/sn83009573/1860-10-23/ed-1/seq-1/; E. Lawrence Abel, *Confederate Sheet Music* (Jefferson, NC: McFarland, 2011), 72.
3. "Mass Meeting."
4. Edward Channing, *A Student's History of the United States* (New York: MacMillan, 1922), 437–438.
5. "Demonstration in Columbia," *Baltimore Daily Exchange*, November 10, 1860, https://chroniclingamerica.loc.gov/lccn/sn83009573/1860-11-10/ed-1/seq-1/.
6. "Charleston, December 2," *Baltimore Daily Exchange*, December 4, 1860, https://chroniclingamerica.loc.gov/lccn/sn83009573/1860-12-04/ed-1/seq-1/.
7. Frank F. White, Jr., *The Governors of Maryland 1777–1970* (Annapolis: The Hall of Records Commission, 1970), 153–157.
8. "City Intelligence. Meeting at the Universalist Church," *Baltimore Daily Exchange*, December 24, 1860, https://chroniclingamerica.loc.gov/lccn/sn83009573/1860-12-24/ed-1/seq-1/.
9. Ibid.
10. "Lincoln to be Waylaid in Baltimore," *Washington Evening Star*, December 12, 1860, https://chroniclingamerica.loc.gov/lccn/sn83045462/1860-12-12/ed-1/seq-3/.
11. Allan Pinkerton, *The Spy of the Rebellion* (New York: G.W. Carleton, 1883), 57.
12. John W. Woods, ed. *Woods' Baltimore City Directory, 1860* (Baltimore: Woods, 1860), 464.
13. Ibid., 63.
14. Edward C. Papenfuse, "Ferrandini, Cipriano," *Archives of Maryland*, 2009, https://msa.maryland.gov/megafile/msa/speccol/sc3500/sc3520/014400/014473/html/14473bio.html.
15. Pinkerton, *The Spy of the Rebellion*, 59.
16. William Wilkins Glenn, *Between North and South* (London: Associated University Press, 1976), 27.
17. Ibid.
18. Thomas M. Myers, *The Norris Family of Maryland* (New York: Clemens, 1916), 42.
19. Richard F. Miller, *States at War*, Vol. 4 (Hanover: University Press of New England, 2015), 476.
20. David Schley, *Steam City* (Chicago: University of Chicago Press, 2020), 229.
21. "The Rachel Parker Case," *Elkton* [MD] *Cecil Whig*, January 8, 1853, https://chroniclingamerica.loc.gov/lccn/sn83016348/1853-01-08/ed-1/seq-2/.
22. Hugh Egan. "The Mackenzie Court-Martial Trial: Cooper's Secret Correspondence with William H. Norris." *Studies in the American Renaissance*, 1990, 149–158. http://www.jstor.org/stable/30227591.
23. Ibid.
24. "Francis Scott Key," *Towsontown* [MD] *Baltimore County Union*, January 5, 1907, https://chroniclingamerica.loc.gov/lccn/sn83016368/1907-01-05/ed-1/seq-1/.
25. Rev. Noah Schenck, *Rev. Mr. Schenck's Introductory Discourse in Emmanuel Church* (Baltimore: John D. Toy, 1860), 7.
26. *Constitution and By Laws of the Christian Labor Union of Emmanuel Church* (Baltimore: John D. Toy, 1860).
27. Ibid.
28. John E Semmes, *John HB Latrobe and His Times 1803–1891* (Baltimore: Norman Remington, 1917), 321.
29. Ibid., 573.
30. Protestant Episcopal Church, *Journal*

of the Seventy-First Annual Convention of the Protestant Episcopal Church in Maryland (Baltimore: Joseph Robinson, 1854), xi.

31. Bel Air (Md) Aegis and Intelligencer, September 18, 1891, https://newscomwc.newspapers.com/image/466024359.

32. Brion McClanahan, "Charles Carroll of Carrollton: The Southern Irish Catholic Planter," March 17, 2016, https://www.abbevilleinstitute.org/.

33. Kate Mason Rowland, *The Life of Charles Carroll of Carrollton, 1737–1832*, Vol. II (New York: G.P. Putnam, 1898), 321.

34. John H.B. Latrobe, *African Colonization: An Address* (Washington: H.S. Bowen, 1862), 10.

35. J.H.B. Latrobe, "Speech of J.H.B. Latrobe," *Thirty-Fifth Annual Report of the American Colonization Society, January 20, 1852* (Washington: C. Alexander, 1852), 54.

36. "John H.B. Latrobe," *New York Daily Tribune*, September 12, 1891, https://newscomwc.newspapers.com/image/78360084/.

37. J.H.B. Latrobe, "Address of J.H.B. Latrobe," *Thirty-Seventh Annual Report of the American Colonization Society* (Washington: C. Alexander, 1854), 25.

38. Frederic P. Stanton, "Address of Frederic P. Stanton," *Thirty-Fifth Annual Report of the American Colonization Society, January 20, 1852* (Washington: C. Alexander, 1852), 13.

39. "American Colonization Society," *Daily Dispatch* (Richmond, VA), January 19, 1860, https://chroniclingamerica.loc.gov/lccn/sn84024738/1860-01-19/ed-1/seq-2/; James Hall to Rev. Wm. McLain, January 16, 1860, *Forty-Third Annual Report of the American Colonization Society, January 17, 1860* (Washington: C. Alexander, 1860), 40–41.

40. "Failure of the African Colonization Society," *New York Daily Herald*, January 20, 1860, https://newscomwc.newspapers.com/image/593956452.

41. Ibid.

42. Charles W. Mitchell and Jean H. Baker, *The Civil War in Maryland Reconsidered* (Baton Rouge: Louisiana State University Press, 2021), 76.

43. "The Free Negro Bills," *Baltimore Daily Exchange*, February 15, 1860, https://chroniclingamerica.loc.gov/lccn/sn83009573/1860-02-15/ed-1/seq-1/.

44. Charles Howard, *Communication from the President of the Maryland State Colonization Society* (Baltimore: Maryland Senate, 1860), 5.

45. Glenn, *Between North and South*, 19–20.

46. Shepard, *History of Baltimore*, 133.

47. Horace Greeley, *The American Conflict: A History of the Great Rebellion in the United States of America*, Vol. 1 (Hartford: O.D. Case, 1864), 462; "Northwestern Young Men's Christian Association," *Baltimore Daily Exchange*, May 28, 1859, https://chroniclingamerica.loc.gov/lccn/sn83009573/1859-05-28/ed-1/seq-1/.

48. "Transit of the Massachusetts Volunteers Through Baltimore," *Alexandria Gazette and Virginia Advertiser*, April 20, 1861, https://chroniclingamerica.loc.gov/lccn/sn85025007/1861-04-20/ed-1/seq-2/.

49. Glenn, *Between North and South*, 29.

50. "Return of General Small's Regiment," *Philadelphia Press*, April 20, 1861, https://panewsarchive.psu.edu/lccn/sn84026296/1861-04-20/ed-1/seq-2/.

51. Maryland General Assembly, *Journal of the Proceedings of the Senate of Maryland, January Session, 1858* (Annapolis: Bull & Tuttle, 1858), 13; Isaac F Nicholson, "The Maryland Guard Battalion, 1860–61," *Maryland Historical Magazine* VI (June 1911), 121.

52. John Lockwood, Charles Lockwood, *Siege of Washington* (New York: Oxford University Press, 2011), 92.

53. Ibid.

54. "The Shooting and Killing of Robert W. Davis, esq," *Rockville [MD] Montgomery County Sentinel*, April 26, 1861, https://chroniclingamerica.loc.gov/lccn/sn83016209/1861-04-26/ed-1/seq-1/.

55. Ibid.

56. "The Battle of Friday," *Richmond Daily Dispatch*, April 24, 1861, https://chroniclingamerica.loc.gov/lccn/sn84024738/1861-04-24/ed-1/seq-3/.

57. Ibid.

58. "Baltimore," *Washington National Republican*, April 23, 1861, https://chroniclingamerica.loc.gov/lccn/sn82014760/1861-04-23/ed-1/seq-2/.

59. Lockwood and Lockwood, *The Siege of Washington*, 176.

60. "Northwestern Young Man's Christian Association," *Baltimore*

Daily Exchange, May 28, 1859, https://chroniclingamerica.loc.gov/lccn/sn83009573/1859-05-28/ed-1/seq-1/.
   61. "Dedication of the Hall of the Northwestern Young Men's Christian Association," *Baltimore Daily Exchange*, April 17, 1860, https://chroniclingamerica.loc.gov/lccn/sn83009573/1860-04-17/ed-1/seq-1/.
   62. "Obituary, John W. Selby."
   63. Abraham Lincoln, *Collected Works of Abraham Lincoln*, Vol. 4 (New Brunswick, NJ: Rutgers University Press, 1953), 341–342.
   64. Michael Burlingame, *Abraham Lincoln: The Observations of John G. Nicolay and John Hay* (Carbondale: Southern Illinois University Press, 2007), 55.
   65. Schenck, *Introductory Discourse*, 7.
   66. "Highly Important," *Chicago Tribune*, July 1, 1861, https://access-newspaperarchive-com.eu1.proxy.openathens.net/us/illinois/chicago/chicago-daily-tribune/1861/07-01/.

Chapter 4

   1. "Music of 'My Maryland,'" *Roanoke Times*, March 25, 1908, https://newscomwc.newspapers.com/image/911739668/.
   2. Lockwood and Lockwood, *The Siege of Washington*, 209.
   3. "Baltimore," *Baltimore Daily Exchange*, May 10, 1861, https://chroniclingamerica.loc.gov/lccn/sn83009573/1861-05-10/ed-1/seq-2/.
   4. Amy Worden, *Lawyers Hill Historic District National Register of Historic Places Inventory Nomination Form* (Washington: National Park Service, 1992), 21.
   5. *Journal of the Seventy First Annual Convention of the Protestant Episcopal Church in Maryland* (Baltimore: Joseph Robinson, 1854), xi; Woods, *Baltimore Directory, 1860*, 227.
   6. Worden, *Lawyers Hill Historic District*, 21.
   7. "Letter From John H.B. Latrobe," *Philadelphia Inquirer*, January 14, 1861, https://newscomwc.newspapers.com/image/167454191/.
   8. John Edward Semmes, *John H.B. Latrobe and His Times* (Baltimore: Norman, Remington, 1917), 452.
   9. Worden, *Lawyers Hill Historic District*, 21.
   10. "The Relay House," *Baltimore Daily Exchange*, May 13, 1861, https://chroniclingamerica.loc.gov/lccn/sn83009573/1861-05-13/ed-1/seq-1/.
   11. McHenry Howard, *Recollections of A Maryland Confederate Soldier and Staff Officer* (Baltimore: Williams & Wilkins, 1914), 13.
   12. *Official Records*, I, Vol. II (Washington: GPO, 1880), 30–31.
   13. "The Capture of the Steam Gun and Its Owner," *Cleveland Morning Leader*, May 17, 1861, https://chroniclingamerica.loc.gov/lccn/sn83035143/1861-05-17/ed-1/seq-2/.
   14. Ibid.
   15. George Wilson Booth, *A Maryland Boy in Lee's Army* (Lincoln: University of Nebraska Press, 2000), 9.
   16. Howard, *Recollections of A Maryland Confederate*, 14.
   17. Ibid., 16.
   18. Ibid., 17.
   19. Andrew Johnson and Paul H. Bergeron, eds., *The Papers of Andrew Johnson*, Vol. 9–10 (Knoxville: University of Tennessee Press, 1991), 420.
   20. "Maryland Furnished Eight Thousand Troops for the War," *New York Herald*, September 20, 1861, https://chroniclingamerica.loc.gov/lccn/sn83030313/1861-09-20/ed-1/seq-2/.
   21. Richard D. Steuart, "Henry A. Steuart - Rebel Spy" *Confederate Veteran* 16 (1908), 332–334.
   22. Ibid.
   23. Ibid.
   24. *Official Records*, II, Vol. II, 279.
   25. *Official Records*, II, Vol. III, 455.
   26. Goldsborough, William W., *The Maryland Line in the Confederate Army* (Baltimore: Guggenheim, Weil & Co, 1900), 296.
   27. Steuart, "Henry A Steuart, Rebel Spy," 333.
   28. *Official Records*, II, Vol. II, 279.
   29. Booth, *A Maryland Boy in Lee's Army*, 10.
   30. "Work of a Confederate Woman," *Confederate Veteran* 9 (July 1901), 321–325; Booth, *A Maryland Boy in Lee's Army*, 10.
   31. *The Whig Standard* (Washington, D.C.), June 3, 1844; "Mr. James Carroll," *Cecil Whig* (Elkton, MD), June 29, 1844,

https://chroniclingamerica.loc.gov/lccn/sn83016348/1844-06-29/ed-1/seq-1/.

32. 1860 U.S. Census, Maryland, 11th Ward Baltimore City, James Carroll, NARA Publication M653, Sheet 84, Page 88, Line 7, https://records.myheritagelibraryedition.com/research/record-10127-8423603/james-carroll-in-1860-united-states-federal-census. Over $7 million in 2020 dollars.

33. Isaac F Nicholson, "The Maryland Guard Battalion, 1860–61," *Maryland Historical Magazine* V6, no. 2 (June 1911), 117–131.

34. "The Brown Veil Club," https://civilwartalk.com/threads/the-brown-veil-club.124445:, accessed August 6, 2023; Lyon Gardiner Tyler, *Encyclopedia of Virginia Biography* (New York: Lewis Historical Publishing, 1915), 850.

35. 1860 U.S. Federal Census, Maryland, 11th Ward Baltimore City, Prudence G Winn in household of James Carroll, NARA Publication M653, Sheet 84, Page 88, Line 8, https://records.myheritagelibraryedition.com/research/record-10127-8423604/prudence-g-winn-in-1860-united-states-federal-census.

36. Woods, *Baltimore Directory, 1860*, 334.

37. Myers, *Norris Family in Maryland*, 42.

38. Thomas Arkle, *Family Tree of Mary Hawkesworth Norris (born Owen)*, https://records.myheritagelibraryedition.com/research/record-1-444033451-1-533111/.

39. Woods, *Baltimore Directory, 1860*, 158.

40. 1850 U.S. Federal Census, Virginia, Clarke County, Riddle Grogan in household of Algernon S Allen, NARA Publication M432, Page 384, https://records.myheritagelibraryedition.com/research/record-10126-22535425/.

41. U.S. Census Record, MD, MSA SM61-226, Slaves 1860, http://slavery2.msa.maryland.gov/.

42. "Music of 'My Maryland.'"

43. Ibid.

44. Ibid.

45. Ibid.

46. "Appointments, Baltimore Conference M.E. Church, 1856," *Alexandria Gazette*, March 22, 1856, https://chroniclingamerica.loc.gov/lccn/sn85025007/1856-03-22/ed-1/seq-2/;

"First Annual Meeting of the East Baltimore Conference," *Baltimore Daily Exchange*, March 10, 1858, https://chroniclingamerica.loc.gov/lccn/sn83009573/1858-03-10/ed-1/seq-2/.

47. "The Episcopal Convention at Baltimore," *Buffalo Courier*, May 30, 1853, https://newscomwc.newspapers.com/image/313007068/.

48. James Edward Armstrong, *History of The Old Baltimore Conference from the Planting of Methodism in 1773 to the Division of the Conference in 1857* (Baltimore: King Brothers, 1907); Robert J. Trout, *They Followed the Plume: The Story of J.E.B. Stuart and His Staff* (Mechanicsburg, PA: Stackpole, 2003), 192.

49. "Reverend Dabney Ball," *Washington Evening Star*, September 11, 1861, https://chroniclingamerica.loc.gov/lccn/sn83045462/1861-09-11/ed-1/seq-2/.

50. Trout, *They Followed the Plume*, 51.

51. Compiled Service Record of Dabney Ball, Captain, First Virginia Cavalry, "Civil War Service Records (CMSR)—Confederate—Officers," NARA M331, RG 109, https://www.fold3.com/image/65648913.

52. "Arrests at Cambridge, MD," *Port Tobacco [MD] Times and Charles County Advertiser*, July 18, 1861, https://chroniclingamerica.loc.gov/lccn/sn89060060/1861-07-18/ed-1/seq-2/; "Further Arrests Under Instructions from Governor Hicks," *Baltimore Daily Exchange*, July 13, 1861, https://chroniclingamerica.loc.gov/lccn/sn83009573/1861-07-13/ed-1/seq-1/.

53. Glenn, *Between North and South*, 34.

54. Ibid., 35.

55. "The Capture of the St. Nicholas—the 'French Lady,'" *Richmond Enquirer*, August 27, 1861, https://chroniclingamerica.loc.gov/lccn/sn84024735/1861-08-27/ed-1/seq-4/.

56. "The Steamer St. Nicholas Seized," *Port Tobacco [MD] Times and Charles County Advertiser*, July 4, 1861, https://chroniclingamerica.loc.gov/lccn/sn89060060/1861-07-04/ed-1/seq-2/.

57. Ibid.

58. "The Piracy of the St. Nicholas," *Washington Evening Star*, July 9, 1861, https://chroniclingamerica.loc.gov/lccn/sn83045462/1861-07-09/ed-1/seq-3/.

59. "A Brave Confederate," *Baltimore Sun*, February 22, 1895, https://baltimoresun.newspapers.com/image/374552942/.
60. *Official Records*, II, Vol. III, 724–725.

Chapter 5

1. William C. Barney to Frederick William Seward, July 7, 1862, *William Henry Seward Papers*, A.S51, Rare Books, Special Collections, and Preservation, River Campus Libraries, University of Rochester, Rochester, New York.
2. William C. Barney to William H. Seward, August 21, 1862, *Seward Papers*.
3. "William Chase Barney."
4. Robert R. Laven, *Major General Philip Kearney* (Jefferson, NC: McFarland, 2020), 18.
5. William C. Barney to William H. Seward, August 21, 1862, *Seward Papers*.
6. George Edward Lowen, *History of the 71st Regiment, N.Y.N.G.* (New York: Eastman, 1919), 93; "For Our Country and For Glory!" *New York Daily Herald*, April 22, 1861, https://chroniclingamerica.loc.gov/lccn/sn83030313/1861-04-22/ed-1/seq-1/.
7. William C. Barney to William H. Seward, August 21, 1862, *Seward Papers*.
8. "The Arrivals This Morning," *Washington Evening Star*, April 27, 1861, https://chroniclingamerica.loc.gov/lccn/sn83045462/1861-04-27/ed-1/seq-2/.
9. James Augustus Armes, *Ups and Downs of an Army Officer* (Washington: 1900), 35.
10. "How They Like It," *Sandusky Daily Commercial Register*, May 21, 1861, https://access-newspaperarchive-com.eu1.proxy.openathens.net/us/ohio/sandusky/sandusky-daily-commercial-register/1861/05-21/page-2/.
11. Ibid.
12. "The Slave Barraccon—Capture of Cavalry," *Washington National Republican*, May 28, 1861, https://chroniclingamerica.loc.gov/lccn/sn82014760/1861-05-28/ed-1/seq-2/.
13. Ibid.
14. "Latest From Manassas Junction, Arrival of an Escaped Negro" *Washington National Republican*, July 29, 1861, https://chroniclingamerica.loc.gov/lccn/sn82014760/1861-07-29/ed-1/seq-2/.
15. *Boyd's Washington and Georgetown Directory, 1860* (Washington: Boyd, 1860), 138; 1860 U.S. Federal Census, Washington, District of Columbia, 5th Ward, Ignatius Smallwood, NARA Publication M653, Sheet 81, Page 491, Line 16, https://records.myheritagelibraryedition.com/research/record-10127-1817898/.
16. William C. Barney to William Seward, August 21, 1862, *Seward Papers*.
17. William C. Barney to William Seward, August 21, 1861, *Seward Papers*.
18. "Letter From Colonel Corcoran, of the Sixty-Ninth" *New York Herald*, July 21, 1861, https://chroniclingamerica.loc.gov/lccn/sn83030313/1861-07-21/ed-1/seq-1/.
19. Lowen, *History of the 71st*, 162.
20. Ibid., 171.
21. Ibid., 864.
22. "The Battle of Manassas," *Port Tobacco Times and Charles County Advertiser*, August 1, 1861, https://chroniclingamerica.loc.gov/lccn/sn89060060/1861-08-01/ed-1/seq-2/.
23. Lowen, *History of the 71st*, 185.
24. *Official Records*, I, Vol. LI, 23.
25. William C. Barney to Frederick Seward, February 18, 1862, *Seward Papers*.
26. Emery M. Thomas, *Bold Dragoon: The Life of J.E.B. Stuart* (Norman: University of Oklahoma Press, 1999), 91.
27. Frank Moore, *The Rebellion Record*, Vol. 2 (New York: G.P. Putnam, 1862), 19.
28. "Latest From Manassas Junction," *Washington National Republican*, July 29, 1861, https://chroniclingamerica.loc.gov/lccn/sn82014760/1861-07-29/ed-1/seq-2/.
29. "8th Regiment, Louisiana Infantry," www.nps.gov; James A Renshaw, "Major John B Prados: A Confederate Officer," *Louisiana Historical Quarterly* 10, no. 1 (January 1927), 241–248.
30. "Latest From Manassas Junction."
31. Ibid.
32. Ibid.
33. "Latest From Manassas Junction."
34. Manhattan [Joseph Alfred Scoville], "America," *Standard* (London), August 10, 1861, https://newscomwc.newspapers.com/image/401670392/.
35. William Gilmore Beymer, "Mrs Greenhow," *Harpers Monthly Magazine* 124 (1911), 565.
36. Edwin C. Fishel, *The Secret War*

for the Union: The Untold Story of Military Intelligence in the Civil War (Boston: Houghton Mifflin, 1996), 58.

37. "House of Representatives, May 24," *Alexandria Gazette*, May 27, 1854, https://chroniclingamerica.loc.gov/lccn/sn85025007/1854-05-27/ed-1/seq-2/.

38. William Gilmore Beymer, "Mrs. Greenhow," *Harper's Monthly Magazine*, March 1912, 563.

39. E.J. Allen to Brigadier General Andrew Porter, November 19, 1861, *Official Records*, II, Vol. II, 567.

40. "News Via Washington," *Baltimore Daily Exchange*, August 26, 1861, https://chroniclingamerica.loc.gov/lccn/sn83009573/1861-08-26/ed-1/seq-1/.

41. E.J. Allen to Brigadier General Andrew Porter, November 19, 1861, *Official Records*, II, Vol. II, 567.

42. "Our Schools," *Washington Evening Star*, August 31, 1861, https://chroniclingamerica.loc.gov/lccn/sn83045462/1861-08-31/ed-1/seq-3/.

43. Thomas Nelson Conrad, *The Rebel Scout: A Thrilling History of Scouting Life in the Southern Army* (Washington: National Publishing, 1904), 26.

44. Horatio King, August 20, 1858, *Diary of Horatio Collins King, 1854–1858*. MC 1999.9, Horatio Collins King Family Papers, Archives and Special Collections, Dickinson College, Carlisle, PA.

45. Thomas Nelson Conrad, *A Confederate Spy* (New York: J.S. Ogilvie, 1892), 7.

46. Ibid.

47. Ibid.

48. Ernest B. Furgurson, "Teacher, Preacher, Soldier, Spy," (2012) https://www.historynet.com/teacher-preacher-soldier-spy/, accessed August 6, 2023.

49. Conrad, *Rebel Scout*, 61.

50. Furgurson, "Teacher, Preacher, Soldier, Spy"; Craig Sodaro, *Civil War Spies* (North Mankato, MN: Capstone Press, 2014), 8.

51. *Washington Evening Star*, July 2, 1861, https://chroniclingamerica.loc.gov/lccn/sn83045462/1861-07-02/ed-1/seq-2/.

52. Woods, *Baltimore Directory, 1860*, 84.

53. Robert J. Trout, *They Followed the Plume* (Mechanicsburg, PA: Stackpole Books, 1993), 50.

54. Dabney Ball to Jefferson Davis, February 5, 1862, *Official Records*, II, Vol. III, 788.

55. U.S. Congress, House of Representatives, "Loyalty of Clerks and Other Persons Employed by the Government," *Reports of Committees of the House of Representatives*, 37th Congress, 2nd Session, 1862 (Washington: GPO, 1862), 23.

56. Ibid. *Reports of Committees*, 16th Congress, 1862 (Washington, GPO, 1862), 22.

57. Eugene Fauntleroy Cordell, *The Medical Annals of Maryland, 1799–1899* (Baltimore: Wilkins & Wilkins, 1903), 360.

58. William C. Barney to Frederick William Seward, July 7, 1862, *Seward Papers*.

59. Carol Wells, "William Ross Postell, Adventurer," *Georgia Historical Quarterly* 57, no. 3 (Georgia Historical Society, Fall, 1973), 390–405.

60. Ibid.

61. William C. Barney to Frederick William Seward, July 7, 1862, *Seward Papers*.

62. Frank Moore, *Rebellion Record* (New York: G.P. Putnam, 1862), 64.

63. File No. B707, William H. Seward to James Lesley, Jr., *Letters Received by the Adjutant General, 1861–1870*, Main Series, National Archives and Records Administration (NARA), M619. https://www.fold3.com/image/299607074.

64. Chas. H. Winder Case File, "Anonymous complaint against Chas. H. Winder," *Union Citizens File*, NARA M345, Record Group (RG) 109, https://www.fold3.com/image/292306097.

65. Fishel, *Secret War*, 293; D.G. McKelvey on C.H. Winder, August 20, 1861, *Union Citizens File*, NARA M345, RG 109, https://www.fold3.com/image/292306096.

66. Chas. H. Winder Case File, "Sketch of Winder's Statement," September 9, 1861, *Union Citizens File*, NARA M345, RG 109, https://www.fold3.com/image/292306100.

67. "The Barney Case Before the Orphan's Court," *Washington Evening Star*, October 30, 1861, https://chroniclingamerica.loc.gov/lccn/sn83045462/1861-10-30/ed-1/seq-3/.

68. "Board of Education," *Brooklyn Daily Times*, November 12, 1862, https://newscomwc.newspapers.com/image/554263528; "New York State Census, 1865," Ward 10, Brooklyn, Kings County, New York, Entry for Ada

Barney, https://www.familysearch.org/ark:/61903/1:1:QVNJ-YBVW.

69. Chas. H. Winder Case File, "Statement of C.H. Winder made on Monday, Sept. 9 at the P. Marshall's," *Union Citizens File*, NARA M345, RG 109, https://www.fold3.com/image/292306124/.

70. Ibid.; "Arrested," *Washington Evening Star*, September 11, 1861, https://chroniclingamerica.loc.gov/lccn/sn83045462/1861-09-11/ed-1/seq-2/.

71. William C. Barney to Frederick William Seward, August 10, 1862, *Seward Papers*.

Chapter 6

1. Conrad, *Rebel Scout*, 42.
2. "The News from Washington," *New Bern [NC] Weekly Progress*, September 3, 1861, https://access-newspaperarchive-com.eu1.proxy.openathens.net/us/north-carolina/new-bern/newbern-weekly-progress/1861/09-03/.
3. *Broad Creek Historic District Preservation Planning Study* (June 2002) located at https://www.mncppcapps.org/; Edward Steers, *Blood on the Moon* (Lexington: University Press of Kentucky, 2001), 66; Simon J. Martenet, *Martenet's Map of Prince George's County, Maryland* (Baltimore, 1861), https://www.loc.gov/item/2002624036/.
4. *Official Records*, II, Vol. II, 868.
5. Robert Pohl, "Lost Capitol Hill: The DC Jail," June 24, 2010, https://thehillishome.com.
6. "A Visit to the 'Blue Jug,' Sometimes Known as the County Jail," *Washington Evening Star*, August 28, 1861, https://chroniclingamerica.loc.gov/lccn/sn83045462/1861-08-28/ed-1/seq-3/.
7. Ibid.
8. Douglass Zevely, "Old Residences and Family History in the City Hall Neighborhood," *Records of the Columbia Historical Society, Washington, D.C.*, Vol. 6 (1903), 104–122.
9. U.S. Congress, House of Representatives, "Loyalty of Clerks and Other Persons Employed by Government," *Reports of Committees of The House of Representatives, 1861–62* (Washington: GPO, 1862), 82.
10. Ibid.

11. Ibid.
12. Ibid.
13. "The Mayor of Washington Arrested for Treason," *Baltimore Daily Exchange*, August 26, 1861, https://chroniclingamerica.loc.gov/lccn/sn83009573/1861-08-26/ed-1/seq-2/; U.S. Congress, *Reports of Committees of the House of Representatives, 1861–62* (Washington: GPO, 1862), 82.
14. "Democratic Conservative Mass Meeting," *Washington Evening Star*, June 3, 1867, https://chroniclingamerica.loc.gov/lccn/sn83045462/1867-06-03/ed-1/seq-1/.
15. U.S. Congress, *Reports of the Committees of the Senate of the United States* (Washington: GPO, 1862), 2.
16. Ibid.
17. Curtis Carroll Davis, "The 'Old Capitol' and Its Keeper: How William P. Wood Ran a Civil War Prison," *Records of the Columbia Historical Society, Washington, D.C.* 52 (1989), 206–234.
18. Curtis Carroll Davis, "The Craftiest of Men: William P. Wood and the Establishment of the United States Secret Service," *Maryland Historical Magazine* 83 (Summer 1988), 111–126.
19. J. Jacob Oswandel, *Notes on the Mexican War* (Philadelphia, 1885), 198.
20. Ibid., 350.
21. Michael Clodfelter, *Warfare and Armed Conflicts* (Jefferson, NC: McFarland, 2017), 249.
22. "Infidelism in Washington," *Washington Evening Star*, December 5, 1857, https://chroniclingamerica.loc.gov/lccn/sn83045462/1857-12-05/ed-1/seq-2/.
23. Ibid.
24. *Reports of the Committees of the Senate of the United States* (Washington: GPO, 1862), 2.
25. "A Visit to the 'Blue Jug,' Sometimes Known as the County Jail," *Washington Evening Star*, August 28, 1861, https://chroniclingamerica.loc.gov/lccn/sn83045462/1861-08-28/ed-1/seq-3/.
26. Ibid.
27. "Arrest of a Chaplain," *Philadelphia Press*, August 27, 1861, https://panewsarchive.psu.edu/lccn/sn84026296/1861-08-27/ed-1/seq-2/.
28. "The Case of the Rev. John M. Green," *Washington Evening Star*, August 29, 1861, https://

chroniclingamerica.loc.gov/lccn/sn83045462/1861-08-29/ed-1/seq-3/.

29. "The Case of the Rev. John M. Green," *Washington Evening Star*, August 30, 1861, https://chroniclingamerica.loc.gov/lccn/sn83045462/1861-08-30/ed-1/seq-3/.

30. Ibid.; Boyd, *Washington and Georgetown Directory, 1860*, 34.

31. "The Case of the Rev. John M. Green," August 30, 1861.

32. Ibid.

33. "Arrest of a Chaplain."

34. James D. Chadwick to his father, August 29, 1861, James D. Chadwick and Jonathan E. Helmreich, *Student as Soldier: The Civil War Letters of James D. Chadwick* (Meadville, PA: Allegany College, 2011), https://sites.allegheny.edu/civilwarletters/.

35. "List of the Military Companies Which Have Tendered Their Services to the State of Pennsylvania," *Philadelphia Press*, May 8, 1861, https://panewsarchive.psu.edu/lccn/sn84026296/1861-05-08/ed-1/seq-4/; John G. White, *A Twentieth Century History of Mercer County, Pennsylvania* (Chicago: Lewis, 1909), 479.

36. *History of Mercer County, It's Past and Present* (Chicago: Brown, Runk & Co, 1888), 486.

37. John G. White, *A Twentieth Century History of Mercer County, Pennsylvania* (Chicago: Lewis, 1909), 479.

38. "Erie Conference Items," *The Advocate* (Buffalo, NY), August 1, 1861, https://newscomwc-newspapers-com.eu1.proxy.openathens.net/image/254527482/.

39. Chadwick, June 25, 1861, *Chadwick Letters*.

40. Chadwick, August 2, 1861, *Chadwick Letters*.

41. Captain A.M. Judson, *History of the Eighty-Third Regiment Pennsylvania Volunteers* (Erie, PA: B.F.H. Lynn, 1865), 22.

42. Chadwick, August 8, 1861, *Chadwick Letters*.

43. Chadwick, August 29, 1861, *Chadwick Letters*.

44. "Toby of Typee."

45. "The Case of the Rev. John M. Green," August 29, 1861.

46. Robert S. Pohl and John R. Wennersten, *Abraham Lincoln and the End of Slavery in the District of Columbia* (Washington: Eastern Branch Press, 2009), 74.

47. "Fashionable Wedding," *Washington Evening Star*, June 23. 1870, https://chroniclingamerica.loc.gov/lccn/sn83045462/1870-06-23/ed-1/seq-4/.

48. Carlton Fletcher, "The Hume Brothers, Confederate Signal Scouts," www.gloverparkhistory.com, accessed August 18, 2023.

49. *Washington: City and Capital* (Washington: GPO, 1937), 56. www.hathitrust.org; "Fashionable Wedding."; "Dem. Jack. Ass," *Washington National Republican*, September 27, 1876, https://chroniclingamerica.loc.gov/lccn/sn86053573/1876-09-27/ed-1/seq-1/.

50. "Acquitted," *Pittsburgh Daily Post*, September 10, 1861, https://panewsarchive.psu.edu/lccn/sn85054562/1861-09-10/ed-1/seq-3/.

51. Letter from John G. Brower, *Warren [PA] Mail*, September 14, 1861, https://access-newspaperarchive-com.eu1.proxy.openathens.net/us/pennsylvania/warren/warren-mail/1861/09-14/page-2/.

52. Chadwick, September 9, 1861, *Chadwick Letters*.

53. "Trials of the Rev. J.S. Green, alias 'Cullison,'" *Hartford Daily Courant*, December 13, 1870, https://newscomwc.newspapers.com/image/368977575/.

54. *Official Records*, II, Vol. II, 354.

55. James Raymond, *Political, or the Spirit of Democracy in 1856* (Baltimore: John W. Woods, 1857), 292; "Trials of the Rev. J.S. Greene, Alias Cullison."

56. David Jonathan Cullison, *Family Tree of Jesse M. Cullison (1816–1889)*, https://records.myheritagelibraryedition.com/site-652925501/cullison; Woods, *Baltimore Directory*, 93.

57. "Married," *Westminster Democratic Advocate*, June 17, 1876, https://access-newspaperarchive-com.eu1.proxy.openathens.net/us/maryland/westminster/the-democratic-advocate/1876/06-17/page-3/; Paul E. Holdcraft, *History of the Pennsylvania Conference of the United Brethren of Christ* (Fayetteville (Pa): Craft Press, 1938), 158.

58. Woods, *Baltimore Directory, 1860*, 93, 344. Selby lived at 136 W. Biddle, while Cullison lived at 263 W. Biddle.

59. F.M. Burrows, "Harper's Ferry in 1861," *Confederate Veteran* 1 (April 1893), 103–104.

60. Woods, *Baltimore Directory, 1860*, 480.

61. Ibid.
62. Lanier Bro & Co, *Confederate Citizens File*, NARA M346, RG 109, https://www.fold3.com/image/43387456.
63. Chadwick, July 24, 1861, *Chadwick Letters*.
64. Woods, *Baltimore Directory, 1860*, 84, 226; Frederick Hatch, *Protecting President Lincoln* (Jefferson, NC: McFarland, 2011), 64.
65. "Arrest on the Charge of Treason," *Augusta Weekly Chronicle and Sentinel*, August 28, 1861, https://access-newspaperarchive-com.eu1.proxy.openathens.net/us/georgia/augusta/augusta-weekly-chronicle-and-sentinel/1861/08-28/page-5/; "Arrival of a United States Prisoner," *American and Commercial Advertiser* (Baltimore, MD), August 15, 1861, https://records.myheritagelibraryedition.com/research/record-10969-710570370/.
66. Conrad, *Rebel Scout*, 44.
67. "Another Military Arrest," *Washington National Republican*, August 16, 1861, https://chroniclingamerica.loc.gov/lccn/sn82014760/1861-08-16/ed-1/seq-2/.
68. John W. Selby Oath of Allegiance, August 16, 1861, *Civil War Service Records (CMSR)—Confederate—Miscellaneous*, NARA M347, RG 109, https://www.fold3.com/image/256999624, accessed August 10, 2023.
69. "Obituary, John W. Selby," *The Dental Cosmos* 43 (1901), 961.
70. "Bargains! Bargains! Bargains!" *Leonardtown [MD] St. Mary's Gazette*, March 31, 1864, https://chroniclingamerica.loc.gov/lccn/sn89060120/1864-03-31/ed-1/seq-4/.
71. *The Local News* (Alexandria, VA), December 7, 1861, https://chroniclingamerica.loc.gov/lccn/sn85025008/1861-12-07/ed-1/seq-1/.
72. "Military Arrests," *St. Mary's Gazette* (Leonardtown, MD), March 31, 1864, https://chroniclingamerica.loc.gov/lccn/sn89060120/1864-03-31/ed-1/seq-2/.
73. "A Serious Accident," *American Telegraph* (Washington, D.C.), May 15, 1851, https://access-newspaperarchive-com.eu1.proxy.openathens.net/us/washington-dc/washington/american-telegraph/1851/05-15/page-11.
74. "It was Begun Here," *Washington Evening Star*, February 12, 1896, https://chroniclingamerica.loc.gov/lccn/sn83045462/1896-02-12/ed-1/seq-10/; "How and Where the Republican Party was Born," *National Republican*, May 31, 1881, https://chroniclingamerica.loc.gov/lccn/sn86053573/1881-05-31/ed-1/seq-1/.
75. Lewis Clephane, *Birth of the Republican Party* (Washington: Gibson, 1889), 8.
76. Thomas Hutchinson, *Boyd's Washington and Georgetown Directory, 1862* (Washington: Taylor and Maury, 1862), 199.

Chapter 7

1. Elodie Todd Dawson and Nathaniel H.R. Dawson, *Practical Strangers, The Courtship Correspondence of Nathaniel Dawson and Elodie Todd, Sister of Mary Todd Lincoln* (Athens: University of Georgia Press, 2017), 51.
2. Matt Jones, "The Confederate President," *Collegiate Times*, www.collegiatetimes.com.
3. Conrad, *Rebel Scout*, 46.
4. Compiled Service Record, Thomas N. Conrad, Chaplain, Third Virginia Cav, NARA M324, RC 109, National Archives, Washington, D.C., https://www.fold3.com/image/6917287.
5. "White's Ferry on the Potomac River," http://www.virginiaplaces.org/transportation/whitesferry.html.
6. Conrad, *Rebel Scout*, 56.
7. U.S. Census Record, MD, MSA SM61–226, Slaves 1860 located at http://slavery.msa.maryland.gov/.
8. Likely Henry Warren. "$50 Reward," *Montgomery County Sentinel*, October 18, 1861, https://chroniclingamerica.loc.gov/lccn/sn83016209/1861-10-18/ed-1/seq-3/.
9. U.S. Congress, House of Representatives, *Report of the Joint Committee on the Conduct of the War* (Washington: GPO, 1863), 280.
10. "Heirs of Samuel C Young v. The United States," *Congressional Serial Set*, Issue 5579 (Washington, GPO, 1909).
11. U.S. Congress, *Report of The Joint Committee on The Conduct of the War*, 343.
12. Ibid., 346.
13. James Battle Averitt, *The Memoirs of General Turner Ashby and His Compeers* (Baltimore: Selby & Dulany, 1867), 256.
14. Clarence Thomas, *General Turner*

Ashby: The Centaur of The South (Winchester: Eddy Press, 1907), 52–53.
 15. "Military Convention of Virginia," *Richmond Enquirer*, January 13, 1860, https://chroniclingamerica.loc.gov/lccn/sn84024738/1860-01-13/ed-1/seq-1/.
 16. "Virginia News," *Alexandria Gazette*, March 26, 1860, https://chroniclingamerica.loc.gov/lccn/sn85025007/1860-03-26/ed-1/seq-2/.
 17. Averitt, *Memoirs of Turner Ashby*, 335.
 18. *American Biography*, Vol. 9 (New York: American Historical Society, 1921), 107–108.
 19. Angus W. McDonald to L.P. Walker, June 25, 1861, *Official Records*, I, Vol. II, 954.
 20. Dawson and Dawson, *Practical Strangers*, 51.
 21. Ida Powell Dulany, *In the Shadow of the Enemy: The Civil War Journal of Ida Dulany* (Knoxville: University of Tennessee Press, 2009), 224; Protestant Episcopal Church, *Journal of The Twenty Ninth Annual Convention of The Protestant Episcopal Church in The Diocese of Alabama* (Mobile: Farrow and Dent, 1860), 10.
 22. "Death of Mr. Averitt," *Raleigh Farmer and Mechanic*, February 20, 1912, https://chroniclingamerica.loc.gov/lccn/sn99061556/1912-02-20/ed-1/seq-5/.
 23. James Battle Averitt, *The Old Plantation: How We Lived in Great House and Cabin Before the War* (New York: F. Tennyson Neely, 1901), 14.
 24. Thomas A. Ashby, *Life of Turner Ashby* (New York: Neale, 1914), 81.
 25. "Highly Interesting Letter," *Marshall County Republican* (Plymouth, IN), July 11, 1861, https://access-newspaperarchive-com.eu1.proxy.openathens.net/us/indiana/plymouth/plymouth-marshall-county-republican/1861/07-11/.
 26. Ibid.
 27. Thomas Wise Durham, *Three Years with Wallace's Zouaves* (Macon: Mercer University Press, 2003), 41.
 28. "The Campaign in Virginia," *Nashville Union and American*, July 10, 1861, http https://newscomwc.newspapers.com/image/83325639/.
 29. Ibid.
 30. Averitt, *Memoirs of Turner Ashby*, 110.
 31. "An Authentic Statement," *Richmond Enquirer*, July 4, 1861, https://chroniclingamerica.loc.gov/lccn/sn84024735/1861-07-04/ed-1/seq-4/.
 32. Averitt, *Memoirs of Turner Ashby*, 114–115.
 33. "Highly Interesting Letter."
 34. Dawson and Dawson, *Practical Strangers*, 120.
 35. "Another Arrest," *Baltimore Daily Exchange*, July 6, 1861, https://chroniclingamerica.loc.gov/lccn/sn83009573/1861-07-06/ed-1/seq-1/.
 36. Harry Gilmor, *Four Years in the Saddle* (New York: Harper, 1866).
 37. Ibid., 14.
 38. J. Thomas Sharff, *A History of Western Maryland*, Vol. 1 (Philadelphia: Louis H. Everts, 1882), 339; "Death of Thomas Sturgis Davis," *Towsontown [MD] Baltimore County Union*, November 10, 1883, https://chroniclingamerica.loc.gov/lccn/sn83016368/1883-11-10/ed-1/seq-3/.
 39. Ibid.
 40. Myers, Frank M., *The Comanches: A History of White's battalion, Virginia Cavalry* (Baltimore: Kelly, Piet & co., 1871), 9; Magnus S. Thompson, "Col. Elijah V White," *Confederate Veteran* 15 (1907), 158.
 41. 1850 U.S. Federal Census, Montgomery County, Maryland, Elijah White in household of Stephen N White, NARA M432, Page 205, https://records.myheritagelibraryedition.com/research/record-10126-1833273/.
 42. "Death of a Valuable Citizen," *Montgomery County Sentinel*, April 13, 1860, https://chroniclingamerica.loc.gov/lccn/sn83016209/1860-04-13/ed-1/seq-3/.
 43. Ibid.
 44. Eugene L. Meyer, *Maryland Lost and Found* (Baltimore: John Hopkins University Press, 1986), 183.
 45. William B Lapham, *My Recollections of The War of The Rebellion* (Augusta: Burleigh & Flynt, 1892), 66. White's father died in 1860, so the man referred to may have been another relative.
 46. Frank M. Myers, *The Comanches: A History of White's battalion, Virginia Cavalry* (Baltimore: Kelly, Piet & Co., 1871), 8–9.
 47. Taylor M. Chamberlin and John M. Sounders, *Between Reb and Yank: A Civil War History of Northern Loudoun County,*

Virginia (Jefferson, NC: McFarland, 2011), 81.
48. "Leesburg, VA," *Alexandria Gazette*, May 28, 1868, https://chroniclingamerica.loc.gov/lccn/sn85025007/1868-05-28/ed-1/seq-2/.
49. James A Morgan, *A Little Short of Boats: The Fights at Ball's Bluff and Edward's Ferry, October 21–22, 1861* (Ft. Mitchell, KY: Ironclad Publishing, 2004), 1.
50. *Official Records*, I, Vol. V, 558.
51. Thompson, "Col Elijah V White," 158.
52. *Official Records*, I, Vol. V, 371.
53. Ibid., 367.
54. Myers, *The Comanches*, 15.
55. Morgan, *Short of Boats*, 198.
56. Ibid., 17.
57. William B Lapham, *My Recollections of The War of The Rebellion* (Augusta: Burleigh & Flynt, 1892), 59.
58. Myers, *The Comanches*, 182.

Chapter 8

1. William C. Barney to Frederick William Seward, August 21, 1862, *Seward Papers*.
2. Charles P. Stone, "Washington on the Eve of War," in Robert Underwood Johnson and Clarence Clough Buell, eds. *Battles and Leaders of the Civil War*, Vol. 1 (New York: Century, 1887), 13.
3. "Members of Congress: Edward D. Baker (1811–1861)," http://www.mrlincolnandfriends.org/members-of-congress/edward-baker; "The Inauguration," *Chicago Daily Tribune*, March 5, 1861, https://chroniclingamerica.loc.gov/lccn/sn84031490/1861-03-05/ed-1/seq-1/.
4. Chas. P. Stone to McClellan, October 29, 1861, *Official Records*, I, Vol. V, 295.
5. Morgan, *Short of Boats*, 70.
6. Stone to McClellan, October 29, 1861, *Official Records*, I, Vol. 5, 295.
7. "The Body of Col. Baker," *Washington Evening Star*, October 29, 1861, https://chroniclingamerica.loc.gov/lccn/sn83045462/1861-11-04/ed-1/seq-2/; U.S. Congress, *Report of the Joint Committee on the Conduct of the War*, 323.
8. "Battle of Leesburg Heights: Statement of Capt. Francis G. Young," *Daily Columbus Ohio Statesman*, October 29,
1861, https://chroniclingamerica.loc.gov/lccn/sn84028645/1861-10-29/ed-1/seq-1/.
9. Laura Stedman, *Life and Letters of Edmund Clarence Stedman*, Vol. 1 (New York: Moffat, Yard & Company, 1910), 248.
10. "Battle of Leesburg Heights: Statement of Capt. Francis G. Young," *Daily Columbus Ohio Statesman*, October 29, 1861, https://chroniclingamerica.loc.gov/lccn/sn84028645/1861-10-29/ed-1/seq-1/.
11. William Marvel, *Mr. Lincoln Goes to War* (Boston: Houghton Mifflin, 2006), 250; Laura Stedman, *Life and Letters of Edmund Clarence Stedman*, Vol. 1 (New York: Moffat, Yard & Company, 1910), 248.
12. "The Battle at Conrad's Ferry," *New York Herald*, October 25, 1861, https://chroniclingamerica.loc.gov/lccn/sn83030313/1861-10-25/ed-1/seq-1/.
13. Morgan, *Short of Boats*, 234.
14. U.S. Congress, *Report of the Joint Committee on the Conduct of the War*, 322.
15. Francis G. Young to Abraham Lincoln, Monday, October 21, 1861, *Abraham Lincoln Papers*, https://www.loc.gov/item/mal1259900/.
16. "Mrs. Abraham Lincoln," *Indianapolis Journal*, July 31, 1887, https://chroniclingamerica.loc.gov/lccn/sn82015679/1887-07-31/ed-1/seq-9/.
17. "The Funeral of Col. Baker," *Washington Evening Star*, October 24, 1861, https://chroniclingamerica.loc.gov/lccn/sn83045462/1861-10-24/ed-1/seq-3/.
18. "Mrs. Abraham Lincoln."
19. U.S. Army of the Potomac, *Index to General Orders Army of The Potomac, 1862* (Washington: Blanchard & Mohun, 1863).
20. Abraham Lincoln to George B. McClellan, December 6, 1861, *Abraham Lincoln Papers*, https://www.loc.gov/item/mal1327200/.
21. Francis G. Young to Abraham Lincoln, December 7, 1861, *Abraham Lincoln Papers*, https://www.loc.gov/item/mal1330100/.
22. Ibid.
23. Morgan, *Short of Boats*, 235.
24. U.S. Army of the Potomac, *Index to the General Orders of the Army of the Potomac, 1862* (Washington: Blanchard & Mohun, 1863), 1.
25. Francis G. Young to Abraham Lincoln, January 7, 1862, *Abraham Lincoln Papers*, https://www.loc.gov/item/mal1388200/.

26. Francis G. Young to Abraham Lincoln, February 7, 1862, *Abraham Lincoln Papers*, https://www.loc.gov/item/mal1442700/.

27. Ibid.

28. Ibid.

29. "Death of Francis G. Young," *Geneva Advertiser*, May 16, 1899, https://nyshistoricnewspapers.org; H. Wilson, *Trow's New York City Directory, 1853–54* (New York: John F. Trow, 1853), 761.

30. "The Young Men's Republican General Committee," *New York Herald*, November 26, 1856, https://chroniclingamerica.loc.gov/lccn/sn83030213/1856-11-26/ed-1/seq-1/.

31. "The Boy and the Skylark," *Geneva Gazette*, April 16, 1880, https://nyshistoricnewspapers.org/.

32. "A Nice Little Estate," *Cleveland Morning Leader*, March 17, 1859, https://newscomwc.newspapers.com/image/78791998/.

33. "Notes and Queries for the People," *New York Dispatch*, October 15, 1854, https://chroniclingamerica.loc.gov/lccn/sn83030364/1854-10-15/ed-1/seq-1/; "Notes and Queries For the People," *New York Dispatch*, January 7, 1855, https://chroniclingamerica.loc.gov/lccn/sn83030364/1855-01-07/ed-1/seq-1/.

34. "American Money Hunters," *Geneva Daily Gazette*, March 26, 1880, https://nyshistoricnewspapers.org/.

35. *Court of Appeals, Francis G. Young against George W. Hunt* (New York: New York Printing, 1870), 74.

36. Morgan, *Short of Boats*, 233.

37. Paul G. Zellar, *The Vermont Brigade in the Seven Days* (Jefferson, NC: McFarland, 2019), 9.

38. Francis G. Young to Abraham Lincoln, Tuesday, June 14, 1864, *Abraham Lincoln Papers: Series 1. General Correspondence. 1833 to 1916*, Library of Congress, https://www.loc.gov/item/mal3374400/.

39. William C. Barney to Frederick William Seward, September 29, 1861, *Seward Papers*.

40. William C. Barney to William H. Seward, August 21, 1862, *Seward Papers*; "William Chase Barney."

41. Manhattan [Joseph Alfred Scoville], "North and South," *Standard* (London), November 11, 1862, https://newscomwc.newspapers.com/image/401694469/; "U.S. Army Military Registers, 1798–1969," https://www.fold3.com/publication/899/army-registers-1798-1969, accessed November 17, 2022.

42. "Another Grand Review," *Washington Evening Star*, September 21, 1861, https://chroniclingamerica.loc.gov/lccn/sn83045462/1861-09-21/ed-1/seq-2/.

43. "The French Princes on McClellan's Staff," *Chicago Daily Tribune*, October 2, 1861, https://chroniclingamerica.loc.gov/lccn/sn84031490/1861-10-02/ed-1/seq-3/.

44. Ibid.

45. Manhattan [Joseph Alfred Scoville], "America," *Standard* (London), August 17, 1861, https://newscomwc.newspapers.com/image/401672963/.

46. Manhattan, "America," September 30, 1861.

47. "Mrs. Lincoln and the Orleans Princes," *New York Daily Herald*, October 8, 1861, https://chroniclingamerica.loc.gov/lccn/sn83030313/1861-10-08/ed-1/seq-3/.

48. "The French Princes in the Federal Army," *New York Daily Herald*, October 27, 1861, https://chroniclingamerica.loc.gov/lccn/sn83030313/1861-10-27/ed-1/seq-2/.

49. Manhattan [Joseph Alfred Scoville], "America," *Standard* (London), December 28, 1861, https://newscomwc.newspapers.com/image/401727111/.

50. Manhattan [Joseph Alfred Scoville], "America," *Standard* (London), January 16, 1862, https://newscomwc.newspapers.com/image/401598437/.

51. William C. Barney to William H. Seward, August 21, 1862, *Seward Papers*.

52. Lowen, *History of the 71st*, 306.

53. U.S. Adjutant General, *Official Army Register for August 1862* (Washington: GPO, 1862), 88.

54. William C. Barney to Frederick William Seward, February 18, 1862, *Seward Papers*.

55. U.S. Adjutant General, *Official Army Register for August 1862* (Washington: GPO, 1862), 88.

56. William C. Barney to William H. Seward, August 21, 1862, *Seward Papers*.

57. William C. Barney to Frederick William Seward, August 21, 1862, *Seward Papers*.

58. C.P. Wolcott to William C. Barney, June 27, 1862, *Official Records*, III, Vol. II, 178.

Notes—Chapter 9

59. William C. Barney to Frederick William Seward, July 7, 1862, *Seward Papers*.
60. Katherine Prescott Wormeley, *The United States Sanitary Commission: A Sketch of Its Purposes and Its Work* (Boston: Little, Brown and Co., 1863), 96–97.
61. Ibid.
62. "The Battle-field of Bull Run," *Bradford* [PA] *Reporter*, September 18, 1862, https://chroniclingamerica.loc.gov/lccn/sn84024558/1862-09-18/ed-1/seq-1/.
63. "Sunday," *Alexandria Gazette*, September 1, 1862, https://chroniclingamerica.loc.gov/lccn/sn85025007/1862-09-01/ed-1/seq-2/.
64. "From the Battle-Field," *Philadelphia Inquirer*, September 3, 1862, https://access-newspaperarchive-com.eu1.proxy.openathens.net/us/pennsylvania/philadelphia/philadelphia-inquirer/1862/09-03/.
65. Francis G. Young to William H. Seward, September 10, 1862, *Seward Papers*.
66. R.C. Lehmann, "Memories of Half a Century," *Chambers Journal* 6, Vol. XI (London: Chambers, 1908), 389.
67. "Personal Intelligence, The French Princes," *New York Daily Herald*, July 6, 1862, https://chroniclingamerica.loc.gov/lccn/sn83030313/1862-07-06/ed-1/seq-4/.
68. "America," September 19, 1861.

Chapter 9

1. Frederic May Holland, *Frederick Douglass: The Colored Orator* (New York: Funk & Wagnalls, 1891), 261.
2. "Work for the Charitable," *Chicago Tribune*, November 9, 1861, https://chroniclingamerica.loc.gov/lccn/sn84031490/1861-11-09/ed-1/seq-2/.
3. "Roger Brooke Taney," Dickinson College Archives, https://archives.dickinson.edu/people/roger-brooke-taney-1777-1864.
4. "The Fugitive Slave Case," *Lancaster Examiner*, September 1, 1847, https://newscomwc.newspapers.com/image/569403926/.
5. Horatio C. King, *History of Dickinson College* (New York: American University, 1896), 16.
6. "Professor Tiffany," *Lancaster Intelligencer*, February 13, 1855, https://newscomwc-newspapers-com.eu1.proxy.openathens.net/image/557085384/.
7. Ibid.
8. King, December 4, 1855, *Diary*.
9. King, December 6, 1855, *Diary*.
10. King, December 7, 1855, *Diary*.
11. King, December 11, 1855, *Diary*.
12. King, February 2, 1856, *Diary*.
13. "Difficulty at Dickinson College," *Shepardstown* [VA] *Register*, February 9, 1856, https://chroniclingamerica.loc.gov/lccn/sn84026824/1856-02-09/ed-1/seq-2/.
14. Dorothy Daneen Volo and James M. Volo, *Daily Life in Civil War America* (Westport: Greenwood Press, 1998), 82.
15. "Rev. Otis Henry Tiffany, D.D.," *Dickinsonian*, November 1891, 9.
16. "Resignation of Rev. Otis H. Tiffany, D.D.," *Newville* [PA] *Star and Enterprise*, September 20, 1860, https://newscomwc.newspapers.com/image/310896929/.
17. "First Methodist Church," n.d., https://greatchicagofire.org/landmarks/first-methodist-church/.
18. "Thanksgiving," *Chicago Tribune*, November 30, 1860, https://chroniclingamerica.loc.gov/lccn/sn84031490/1860-11-30/ed-1/seq-1/.
19. "Rev. Otis Henry Tiffany, D.D."
20. "The Soldiers Aid Sociable," *Chicago Tribune*, December 20, 1861, https://chroniclingamerica.loc.gov/lccn/sn84031490/1861-12-20/ed-1/seq-4/.
21. "Our Cairo Dispatches," *Cleveland Morning Leader*, May 3, 1861, https://chroniclingamerica.loc.gov/lccn/sn83035143/1861-05-03/ed-1/seq-3/.
22. "Resignation of Rev. Dr. Tiffany," *Chicago Tribune*, May 17, 1862, https://chroniclingamerica.loc.gov/lccn/sn84031490/1862-05-17/ed-1/seq-4/.
23. Ibid.
24. "Temperance Lecture," *Chicago Tribune*, November 9, 1861, https://chroniclingamerica.loc.gov/lccn/sn84031490/1861-11-09/ed-1/seq-4/.
25. "The Withdrawal of the Rev. Dr. Tiffany from the Methodist Episcopal Church," *Daily Missouri Republican* (St. Louis), May 21, 1862, https://newscomwc.newspapers.com/image/666812923/.
26. *Minutes of the Annual Conference of the Methodist Episcopal Church, 1862* (New York: Carleton & Porter, 1862), 182.
27. Otis H. Tiffany, "Dr. Dempster as a

Man of Progress," *John Dempster, Lectures and Addresses* (Cincinnati: Poe 8: Hitchcock, 1864), 67.

28. "Sound and Stirring Doctrine," *Wheeling [VA] Daily Intelligencer*, July 26, 1862, https://newscomwc.newspapers.com/image/171197925/.

29. Ibid.

30. William W. Patton, *The American Board and Slaveholding* (Hartford: William H. Burleigh, 1846), 4–5.

31. "Sang an Army into Being," *Boston Evening Transcript*, January 24, 1912, https://newscomwc.newspapers.com/image/735628623/.

32. "The Battle Cry of Freedom," *Chicago Tribune*, July 28, 1862, https://chroniclingamerica.loc.gov/lccn/sn84031490/1862-07-28/ed-1/seq-4/.

33. "Interview Between President Lincoln and a Committee of Colored Men," *Washington Evening Star*, August 15, 1862, https://chroniclingamerica.loc.gov/lccn/sn83045462/1862-08-15/ed-1/seq-2/.

34. Allen Thorndike Rice, ed., *Reminiscences of Abraham Lincoln by Distinguished Men of His Time* (New York: North American Publishing, 1886), 193.

35. Patton, *President Lincoln and the Chicago Memorial on Emancipation*, 12.

36. "The Meeting on Saturday Night," *Chicago Daily Tribune*, June 9, 1862, https://chroniclingamerica.loc.gov/lccn/sn84031490/1862-06-09/ed-1/seq-1/.

37. . Earl Schenck Miers, *Lincoln Day by Day, 1861–1865*, Vol. 3 (Washington: C Percy Powell, 1960), 139.

38. Gideon Welles, *Diary of Gideon Welles*, Vol. 1 (Boston: H. Mifflin Co. 1911), 130.

39. Isaac Newton Arnold, *The Life of Abraham Lincoln* (Chicago: Jansen, McClurg, 1885) 452.

40. James B. Conroy, *Lincoln's White House: The People's House in Wartime* (Lanham, MD: Rowman & Littlefield, 2016), 96.

41. Patton, *President Lincoln and the Chicago Memorial on Emancipation*, 18.

42. Gideon Welles, *Diary of Gideon Welles*, Vol. 1 (Boston: H. Mifflin Co., 1911), 70.

43. Patton, *President Lincoln and the Chicago Memorial on Emancipation*, 18.

44. Ibid., 19.

45. Abraham Lincoln, *Collected Works of Abraham Lincoln*, Vol. 5 (New York: H. Wolff, 1953), 420.

46. Ibid.

47. Horace Greely, *The American Conflict*, Vol. 2 (Hartford: Case, 1866), 252.

48. Ibid.

49. Unknown to Gen. George B. McClellan, January 19, 1862, *George Brinton McClellan Papers: Correspondence II, 1823–1898; Jan. 13, 1862–Mar. 2, 1862*, Library of Congress, https://www.loc.gov/item/mss318980128/.

50. Ibid.

51. Unknown to Gen. George B. McClellan, February 1, 1862, *George Brinton McClellan Papers: Correspondence II, 1823–1898; Jan. 13, 1862–Mar. 2, 1862*, Library of Congress, https://www.loc.gov/item/mss318980128/.

52. Ibid.

53. Ibid. Ellen Hutchinson Stanton was the member of a prominent Pittsburgh family.

54. "Special Orders No. 191," National Park Service, https://www.nps.gov/mono/learn/historyculture/so191.htm.

55. Patton, *President Lincoln and the Chicago Memorial on Emancipation*, 34.

56. Salmon P. Chase, *Diary and Correspondence of Salmon P. Chase* (Washington: 1903).

57. Ibid.

58. Welles, *Diary of Gideon Welles*, 143.

59. Manhattan [Joseph Alfred Scoville], "America," *Standard* (London), December 10, 1861, https://newscomwc.newspapers.com/image/401711422/.

60. Ibid.

61. George B. McClellan and Stephen W. Sears, ed., *The Civil War Papers of George B. McClellan: Selected Correspondence, 1860–1865* (Boston: Ticknor & Fields, 1989), 482.

62. Frank Abial Flower, *Edwin McMasters Stanton: The Autocrat of Rebellion Emancipation and Reconstruction* (Akron: Saalfield, 1905), 193.

63. William C. Barney to Unknown, November 30, 1862, *Abraham Lincoln Papers*, https://www.loc.gov/item/mal1981500/.

Chapter 10

1. "North and South," November 11, 1862.

2. "Unwritten History of the War," *New York Tribune*, March 14, 1880, https://newscomwc.newspapers.com/image/467174051/.
3. Ibid.
4. Ibid.
5. "Unwritten History of our Civil War, A Chance for Peace After Sharpsburg," *Nashville Union and American*, March 8, 1872, https://newscomwc.newspapers.com/image/80862341/.
6. Unknown to Gen George B. McClellan, September 1862, *George Brinton McClellan Papers: Correspondence II, 1823-1898, Sept. 20, 1862-Aug. 7, 1863*, Library of Congress, https://www.loc.gov/item/mss318980131/.
7. Ibid.
8. William Roscoe Thayer, *John Hay*, Vol. 2 (Boston: Riverside, 1915), 131.
9. Ibid.
10. Ibid.
11. "An Old Time Telegrapher," *Pittsburg [sic] Dispatch*, December 21, 1890, https://chroniclingamerica.loc.gov/lccn/sn84024546/1890-12-21/ed-1/seq-18/.
12. John F. Stegeman, *These Men She Gave: Civil War Diary of Athens, Georgia* (Athens: University of Georgia Press, 2009), 63.
13. General R.E. Lee to General George B. McClellan, June 13, 1862, *Official Records*, II, Vol. IV, 14.
14. "Unwritten History of our Civil War," *Nashville Union and American*, March 8, 1872, https://newscomwc.newspapers.com/image/80862341/.
15. Ibid.
16. "Gen. McClellan for Peace," *Baltimore Sun*, January 11, 1904, https://baltimoresun.newspapers.com/image/372491337/.
17. "Gen. McClellan for Peace."
18. Ibid.
19. Ibid.
20. "Bishop Keiley, Beloved in South, Dies Suddenly," *Wichita Catholic Advance*, June 27, 1925, https://newscomwc.newspapers.com/image/180102983.
21. Ibid.
22. Ibid.
23. James Longstreet to Osmun Latrobe, February 27, 1886, *Osmun Latrobe Papers*, Virginia Museum of History and Culture, Richmond, Virginia.
24. James Longstreet to Osmun Latrobe, March 27, 1886, *Latrobe Papers*.
25. "How They Were Captured," *Washington Evening Star*, October 11, 1862, https://chroniclingamerica.loc.gov/lccn/sn83045462/1862-10-11/ed-1/seq-2/.
26. "Important from Washington, Rebel Overtures for Peace," *New York Tribune*, December 5, 1862, https://chroniclingamerica.loc.gov/lccn/sn83030213/1862-12-05/ed-1/seq-1/.
27. William C. Barney to Frederick William Seward, August 10, 1862, *Seward Papers*.
28. "North and South."
29. William C. Barney to Frederick William Seward, February 18, 1862, *Seward Papers*
30. William C. Barney to William H. Seward, August 21, 1862, *Seward Papers*; "William Chase Barney."FULL CITE?
31. "Georgetown affairs," *Washington Evening Star*, August 8, 1862, https://chroniclingamerica.loc.gov/lccn/sn83045462/1862-08-08/ed-1/seq-3/.
32. "North and South," November 11, 1862.
33. Miller, *Maryland Reports*, Vol. XI, 204.
34. "North and South," November 11, 1862; "William Chase Barney."
35. U.S. Congress, *Journal of The Executive Proceedings of The Senate*, Vol. 4 (Washington: GPO, 1887), 512; Rosa Postall to Mrs. Baber, March 13, 1863, Baber-Blackshear Collection, ms11, Hargrett Rare Book and Manuscript Library, University of Georgia Libraries.
36. Roy P. Basler, ed. *Collected Works of Abraham Lincoln*, Vol. 5 (Springfield: Abraham Lincoln Association, 1953), 60.
37. Miers, *Lincoln Day by Day*, 81.
38. "Latest Southern News," *Alexandria Gazette*, September 24, 1862, https://chroniclingamerica.loc.gov/lccn/sn85025007/1862-09-24/ed-1/seq-2/.
39. "How They Were Captured."
40. Ibid.
41. *Alexandria Gazette*, October 10, 1862, https://chroniclingamerica.loc.gov/lccn/sn85025007/1862-10-10/ed-1/seq-3/.
42. "A Trip to Richmond," *Chambersburg Valley Spirit*, October 22, 1862, https://newscomwc.newspapers.com/image/346627874/.
43. Ibid.

44. http://www.thelincolnlog.org/
45. Shelby Moore Cullom, *Fifty Years of Public Service* (Chicago: McClurg, 1911), 91.
46. Richard Slotkin, *The Long Road to Antietam* (New York: Liveright, 2012), 99.

Chapter 11

1. Major General John A. Dix to Hon. Edwin Stanton, October 31, 1862, *Official Records*, II, Vol. IV, 670.
2. Case File 1150, William P. Wood, John P. Sherburne to William P. Wood, September 28, 1862, *Case Files of Levi C. Turner and Lafayette C. Baker, 1861–1866* (*Turner-Baker Files*), https://www.fold3.com/image/257035305/257035282.
3. Case File 1150, William P. Wood, William P. Wood to Brig Gen Wadsworth, November 17, 1862, *Turner-Baker Files*, https://www.fold3.com/image/257035305/257035455.
4. "The 'Old Capitol' and Its Keeper."
5. Ibid.
6. Wood to Wadsworth, November 17, 1862, *Turner-Baker Files*.
7. Ibid.
8. "The 'Old Capitol' and Its Keeper."
9. Ibid.
10. *Alexandria Gazette*, October 10, 1862, https://chroniclingamerica.loc.gov/lccn/sn85025007/1862-10-10/ed-1/seq-3/.
11. Ibid.
12. "Arrival From Richmond," *The Evansville Daily Journal*, October 10, 1862, https://newscomwc.newspapers.com/image/354148037/.
13. "A Trip to Richmond."
14. Ibid.
15. Ibid.
16. Ibid.
17. Morgan, *Short of Boats*, 233–236.
18. Francis G. Young to Edmund C. Stedman, September 3, 1863, *Edmund Clarence Stedman Papers*, Rare Book and Manuscript Library, Columbia University, New York City.
19. Turner to Stanton, October 25, 1862, *Turner-Baker Files*.
20. Turner to Stanton, October 22, 1862, *Turner-Baker Files*.
21. Osmun Latrobe, August 21, 1862, *Diary of Osmun Latrobe*, Osmun Latrobe Papers, Virginia Museum of History and Culture, Richmond, Virginia.
22. *Reports Of Committees of The House of Representatives, First Session of the Fifty Second Congress, 1891–92* (Washington: GPO, 1892).
23. Conrad, *The Rebel Scout*, 72–73.
24. Turner to Stanton, October 22, 1862, *Turner-Baker Files*.
25. "Congressional," *Washington Union*, January 25, 1859, https://chroniclingamerica.loc.gov/lccn/sn82006534/1859-01-25/ed-1/seq-1/.
26. *Official Records*, II, Vol. IV, 908.
27. Ibid.
28. Ibid.
29. Wilfred B. Yearns, Jr., "The Peace Movement in the Confederate Congress," *Georgia Historical Quarterly* 41, no. 1 (March 1957), 1–18.
30. *Alexandria Gazette and Virginia Advertiser*, November 19, 1860, https://chroniclingamerica.loc.gov/lccn/sn85025007/1860-11-19/ed-1/seq-2/.
31. Ibid., 911.
32. Major General John A. Dix to Hon. Edwin Stanton, October 31, 1862, *Official Records*, II, Vol. IV, 670.
33. Case File 3879, William P. Wood, L.C. Turner to Edwin M. Stanton, November 7, 1865, *Turner-Baker Files* https://www.fold3.com/image/257045312/25704 5601.
34. Conrad, *The Rebel Scout*, 28.
35. Ibid., 27.
36. Thomas Nelson Conrad, *A Confederate Spy: A Story of the Civil War* (New York: J.S. Ogilvie, 1892), 83.
37. Ibid.
38. Dennis A. Mahoney, *The Prisoner of State* (New York: Carleton, 1863), 394.
39. Ibid., 395.
40. "The 'Old Capitol' and its Keeper."
41. Wm. Chase Barney to Gen. J.H. Winder, October 13, 1862, *Official Records*, II, Vol. IV, 916.
42. William H. Ludlow to Hon. Edwin M. Stanton, October 25, 1862, *Official Records*, II, Vol. IV, 654.
43. William H. Ludlow to L. Thomas, October 26, 1862, *Official Records*, II, Vol. IV, 656.
44. "By Telegraph," *Daily Gate City* (Keokuk, IA), October 28, 1862, https://newscomwc-newspapers-com.eu1.proxy.openathens.net/image/843111761/.
45. Case File 1150, William P. Wood, L. Thomas to W.H. Ludlow by telegram,

October 27, 1862, *Turner-Baker Files,* https://www.fold3.com/image/257035305/257035377.
46. "Rebel Overtures for Peace."
47. "Peace Rumors," *New York Daily Tribune,* December 8, 1862, https://chroniclingamerica.loc.gov/lccn/sn83030213/1862-12-08/ed-1/seq-4/.
48. "Our Fortress Monroe Correspondence," *New York Daily Herald,* October 31, 1862, https://newscomwc.newspapers.com/image/329335930/.
49. Major General John A. Dix to Hon. E.M. Stanton, October 31, 1862, *Official Records,* II, Vol. IV, 670.
50. Hon. Edwin M. Stanton to Major General John A. Dix, October 31, 1862, *Official Records,* II, Vol. IV, 670.
51. Gideon Welles, *Diary of Gideon Welles,* Vol. 1 (Boston: Houghton, Mifflin, 1911), 179.
52. Frank A. Flower, *Edwin McMasters Stanton: The Autocrat of Rebellion Emancipation and Reconstruction* (Akron: Saalfield, 1905), 180.
53. William B. Styple, *McClellan's Other Story* (Kearney, NJ: Belle Grove, 2012), 252.
54. Ibid., 253.
55. Abraham Lincoln, *Abraham Lincoln: Complete Works: Comprising His Speeches, Letters, State Papers, and Miscellaneous Writings* (New York: The Century Co., 1894), 2:252.
56. "Extremely Important: Peace Propositions from Richmond," January 11, 1863, *New York Daily Herald,* https://chroniclingamerica.loc.gov/lccn/sn83030313/1863-01-11/ed-1/seq-5/.

Chapter 12

1. "The Peace Propositions from Richmond," *Pittsburgh Daily Post,* December 12, 1862, https://panewsarchive.psu.edu/lccn/sn85054562/1862-12-12/ed-1/seq-2/.
2. John Wesley Greene to Abraham Lincoln, Tuesday, November 11, 1862, *Abraham Lincoln Papers,* https://www.loc.gov/item/mal1949700/.
3. Ibid.
4. "J Wesley Greene—How He Got the Furs—His Escape to Canada," *Pittsburg Gazette,* December 17, 1862, https://panewsarchive.psu.edu/lccn/sn85054513/1862-12-17/ed-1/seq-3/.
5. Ibid.
6. Case File 739, J Wesley Green, E.J. Allen to P.H. Watson, December 13, 1862, *Turner-Baker Files,* NARA 797, RG 94, https://www.fold3.com/image/257185143/257185129.
7. "J. Wesley Greene—His Standing and Career Here," *Pittsburg Daily Post,* December 13, 1862, https://panewsarchive.psu.edu/lccn/sn85054562/1862-12-13/ed-1/seq-3/.
8. Josiah Rhinehart Syphur, *History of the Pennsylvania Reserve Corps* (Lancaster: Elias Barr, 1865), 671.
9. Edwin M. Stanton to Abraham Lincoln, November 19, 1862, *Abraham Lincoln Papers,* https://www.loc.gov/item/mal1960000/.
10. "The Peace Proposals," *New York Times,* December 13, 1862, www.nytimes.com/1862/12/13/archives.
11. Ibid.
12. John Wesley Greene to Abraham Lincoln, Tuesday, November 11, 1862, *Abraham Lincoln Papers.*
13. "The Peace Propositions from Richmond."
14. Ibid.
15. Ibid.
16. Ibid.
17. Ibid.
18. Ibid.
19. Miers, *Lincoln Day by Day,* 150.
20. Ibid., 151.
21. "The Peace Propositions from Richmond."
22. "The 'Peace Commissioner' Under Arrest," *Washington Evening Star,* December 13, 1862, https://chroniclingamerica.loc.gov/lccn/sn83045462/1862-12-13/ed-1/seq-3/.
23. Case File 739, J Wesley Green, Affidavit of Walter Ker, December 8, 1862, *Turner-Baker Files,* https://www.fold3.com/image/257185143/257185158; Case File 739, J Wesley Green, *Turner-Baker Files,* J. Wesley Greene to Secy of Treasury, November 22, 1862, https://www.fold3.com/image/257185143/257185149.
24. Ibid.
25. "The 'Peace Commissioner' Under Arrest."
26. Case File 739, J Wesley Green, W.B. Webb to P.H. Watson, December 8, 1862,

Turner-Baker Files, https://www.fold3.com/image/257185143/257185189.

27. Miers, *Lincoln Day by Day,* 151.

28. Case File 739, J Wesley Green, Affidavit of B.H. Steinmetz, December 8, 1862, *Turner-Baker Files,* https://www.fold3.com/image/257185143/257185158.

29. John Wesley Greene to Abraham Lincoln, November 22, 1862, *Abraham Lincoln Papers,* https://www.loc.gov/item/mal1970600/.

30. Case File 161B, Collision and J W Green, W.S. Radle, "Report of W.S. Radle in Relation to the Movement of J.W. Green," November 25, 1862, *Turner-Baker Files,* https://www.fold3.com/image/257123288/257123525.

31. Case File 161B, Collision and J W Green, Segt Jno Lee to Col Baker by telegraph, November 22, 1862, 11:20 p.m., *Turner-Baker Files,* https://www.fold3.com/image/257123288/257123204.

32. Cullison, *Family Tree of Jesse M. Cullison (1816-1889),* https://records.myheritagelibraryedition.com/site-652925501/cullison

33. "Trials of the Rev. J.S. Green, alias 'Cullison.'" Greene's brother-in-law was Micajah M. Cullison.

34. Case File 161B, Collision and J W Green, Sgt. Jno Lee to Col. LC Baker by telegraph, November 22, 1862, *Turner-Baker Files,* https://www.fold3.com/image/257123288/257123243.

35. Case File 161B, Collision and J W Green, Baker to Lee by telegraph, November 22, 1862, *Turner-Baker Files,* https://www.fold3.com/image/257123288/257123335.

36. Case File 161B, Collision and J W Green, Lee to Baker by telegraph, November 22, 1862, 12:40 p.m. (actually 12:40 a.m.), *Turner-Baker Files,* https://www.fold3.com/image/257123288/257123288.

37. Case File 161B, Collision and J W Green, Baker to Lee, November 23, 1862, by telegraph, *Turner-Baker Files,* https://www.fold3.com/image/257123288/257123349.

38. Radle, "Report of W.S. Radle," *Turner-Baker Files.*

39. Ibid.

40. Lee to Baker by telegraph, November 24, 1862, *Turner-Baker Files.*

41. "The Peace Proposals."

42. "J. Wesley Greene—His Standing and Career Here."

43. "Arrest of Greene, the Chicago Times Tinker."

44. "From Washington," *Chicago Times,* March 4, 1862, https://newscomwc.newspapers.com/image/897541051/.

45. "J. Wesley Greene," *Chicago Tribune,* July 27, 1867, https://chroniclingamerica.loc.gov/lccn/sn82014064/1867-07-27/ed-1/seq-2/.

46. "Toby of Typee."

Chapter 13

1. Edward A. Pollard, *Life of Jefferson Davis, With a Secret History of the Confederacy* (Philadelphia: National Publishing, 1869), 238.

2. Ibid.

3. "Gen. Foote as a Peacemaker," *New York Times,* September 29, 1862, https://www.nytimes.com/1862/09/29/archives.

4. "Jefferson Davis During the War—Letter from Hon. H.S. Foote," *New York Times,* May 19, 1869, https://www.nytimes.com/1869/05/19/archives.

5. *The Papers of Jefferson Davis,* Vol. 8 (Baton Rouge: Louisiana State University Press, 1995), 384.

6. "Jefferson Davis During the War."

7. "The Peace Propositions," *Richmond Enquirer,* September 30, 1862, https://chroniclingamerica.loc.gov/lccn/sn84024735/1862-09-30/ed-1/seq-4/.

8. Pollard, *Life of Jefferson Davis,* 239.

9. "Speech of Hon. Charles W. Russell," *Richmond Enquirer,* October 10, 1862, https://chroniclingamerica.loc.gov/lccn/sn84024735/1862-10-10/ed-1/seq-1/.

10. J.J. Haley, *Debates That Made History: The Story of Alexander Campbell's Debates* (St. Louis: Christian Board, 1920), 185–222; "Married." *Cincinnati Daily Press,* January 9, 1860, https://newscomwc.newspapers.com/image/47624007/.

11. "Toby of Typee"; Haley, *Debates That Made History,* 185–222.

12. "Toby of Typee"; "The Democratic Peace Envoy," *Chicago Daily Tribune,* December 16, 1862, https://chroniclingamerica.loc.gov/lccn/sn84031490/1862-12-16/ed-1/seq-4/.

13. Virginia General Assembly, House

of Delegates, *Journal of the House of Delegates of the State of Virginia* (Richmond: Ritchie, 1862), x.

14. Festus P. Summers, *The Baltimore and Ohio in the Civil War* (Gettysburg: Stan Clark, 1993), 120.

15. Charles W. Ramsdell, "General Robert E. Lee's Horse Supply, 1862–1865," *The American Historical Review* 35 (July 1930): 758–777.

16. G.W. Randolph to R.E. Lee, November 14, 1862, *Official Records*, I, Vol. XIX, Part II, 714.

17. Conrad, *Rebel Scout*, 67.

18. "Senator Swanson Delivers Address at Memorial Unveiling, Blacksburg Va.," *Washington Evening Star*, June 12, 1912, https://chroniclingamerica.loc.gov/lccn/sn83045462/1912-06-12/ed-1/seq-10/.

19. "William Chase Barney."

20. Nathaniel C. Hughes, *Yale's Confederates* (Knoxville: University of Tennessee Press, 2008), 151.

21. Charles W. Stewart, ed. *Official Records of the Union and Confederate Navies in the War of the Rebellion*, II, Vol. 3 (Washington: GPO, 1922), 455.

22. George Washington Cullum, *Biographical Register of the Officers and Graduates of the U.S. Military Academy*, Vol. II (New York: James Miller, 1879), 352–366.

23. Tunstall Smith, *Richard Snowden Andrews* (Baltimore: Sun, 1910), 37.

24. Major General John A. Dix to Edwin Stanton, February 21, 1862, *Official Records*, II Vol. I, 618.

25. Thomas D. Gold, *History of Clarke County, Virginia* (C.R. Hughes, 1914), 118.

26. Mary Norris, *Confederate Papers Relating to Citizens or Business Firms*, NARA M346, RG 109, https://www.fold3.com/image/46474824/.

27. Compiled Service Record of James William Lyon, *Compiled Service Records of Confederate General and Staff Officers, and Nonregimental Enlisted Men*, NARA M331, RG 109, https://www.fold3.com/image/78266742.

28. Michaela Riva Gaaserud, *Moon Virginia & Maryland* (Berkeley: Hachette, 2020).

29. "Obituary," *Daily Dispatch* (Richmond, VA), May 25, 1863, https://chroniclingamerica.loc.gov/lccn/sn84024738/1863-05-25/ed-1/seq-2/.

30. Dawn F. Thomas, *The Green Spring Valley: Its History and Heritage* (Baltimore: Maryland Historical Society, 1978), 134.

31. *Official Records*, II, Vol. II, 277.

32. Ibid.

33. "The Craftiest of Men."

34. *Official Records*, II, Vol. IV, 934.

35. *Official Records*, II, Vol. II, 292.

36. J.P. Benjamin to the President, October 16, 1862, Compiled Service Record of William Henry Norris, *Compiled Service Records of Confederate General and Staff Officers, and Nonregimental Enlisted Men*, NARA M331, RG 109, https://www.fold3.com/image/72364863

37. Samuel H. Lyon to President Andrew Johnson, August 3, 1865, *Case Files for Former Confederates for Presidential Pardons*, NARA M1003, RG 94, https://www.fold3.com/image/21568272, accessed August 11, 2023.

38. Mary Norris, *Confederate Papers Relating to Citizens or Business Firms*, NARA M346, RG 109, https://www.fold3.com/image/46474782.

39. "The Peace Propositions from Richmond."

40. Compiled Service Record of Charles Howard, *Civil War Service Records (CMSR)—Confederate—Maryland, 1861–1865*, NARA M321, RG 109, https://www.fold3.com/image/109770664.

41. John M. Strother to Charles Howard, March 11, 1865, Elizabeth Phoebe Key Howard (1803–1897), Correspondence, MS 1839, Maryland Museum of History and Culture, Baltimore, MD.

42. Compiled Service Record of B.H. Latrobe, *Civil War Service Records (CMSR)—Confederate*, NARA M347, RG 109, https://www.fold3.com/image/254788603.

43. "Reported 'Interviews,'" *Alexandria Gazette*, September 5, 1873, https://chroniclingamerica.loc.gov/lccn/sn85025007/1873-09-05/ed-1/seq-2/.

44. *Alexandria Gazette and Virginia Advertiser*, September 8, 1873, https://chroniclingamerica.loc.gov/lccn/sn85025007/1873-09-08/ed-1/seq-2/.

45. Conrad, *Rebel Scout*, 22–23.

46. King, December 22, 1856, *Diary*.

47. Ibid.

48. Ibid.

49. Ibid.

50. King, November 11, 1857, *Diary*.
51. Compiled Service Record of DM Cloud, Sergeant, Seventh Virginia Cavalry, *Civil War Service Records (CMSR)—Confederate—Virginia*, NARA M324, RG 109, https://www.fold3.com/image/7515368.
52. Compiled Service Record of Thomas H. Buck, Captain, Seventh Virginia Cavalry, *Civil War Service Records (CMSR)—Confederate—Virginia*, NARA M324, RG 109, https://www.fold3.com/image/7514334.
53. Averitt, *Memoirs of Turner Ashby*, 248.
54. "Thomas H. Harbin," MSA SC 5496-018954, Maryland State Archives, Biographical Series, http://www.msa.md.gov.
55. Case file of Thomas H. Harbin, C.A. Beall to Unknown, November 29, 1862, *Union Citizen Files*, NARA M345, RG 109, https://www.fold3.com/image/286687709.
56. Susan King, George Francis Harbin Family Tree, https://records.myheritagelibraryedition.com/site-309336861/king-family-site-23andme; *Official Records*, II, Vol. II, 857–858.
57. Compiled Service Record of Thomas H. Harbin, First Maryland Cavalry, *Civil War Service Records (CMSR)—Confederate—Maryland*, NARA M321, RG 109, https://www.fold3.com/image/1133254 35.
58. Harry Gilmor, *Four Years in the Saddle* (New York: Harper, 1866), 49.
59. Ibid., 49–50.
60. King, April 9, 1858, *Diary*.
61. Lucy Rebecca Buck, *Shadows on My Heart* (Athens: University of Georgia Press, 2012), 155.
62. John Wesley Greene to Abraham Lincoln, November 22, 1862, *Abraham Lincoln Papers*, https://www.loc.gov/item/mal1970600/.
63. Ibid., 42.
64. Compiled Service Record of John N. Buck, Seventh Virginia Cavalry, *Civil War Service Records (CMSR)—Confederate—Virginia*, NARA M324, RG 109, https://www.fold3.com/image/7514308.
65. Conrad, *Rebel Scout*, 172.
66. Peachy R. Grattan, *Cases Decided in the Supreme Court of Appeals of Virginia*, Vol. XXII (Richmond: R.F. Walker, 1873), 514.
67. Averitt, *Memoirs of Turner Ashby*, 189.
68. King, April 9, 1858, *Diary*.

Chapter 14

1. Conrad, *Rebel Scout*, 43.
2. Laura Virginia Hale, "Capt. Daniel Mountjoy Cloud Memorial," *Warren Sentinel*, June 16, 1955, https://virginiachronicle.com/.
3. Protestant Episcopal Church, *Journal of the Seventy-Sixth Annual Convention of the Protestant Episcopal Church in Maryland* (Baltimore: P.E. Church, 1859), vii.
4. Elizabeth Janney, *Elkridge* (Charleston: Arcadia, 2013), 60–61.
5. George D. Fisher, *History and Reminiscences of the Monumental Church* (Richmond: Whittet & Shepperson, 1880), 125–128.
6. Edward J. Swords, *Sword's Pocket Almanack, 1832* (New York: T. and J. Swords 1832), 44.
7. Charles W. Mitchell, *Maryland Voices* (Baltimore: John Hopkins University Press, 2007), 145.
8. Case File 161B, Collision and J W Green, Wm S. Radle, "Notes of J.W. Green," *Turner-Baker Files*, https://www.fold3.com/image/257123559/257123535.
9 John Edward Semmes, *John H.B. Latrobe and His Times* (Baltimore: Norman, Remington, 1917), 258, 385, 545.
9. John H.B. Latrobe to William Seward, December 5, 1861, *Abraham Lincoln Papers*, https://www.loc.gov/item/mal1325500/.
10. John Jennings Moorman, *The Virginia Springs* (Richmond: J.W. Randolph, 1855), 268–275; J.N. Buck, "The Mountain House, Capon Springs, Virginia," *Alexandria Gazette*, June 26, 1857, https://chroniclingamerica.loc.gov/lccn/sn85025007/1857-06-26/ed-1/seq-2/.
11. David Blackford, *Family Tree of Frank Latrobe Buck (1861–1909)*, https://records.myheritagelibraryedition.com/site-139175952/my-family.
12. "Married," *Baltimore Daily Exchange*, November 8, 1860, https://chroniclingamerica.loc.gov/lccn/sn83009573/1860-11-08/ed-1/seq-2/.
13. Harrison S. Van Waes, "Together

Again: Reuniting the Silver Tureens of Judge George Washington Dobbin," December 17, 2021, https://www.mdhistory.org/.

14. Ibid.

15. Ibid.

16. Michael Andrew Hoffman, Elizabeth Swan Key Dobbin Family Tree, https://records.myheritagelibraryedition.com/site-1004053401/hoffman.

17. Compiled Service Record of Robert A. Dobbin, Robert A. Dobbin to G.W. Randolph, September 26, 1862, *Civil War Service Records (CMSR)—Confederate—Virginia, 1861–1865*, NARA M324, RG 109, https://www.fold3.com/image/11902314.

18. Conrad, *Rebel Scout*, 119.

19. James I. Robertson, Jr., *Proceedings of the Advisory Council of the State of Virginia, April 21–June 19, 1861* (Richmond: Virginia State Library, 1977), 102.

20. Richard Steuart Latrobe to Mrs. J.H.B. Latrobe, March 21, 1863, John H.B. Latrobe Papers, MS 0526, Maryland Center for History and Culture, Baltimore, MD.

21. James McLachlan, ed., "Civil War Diary of Joseph H. Coit," *Maryland Historical Magazine* 60 (September 1965), 249; Goldsborough, *Maryland Line*, 232.

22. Ferdinand C. Latrobe, *Iron Men and Their Dogs* (Baltimore: Drechsler, 1941), 9; Brenda McCormick Penepent, Family Tree of Nehemiah Hayward, https://records.myheritagelibraryedition.com/research/record-1-433543211-1-512912/, accessed September 11, 2023.

23. "Confederate Prisoners," *Washington Evening Star*, July 9, 1863, https://chroniclingamerica.loc.gov/lccn/sn83045462/1863-07-09/ed-1/seq-2/.

24. Compiled Service Record of Richard Stewart Latrobe, Edwin M. Stanton to Gen. R.S. Schenck, July 8, 1863, *Civil War Service Records (CMSR)—Confederate—Miscellaneous, 1861–1865*, NARA M345, RG 109, https://www.fold3.com/image/254788632.

25. Compiled Service Record of Richard Stewart Latrobe, R. Stewart Latrobe, October 13, 1863, *Civil War Service Records (CMSR)—Confederate—Miscellaneous, 1861–1865*, NARA M345, RG 109, https://www.fold3.com/image/254788620.

26. "Dr. Schenck," *Brooklyn Daily Eagle*, January 5, 1885, https://newscomwc.newspapers.com/image/50425624/.

27. *Catalogue of Dickinson College for the Academical Year, 1854–55* (1855), Dickinson College Archives, https://archives.dickinson.edu/; King, *History of Dickinson College*, 35, 43.

28. Cullison's daughter, Laura Cullison, was married there in 1876. "Married," *Westminster Democratic Advocate*, June 17, 1876, https://newscomwc.newspapers.com/image/348124604/; Susanna A. Forsyth, *Compiled History of Strawbridge M.E. Church* (Baltimore: American Methodist Historical Society, 1932), 6.

29. Ibid.

30. "Following His Leader," *Memphis Public Ledger*, March 15, 1872, https://newscomwc.newspapers.com/image/587390304/.

31. "A Church Difficulty," *Alexandria Gazette*, February 16, 1863, https://chroniclingamerica.loc.gov/lccn/sn85025007/1863-02-16/ed-1/seq-2/.

32. John H. Dashiell Case File, Lt. J. Emory Gault to Maj. Wm. S. Fish, February 15, 1863, *Union Citizens File*, NARA M345, RG 109, https://www.fold3.com/image/281948784/.

33. John H. Dashiell Case File, Letter to Editors of the *Baltimore American*, February 16, 1863, *Union Citizens File*, NARA M345, RG 109, https://www.fold3.com/image/281948799/.

34. "J. Wesley Greene—His Standing and Career Here."

35. Elizabeth Anderson, *Family Tree of James M. Cullison (1838–1889)*, https://records.myheritagelibraryedition.com/site-1498070572/anderson; Woods, *Baltimore Directory*, 70.

36. James Cullison Case File, Affidavit of Maximillian Plitt, August 6, 1864, *Union Citizens File*, NARA M345, RG 109, https://www.fold3.com/image/280342692.

37. James M. Cullison Case File, James Cullison to Unknown, July 27, 1864, *Union Citizens File*, NARA M345, RG 109, https://www.fold3.com/image/280342699/.

38. Ibid.

39. Compiled Service Record of Micajah M. Cullison, Private, Thirteenth Maryland Infantry, *Civil War Service Records (CMSR)—Union—Maryland*, NARA M384, RG 94, https://www.fold3.com/image/268990072/.

40. Ibid.

41. Compiled Service Record of Alex G. Babcock, 4th Sergt, 71st N.Y. State Militia, *Civil War Service Index (CMSR)—Union—New York*, NARA M551, RG 94, https://www.fold3.com/image/289021496/; Lowen, *History of the 71st*, 157; Peter Morris and William J. Ryczek, *Base Ball Founders* (Jefferson, NC: McFarland, 2013), 129.
42. "Capt. A.G. Babcock," *Richmond Dispatch*, October 8, 1897, https://chroniclingamerica.loc.gov/lccn/sn85038614/1897-10-08/ed-1/seq-7/.
43. Compiled Service Record of Micajah M. Cullison.
44. Summers, *Baltimore and Ohio*, 126.
45. Compiled Service Record of DM Cloud, Sergeant, Seventh Virginia Cavalry, *Civil War Service Records (CMSR)—Confederate—Virginia*, NARA M324, RG 109, https://www.fold3.com/image/7515368; Compiled Service Record of Kennedy Grogan, Sergeant, Thirty-Fifth Virginia Battalion, *Civil War Service Records (CMSR)—Confederate—Virginia*, NARA M324, RG 109, https://www.fold3.com/image/7808364.
46. Philip Ensley, *Dear Esther: The Civil War Letter of Aungier Dobbs* (Apollo, PA: Closson Press, 1991), 144.
47. Joseph G.W. Marriott to Secretary of War, *Letters Received by the Confederate Adjutant and Inspector General's Office*, NARA M474, RG 109, https://www.fold3.com/image/643005814.
48. Darrell L. Collins, *The Jones-Imboden Raid* (Jefferson, NC: McFarland, 2007).
49. Roy Bird Cook, *Lewis County in the Civil War, 1861–1865* (Charleston, WV: Jarrett, 1924), 97.
50. "An Italianate Beauty in Baltimore," February 2, 2018, https://www.bhchimneys.com/, accessed August 20, 2023.
51. Compiled Service Record of A.J. Albert Jr., Private, First Maryland Artillery, *Civil War Service Records (CMSR)—Confederate—Maryland*, NARA M347, RG 109, https://www.fold3.com/image/109437176.
52. Case File 62B, Kirby, J T and E H Stein, Affidavit of E.H. Stein, September 15, 1862, *Turner-Baker Files*, NARA M797, RG 94, https://www.fold3.com/image/260188508/260188508/; Douglas Waller, *Lincoln's Spies: Their Secret War to Save a Nation* (New York: Simon and Schuster, 2020), 115.
53. "Kirby the Alleged Spy and a Brief History of Him," *Atlanta Southern Confederacy*, November 18, 1862, https://newscomwc.newspapers.com/image/604357851/.
54. Ibid.
55. Ibid.
56. Major Charles Marshall to General R.E. Lee, November 10, 1862, *Official Records*, II, Vol. V, 708.
57. Unknown to Major Charles Marshall, October 29, 1862, *Official Records*, Series II, Vol. V (Washington, GPO, 1887), 708.
58. *Official Records*, I, Vol. XIX, 890.
59. *Official Records*, II, Vol. V, 697.
60. Case File 62B, Kirby, J T and E H Stein, Affidavit of E.H. Stein, September 15, 1862, *Turner-Baker Files*, NARA M797, RG 94, https://www.fold3.com/image/260188508/260188508/.
61. 1860 U.S. Federal Census, Baltimore, Maryland, 11th Ward, Charles Marshall, NARA Publication M653, Sheet: 227, Page 231, Line 11 https://records.myheritagelibraryedition.com/research/record-10127-8429294/.

Chapter 15

1. George H Pendleton, *The Copperhead Candidate for Vice President* (Washington: Union Congressional Committee, 1864), 8.
2. William C. Barney to Unknown, November 30, 1862, *Abraham Lincoln Papers*, https://www.loc.gov/item/mal1981500/.
3. Ibid. The November 17, 1862, letter from Barney to Seward cannot be found.
4. George B. McClellan, *McClellan's Own Story* (London: Sampson Low Marston Searle & Rivington, 1887), 655.
5. Ibid., 657–658.
6. *Court of Appeals, Francis G. Young against George W. Hunt* (New York: New York Printing, 1870), 61.
7. William C. Barney to Unknown, November 23, 1862, *Abraham Lincoln Papers*, https://www.loc.gov/item/mal1972600/.
8. "William Chase Barney."
9. "John Van Buren's Plan," *Windsor*

Notes—Chapter 15

Vermont Journal, November 22, 1862, https://newscomwc.newspapers.com/image/491198631/.

10. "The Detective and Spy System," *New York Herald*, November 28, 1862, https://chroniclingamerica.loc.gov/lccn/sn83030313/1862-11-28/ed-1/seq-6/.

11. E.J. Allen to George B. McClellan, November 28, 1862, *George Brinton McClellan Papers: Correspondence II, 1823–1898, Sept. 20, 1862–Aug. 7. 1863*, https://www.loc.gov/item/mss318980131/.

12. G.H. Eldridge to Dr. McClellan, November 28, 1862, *George Brinton McClellan Papers: Correspondence II, 1823–1898, Sept. 20, 1862–Aug. 7. 1863*, https://www.loc.gov/item/mss318980131/.

13. "Samuel L.M. Barlow," *New York Times*, July 11, 1889, https://www.nytimes.com/1889/07/11/archives.

14. Stephen W. Sears, *George B. McClellan: The Young Napoleon* (Boston: Ticknor & Fields, 1988), 51.

15. McClellan and Sears, ed., *The Civil War Papers of George B. McClellan*, 128.

16. Ibid., 361.

17. "The Rumors of Peace Propositions," *Brooklyn Daily Eagle*, December 2, 1862, https://newscomwc.newspapers.com/image/50421515/.

18. William C. Barney to Unknown, November 30, 1862, *Abraham Lincoln Papers*.

19. "Rebel Overtures for Peace."

20. "Gov. Letcher and Fernando Wood," *Pittsburgh Daily Post*, December 17, 1862, https://newscomwc.newspapers.com/image/87565306/.

21. "The Naval Court of Inquiry," *Richmond Enquirer*, November 10, 1857, https://chroniclingamerica.loc.gov/lccn/sn84024735/1857-11-10/ed-1/seq-2/.

22. "The Rumors of Overtures for Peace," *Brooklyn Daily Eagle*, December 6, 1862, https://newscomwc.newspapers.com/image/50421766/.

23. Ibid.

24. Cooper Wingert, "1850 Fugitive Slave Law," https://blogs.dickinson.edu/hist-wingert/uscommissioners/philip-a-hoyne/.

25. Dennis Rodkin, "When a Chicago Street Mob Rescued a Fugitive from Slavery," *Chicago Magazine*, June 24, 2019, https://www.chicagomag.com/chicago-magazine/june-july-2019/when-a-chicago-street-mob-rescued-a-fugitive-from-slavery/.

26. Ibid., "The Eliza Grayson Rescue Case," *Chicago Tribune*, December 5, 1860, https://chroniclingamerica.loc.gov/lccn/sn84031490/1860-12-05/ed-1/seq-1/.

27. J. Wesley Greene, "To the Editors of the Chicago Times," *Chicago Times*, December 10, 1862, Rpt. in "A New Sensation Story!" *Daily Milwaukee News*, December 11, 1862, https://newscomwc.newspapers.com/image/7815869/.

28. Ibid.

29. Ibid.

30. Ibid.

31. "Another Peace Canard," *New York Times*, December 11, 1862, https://www.nytimes.com/1862/12/11/archives/another-peace-canard-mr-j-wesley-greene-otherwise-verdant-greene.html.

32. Basler, *Collected Works*, Vol. 5, 517.

33. "The Rumors of Overtures for Peace—J. Wesley Greene and the Administration," *Brooklyn Daily Eagle*, December 15, 1862, https://newscomwc.newspapers.com/image/50422405/.

34. "Arrest of J. Wesley Greene," *Brooklyn Daily Eagle*, December 16, 1862, https://newscomwc.newspapers.com/image/50422484/.

35. "Arrest of Greene, the Chicago Times Tinker," *Chicago Tribune*, December 13, 1862, https://chroniclingamerica.loc.gov/lccn/sn84031490/1862-12-13/ed-1/seq-4/.

36. "Death of Senator Douglas," *Kenosha Telegraph*, June 6, 1861, https://chroniclingamerica.loc.gov/lccn/sn85033123/1861-06-06/ed-1/seq-2/; "An Atrocious Libel," *Chicago Tribune*, April 19, 1864, https://chroniclingamerica.loc.gov/lccn/sn84031490/1864-04-19/ed-1/seq-4/.

37. "Arrest of J. Wesley Greene," *Brooklyn Daily Eagle*, December 16, 1862, https://newscomwc.newspapers.com/image/50422484/.

38. "Trials of Rev. J.S. Greene, Alias Cullison."

39. "Capt. Daniel Mountjoy Cloud Memorial."

40. "Highly Important."

41. George H. Pendleton, https://www.wikitree.com/wiki/Pendleton-1255.

42. Virginia Clay-Clopton, *Belle of the Fifties* (New York: Doubleday Page & Co., 1904), 146.

43. George H Pendleton, *The Copperhead Candidate*, 8.
44. Ibid., 4–7.
45. "Political," *Chicago Daily Tribune*, August 11, 1864, https://chroniclingamerica.loc.gov/lccn/sn84031490/1864-08-11/ed-1/seq-3/.
46. "At Ilion, Astounding Rascalities" *Utica Daily Observer*, March 29, 1873, https://nyshistoricnewspapers.org/lccn/sn83031899/1873-03-29/ed-1/seq-8/ .
47. *Our Excellent Women of the Methodist Church in England and America* (New York: J.C. Buttre, 1861), 216–219.
48. Geni World Family Tree, *Family Tree of Henry Slicer*, https://records.myheritagelibraryedition.com/research/collection-40000/geni-world-family-tree, accessed October 7, 2023.
49. Henry Slicer, *Speech of Rev Henry Slicer* (Washington: H. Polkinhorn, 1856), 8.
50. *Boston Liberator*, April 23, 1858, https://newscomwc.newspapers.com/image/34576699/.
51. "The Power of the Press," *Lancaster Daily Evening Express*, March 11, 1858, https://newscomwc.newspapers.com/image/566039045/.
52. "Death of Rev. Dr. Henry Slicer," *Washington Evening Star*, April 24, 1874, https://chroniclingamerica.loc.gov/lccn/sn83045462/1874-04-24/ed-1/seq-4/.
53. "Trouble Among the Northern Churchmen," *Charleston Mercury*, March 29, 1862, https://newscomwc.newspapers.com/image/605542326/.
54. "Strong Signs of Anti-Slavery Reaction," *Keokuk* [IA] *Daily Gate City*, March 31, 1862, https://newscomwc.newspapers.com/image/843102349/.
55. Ibid.
56. Henry Slicer, Journal, Lovely Lane Museum & Archives, Methodist Historical Society Collection, Baltimore, MD.
57. Kathleen Minnix, *Laughter in the Amen Corner* (Athens: University of Georgia Press, 1993), 21–22.

Chapter 16

1. Melville, *The Confidence-Man*, 261.
2. "The Overtures of Peace," *New York Tribune*, December 11, 1862, https://newscomwc.newspapers.com/image/78346649/.
3. "J. Wesley Greene's Story," *Pittsburg Gazette*, December 13, 1862
4. "Overtures For Peace," *Memphis Appeal*, December 22, 1862, https://newscomwc.newspapers.com/image/39803668/.
5. "J. Wesley Greene—His Standing and Career Here."
6. "The Greatest Humbug of the Day," *Pittsburgh Daily Gazette*, December 13, 1862, https://panewsarchive.psu.edu/lccn/sn85054513/1862-12-13/ed-1/seq-3/ .
7. Ibid.
8. "J. Wesley Greene—His Standing and Career Here."
9. *Directory of Pittsburgh and Allegheny Cities*, 1862–63 (Pittsburgh: George H. Thurston, 1862), 130, 360.
10. "Greatest Humbug of the Day."
11. Ibid.
12. 1860 U.S. Federal Census, Cincinnati, Ohio, Martha Green in household of Peobe Borland, NARA Publication: M653, Sheet 52, Page 244, Line: 23, https://records.myheritagelibraryedition.com/research/record-10127-19248249/; *Williams Cincinnati Directory and Business Advertiser, 1849–1850* (Cincinnati: C.S. Williams, 1849), 40.
13. J.H. Woodruff, ed., *Cincinnati Directory Advertiser, 1836–37* (Cincinnati: J.H. Woodruff, 1836).
14. "The Democratic Peace Envoy."
15. "Methodist Contributions," *New Orleans Daily Crescent*, November 17, 1848, https://newscomwc.newspapers.com/image/321495376/.
16. "The Democratic Peace Envoy."
17. "Toby of Typee."
18. *Williams Cincinnati Directory*, 40.
19. "Toby of Typee."
20. *Williams Cincinnati Directory*, 115.
21. "Toby of Typee."
22. "A Circumstantial and Palpable Lie," *Little Rock True Democrat*, December 24, 1862, https://chroniclingamerica.loc.gov/lccn/sn84023190/1862-12-24/ed-1/seq-1/.
23. "Toby of Typee."
24. "West End Park," *Cincinnati Daily Press*, June 24, 1859, https://newscomwc.newspapers.com/image/64296554/; *History of Council, 1802–1902 City of*

Cincinnati (Cincinnati: Board of Legislation, 1902), 33.
25. David L. Mowrey, *Cincinnati in the Civil War: The Union's Queen City* (Charleston: History Press, 2021), 134.
26. William Henry Venable, *Centennial History of Christ Church Cincinnati* (Cincinnati: Stewart & Kidd, 1918), 137–140.
27. "Trials of the Rev. J.S. Green, alias Cullison."
28. 1860 U.S. Federal Census, Cincinnati, Ohio, Anna Green in household of Peobe Borland, NARA Publication: M653, Sheet 52, Page 244, Line: 26, https://records.myheritagelibraryedition.com/research/record-10127-19248252/.
29. "Dr. Schenck."
30. "Toby of Typee."
31. Ibid.
32. Bernard Whelen, Philip Messing and Robert Mladinich, *Case Files of the NYPD* (New York: Hachette, 2016).
33. "J. Wesley Greene."
34. Ibid.
35. "Freaks of a 'Loyal' Clergyman," *Clearfield* [PA] *Republican*, August 22, 1867, https://panewsarchive.psu.edu/lccn/sn83032199/1867-08-22/ed-1/seq-1/.
36. "J. Wesley Greene."
37. "Greatest Humbug of the Day."
38. "Who is J. Wesley Greene?" *Chicago Tribune*, December 13, 1862, https://chroniclingamerica.loc.gov/lccn/sn84031490/1862-12-13/ed-1/seq-1/.
39. "Editorial Summary," *Washington National Republican*, December 15, 1862, https://chroniclingamerica.loc.gov/lccn/sn86053570/1862-12-15/ed-1/seq-2/.
40. "Ubiquitous," *Burlington* [IA] *Weekly Hawk-Eye*, December 20, 1862, https://chroniclingamerica.loc.gov/lccn/sn84027060/1862-12-20/ed-1/seq-4/.
41. "'Rev. J. Wesley Greene Again," *Buffalo Weekly Courier*, April 9, 1873, https://newscomwc.newspapers.com/image/494828921/.
42. Alfred T. Andreas, *History of Chicago*, Vol. 3 (Chicago: Andreas, 1886); "Trials of the Rev. J.S. Green, Alias Cullison."; "The King of the Confidence Men," *New York Dispatch*, January 20, 1856, https://www.loc.gov/item/sn83030364/1856-01-20/ed-1/.
43. "The King of the Confidence Men."
44. "The Great West," *New York Tribune*, February 14, 1851, https://newscomwc.newspapers.com/image/50640802/.
45. "The Romance of Diplomacy," *Ottumwa* [IA] *Weekly Courier*, January 1, 1863, https://chroniclingamerica.loc.gov/lccn/sn84027352/1863-01-01/ed-1/seq-1/.
46. "Who is J. Wesley Greene?"
47. Ibid.
48. "The Adventures of a Gentleman by the Name of Greene," *Philadelphia Press*, December 12, 1862, https://panewsarchive.psu.edu/lccn/sn84026296/1862-12-12/ed-1/seq-4/.
49. "Brief Sketch of a Criminal," *Philadelphia Press*, December 17, 1862, https://panewsarchive.psu.edu/lccn/sn84026296/1862-12-13/ed-1/seq-4.
50. *New York Times*, March 18, 1852, https://www.nytimes.com/1852/03/18/archives.
51. "Brief Sketch of a Criminal."
52. "Arrest of Rev. J.W. Green, the Imposter," *New York Times*, March 22, 1852, https://www.nytimes.com/1852/03/22/archives.
53. "Editors' Correspondence," *Washington Daily American Telegraph*, April 5, 1852, https://newscomwc.newspapers.com/image/320662462/.
54. "Baltimore Correspondence," *Washington Daily Republic*, March 24, 1852, https://newscomwc.newspapers.com/image/320662433/.
55. "Editors' Correspondence."
56. "The Adventures of a Gentleman by the Name of Greene."
57. "Toby of Typee."
58. Ibid.
59. Ibid.
60. "Miscellany," *Brookville Indiana American*, December 8, 1854, https://newscomwc.newspapers.com/image/171661615/; Henry Tanner, *Louisville Directory and Business Advertiser, 1859–60* (Louisville: Maxwell & Co, 1860), 276.
61. "Miscellany."
62. Heflin, Edwards, and Heffernan, *Whaling Years*, 213.
63. "Wesley Greene, Tinker."
64. "Toby of Typee."
65. J. Wesley Greene, "The World's Not Shrouded," *Salt Lake Deseret News*, February 15, 1860, https://newscomwc.newspapers.com/image/286313142/.
66. Latrobe, February 16, 1862, *Diary of Osmun Latrobe*.

67. "Retaliatory Proclamation of Jefferson Davis," *Philadelphia Press*, December 27, 1862, https://panewsarchive.psu.edu/lccn/sn84026296/1862-12-27/ed-1/seq-2.

68. "John Van Buren on the War," *The Globe* (Huntingdon, PA), February 25, 1862, https://panewsarchive.psu.edu/lccn/sn83032114/1863-02-25/ed-1/seq-2/.

69. "Propositions For Peace—Orpheus C. Kerr in Diplomacy" *Worcester* [MA] *Daily Spy*, December 12, 1862, https://chroniclingamerica.loc.gov/lccn/sn83021205/1862-12-12/ed-1/seq-1/.

70. William C. Barney to Unknown, November 30, 1862, *Abraham Lincoln Papers*, https://www.loc.gov/item/mal1981500/.

71. Alfred T. Andreas, *History of Chicago*, Vol. 2 (Chicago: Andreas, 1886), 495.

72. "Trials of the Rev. J.S. Green, alias Cullison."

Postscript

1. "William Chase Barney"; "Congressional," *Columbia* [SC] *Daily Phoenix*, November 27, 1867, https://chroniclingamerica.loc.gov/lccn/sn84027008/1867-11-27/ed-1/seq-3/.

2. "Capt. Daniel Mountjoy Cloud Memorial."

3. "Teacher, Preacher, Soldier, Spy."

4. *Army Register of Enlistments, 1798–1914*, NARA M233, RG 94, National Archives, https://www.fold3.com/image/310833513; *Congressional Medal of Honor, the Distinguished Service Cross, and the Distinguished Service Medal*, 1919 (Washington: GPO, 1920), 257.

5. Compiled Service Record of Micajah M. Cullison, Private, Thirteenth Maryland Infantry, NARA M384, RG 94, National Archives, https://www.fold3.com/image/268990072.

6. "His Long Career as Crime," *Chicago Tribune*, September 6, 1888, https://chicagotribune.newspapers.com/.

7. "Relatives See End of Murat Halstead," *San Francisco Call*, July 3, 1908, https://chroniclingamerica.loc.gov/lccn/sn85066387/1908-07-03/ed-1/seq-3/.

8. "Dr Schenck."

9. "Following His Leader"; "Obituary, John W. Selby."

10. "Colored Man Drops Dead," *Washington Evening Star*, February 17, 1902, https://chroniclingamerica.loc.gov/lccn/sn83045462/1902-02-17/ed-1/seq-7/; "Major John B Prados."

11. "The 'Old Capitol' and Its Keeper."

12. "Mrs. Abraham Lincoln," *Indianapolis Journal*, July 31, 1887, https://chroniclingamerica.loc.gov/lccn/sn82015679/1887-07-31/ed-1/seq-9.

Bibliography

Abel, E. Lawrence. *Confederate Sheet Music.* Jefferson, NC: McFarland, 2011.
The African Repository. Washington: Dunn, 1827.
American Biography 9. New York: American Historical Society, 1921.
Anderson, Elizabeth. *Family Tree of James M. Cullison (1838–1889),* https://records.myheritagelibraryedition.com/site-1498070572/anderson, accessed August 18, 2023.
Andreas, Alfred T. *History of Chicago.* Chicago: Andreas, 1886.
Anema, Elizabeth Ann. *Family Tree of Elizabeth Ada Flower (1835–?),* https://records.myheritagelibraryedition.com/site-545244791/hackett.
Arkle, Thomas. *Family Tree of Mary Hawkesworth Norris (born Owen),* https://records.myheritagelibraryedition.com/research/record-1-444033451-1-533111 accessed August 18, 2023.
Armes, James Augustus. *Ups and Downs of an Army Officer.* Washington: 1900.
Armstrong, James Edward. *History of The Old Baltimore Conference from the Planting of Methodism in 1773 to the Division of the Conference in 1857.* Baltimore: King Brothers, 1907.
Arnold, Isaac Newton. *The Life of Abraham Lincoln.* Chicago: Jansen, McClurg, 1885.
Ashby, Thomas A. *Life of Turner Ashby.* New York: Neale, 1914.
Averitt, J. B., *The Memoirs of General Turner Ashby and His Compeers.* Baltimore: Selby & Dulany, 1867.
_____. *The Old Plantation: How We Lived in Great House and Cabin Before the War.* New York: F. Tennyson Neely, 1901.
Baltimore: Its History and Its People II. New York: Lewis Historical Publishing, 1912.
Barney, Blaine. *Family Tree of William Chase Barney (1814–1892),* https://records.myheritagelibraryedition.com/site-245203301/barney, accessed August 18, 2023.
Barney, John. Letters to Lewis Cass, 1843. *Lewis Cass Papers, 1774–1924.* William L. Clements Library, University of Michigan, Ann Arbor, Michigan.
Barney, Mary. *A Biographical Memoir of the late Commodore Barney.* Boston: Gray and Bowen, 1832.
Barney, William C. Letters, 1861–62. *Abraham Lincoln Papers, Series 1, General Correspondence, 1833–1916.* Manuscript Division, Library of Congress.
_____. Letters, 1861–63. *William Henry Seward Papers.* A.S51, Rare Books, Special Collections, and Preservation, River Campus Libraries, University of Rochester, Rochester, New York.
_____. "Ocean Steamers from New Orleans to France." *De Bow's Review* 22 (1857): 318–320.
_____. "Steamships at the South." *De Bow's Review* 22 (1857): 410–414.
Basler, Roy P., ed. *Collected Works of Abraham Lincoln,* Vol. 5. Springfield: Abraham Lincoln Association, 1953.
Bergeron, Paul H., and Johnson, Andrew. *The Papers of Andrew Johnson,* Vol. 9–10. Knoxville: University of Tennessee Press, 1991.
Beymer, William G. "Mrs. Greenhow." *Harpers Monthly Magazine* 124 (March 1912): 565.
Blackford, David. *Family Tree of Frank Latrobe Buck (1861–1909),* https://records.myheritagelibraryedition.com/site-139175952/my-family, accessed August 18, 2023.

Booth, George Wilson. *A Maryland Boy in Lee's Army.* Lincoln: University of Nebraska Press, 2000.
Boyd, William H. *Boyd's Washington and Georgetown Directory, 1860.* Washington: Taylor and Maury, 1860.
Branch, Watson, Hershel Parker, and Harrison Hayford. "Historical Note." *The Confidence-Man: His Masquerade.* Evanston: Northwestern University Press, 1984.
Broad Creek Historic District Preservation Planning Study (June 2002), https://www.mncppcapps.org/
Buck, Lucy Rebecca. *Shadows on My Heart.* Athens: University of Georgia Press, 2012.
Burlingame, Michael. *Abraham Lincoln: The Observations of John G. Nicolay and John Hay.* Carbondale: Southern Illinois University Press, 2007.
Burrows, F. M. "Harper's Ferry in 1861." *Confederate Veteran* 1 (April 1893): 103–104.
Case Files of Investigations by Levi C. Turner and Lafayette C. Baker, compiled 1861–1866. National Archives and Records Administration, M797, Washington, D.C.
Chadwick, James D., and Jonathan E. Helmreich. *Student as Soldier: The Civil War Letters of James D. Chadwick.* Meadville, PA: Allegheny College, 2011, https://sites.allegheny.edu/civilwarletters/. Excerpts from the letters courtesy of Allegheny College.
Chamberlin, Taylor M., and John M. Sounders. *Between Reb and Yank: A Civil War History of Northern Loudoun County, Virginia.* Jefferson, NC: McFarland, 2011.
Channing, Edward. *A Student's History of the United States.* New York: Macmillan, 1922.
Chase, Salmon P. *Diary and Correspondence of Salmon P. Chase.* Washington: 1903.
Cincinnati City Council. *History of Council, 1802–1902.* Cincinnati: Board of Legislation, 1902.
Civil War Service Records. National Archives and Records Administration, Washington, D.C., https://www.fold3.com.
Clay-Clopton, Virginia. *Belle of the Fifties.* New York: Doubleday, Page, 1904.
Clephane, Lewis. *Birth of the Republican Party.* Washington: Gibson, 1889.
Clodfelter, Micheal. *Warfare and Armed Conflicts,* 4th ed. Jefferson, NC: McFarland, 2017.
Cluskey, Michael W. *Speeches Messages and Other Writings of The Hon. Albert Gallatin Brown.* Philadelphia: James B. Smith, 1859.
Collins, Darrell L. *The Jones-Imboden Raid.* Jefferson, NC: McFarland, 2007.
Confederate Citizens File. National Archives and Records Administration, M346, RG 109, Washington, D.C., https://www.fold3.com.
Confederate Papers Relating to Citizens or Business Firms. National Archives and Records Administration, M346, RG 109, Washington, D.C., https://www.fold3.com.
Connery, William S. *Moseby's Raids in Civil War Northern Virginia.* Charleston, SC: History Press, 2013.
Conrad, Thomas N. *A Confederate Spy, A Story of the Civil War.* New York: J. S Ogilvie, 1892.
_____. *The Rebel Scout: A Thrilling History of Scouting Life in the Southern Army.* Washington: National Publishing, 1904.
Conroy, James B. *Lincoln's White House: The People's House in Wartime.* Lanham, MD: Rowman & Littlefield, 2016.
Constitution and By Laws of the Christian Labor Union of Emmanuel Church. Baltimore: John D. Toy, 1860.
Cook, Roy Bird. *Lewis County in the Civil War, 1861–1865.* Charleston, WV: Jarrett, 1924.
Cordell, Eugene Fauntleroy. *The Medical Annals of Maryland, 1799–1899.* Baltimore: Williams & Wilkins, 1903.
_____. *University of Maryland, 1807–1907: Its History, Influence, Characteristics and Equipment,* Vol. II. New York: Lewis, 1907.
Court of Appeals, Francis G. Young against George W. Hunt. New York: New York Printing, 1870.
Cullison, David Jonathon. Cullison website, https://records.myheritagelibraryedition.com/site-652925501/cullison.
Cullom, Shelby Moore. *Fifty Years of Public Service.* Chicago: McClurg, 1911.
Cullum, George Washington. *Biographical Register of the Officers and Graduates of the US Military Academy,* Vol. II. New York: James Miller, 1879.

Cutler, Josh S. *Mobtown Massacre: Alexander Hanson and the Baltimore Newspaper War of 1812*. Charleston, SC: History Press, 2019.
Davis, Curtis Carroll. "The Craftiest of Men: William P. Wood and the Establishment of the United States Secret Service." *Maryland Historical Magazine* 83 (Summer 1988): 111–126.
_____. "The 'Old Capitol' and Its Keeper: How William P. Wood Ran a Civil War Prison." *Records of the Columbia Historical Society, Washington, D.C.* 52 (1989): 206–34.
Dawson, Elodie Todd, and Nathaniel Dawson. *Practical Strangers, The Courtship Correspondence of Nathaniel Dawson and Elodie Todd, Sister of Mary Todd Lincoln*. Athens: University of Georgia Press, 2017.
Dexter, Gary. *Why Not Catch-21? The Stories Behind the Titles*. London: Francis Franklin Limited, 2007.
Disosway, Gabriel Poillon. *Our Excellent Women of the Methodist Church in England and America*. New York: J. C. Buttre, 1861.
Dulany, Ida P. *In the Shadow of the Enemy: The Civil War Journal of Ida Dulany*. Knoxville: University of Tennessee Press, 2009.
Durham, Thomas Wise. *Three Years with Wallace's Zouaves*. Macon: Mercer University Press 2003.
Egan, Hugh. "The Mackenzie Court-Martial Trial: Cooper's Secret Correspondence with William H. Norris." *Studies in the American Renaissance* (1990): 149–158.
Ensley, Philip. *Dear Esther: The Civil War Letter of Aungier Dobbs*. Apollo, PA: Closson Press, 1991.
Fishel, Edward G. *The Secret War for the Union*. Boston: Houghton Mifflin, 1996.
Fisher, George D. *History and Reminiscences of the Monumental Church*. Richmond: Whittet & Shepperson, 1880.
Fletcher, Carlton. "The Hume Brothers, Confederate Signal Scouts," https://gloverparkhistory.com/civil-war/local-people-in-the-civil-war/confederate-signal-scouts/.
Flower, Frank A. *Edwin McMasters Stanton: The Autocrat of Rebellion Emancipation and Reconstruction*. Akron: Saalfield, 1905.
Forsyth, Susanna A. *Compiled History of Strawbridge M.E. Church*. Baltimore: American Methodist Historical Society, 1932.
Furgurson, Ernest B. "Teacher, Preacher, Soldier, Spy" (2012), https://www.historynet.com/teacher-preacher-soldier-spy/, accessed August 6, 2023.
Gaaserud, Michaela Riva. *Moon Virginia & Maryland*. Berkeley: Hachette, 2020.
Geni World Family Tree. *Family Tree of Henry Slicer,* https://records.myheritagelibraryedition.com/research/collection-40000/geni-world-family-tree, accessed October 7, 2023.
George H Pendleton, The Copperhead Candidate for Vice President. Washington: Union Congressional Committee, 1864.
Gilmor, Harry. *Four Years in the Saddle*. New York: Harper, 1866.
Glenn, William Wilkins. *Between North and South*. London: Associated University Press, 1976.
Gold, Thomas D. *History of Clarke County, Virginia*. C. R. Hughes, 1914.
Goldsborough, William W. *The Maryland Line in the Confederate Army*. Baltimore: Guggenheimer & Weil, 1900.
Grattan, Peachy. *Cases Decided in the Supreme Court of Appeals of Virginia*, Vol. XXII. Richmond: R. F. Walker, 1873.
Greeley, Horace. *The American Conflict: A History of the Great Rebellion in the United States of America*, Vol. 1. Hartford: O. D. Case, 1864.
Gross, John J. "Melville's 'The Confidence-Man': The Problem of Source and Meaning." *Modern Language Society* 60 (1959): 299–310.
Hale, Laura Virginia. "Capt. Daniel Mountjoy Cloud Memorial." *Warren Sentinel*, June 16, 1955, https://virginiachronicle.com/.
Haley, J. J. *Debates That Made History: The Story of Alexander Campbell's Debates*. St. Louis: Christian Board, 1920.
Hall, James. Letter to Rev. Wm. McLain, January 16, 1860, *Forty-Third Annual Report of the American Colonization Society, January 17, 1860*. Washington: C. Alexander, 1860.

Bibliography

Hatch, Frederick. *Protecting President Lincoln.* Jefferson, NC: McFarland, 2011.
Heflin, Wilson, Mary K. Bercaw Edwards, and Thomas Farel Heffernan. *Herman Melville's Whaling Years.* Nashville: Vanderbilt University Press, 2004.
"Heirs of Samuel C Young v. The United States." *Congressional Serial Set* 5579. Washington: GPO, 1909.
History of Mercer County, Pennsylvania: Its Past and Present. Chicago: Brown, Runk & Company, 1888.
Hoffman, Michael Andrew. Elizabeth Swan Key Dobbin Family Tree, https://records.myheritagelibraryedition.com/site-1004053401/hoffman.
Holdcraft, Paul E. *History of the Pennsylvania Conference of the United Brethren of Christ.* Fayetteville, PA: Craft Press, 1938.
Holland, Frederic May. *Frederick Douglass: The Colored Orator.* New York: Funk & Wagnalls, 1891.
Howard, Charles. *Communication from the President of the Maryland State Colonization Society.* Baltimore: Maryland Senate, 1860.
Howard, Elizabeth Phoebe Key. Correspondence. Special Collections, MS 1839, Maryland Museum of History and Culture, Baltimore, MD.
Howard, McHenry. *Recollections of A Maryland Confederate Soldier and Staff Officer.* Baltimore: Williams & Wilkins, 1914.
Hughes, Nathaniel C. *Yale's Confederates.* Knoxville: University of Tennessee Press, 2008.
Hutchinson, Thomas. *Boyd's Washington and Georgetown Directory, 1862.* Washington: Taylor and Maury, 1862.
In Memoriam, John E Norris. Washington: Polkinhorn, 1887.
"An Italianate Beauty in Baltimore." February 2, 2018, https://www.bhchimneys.com/, accessed August 20, 2023.
Janney, Elizabeth. *Elkridge.* Charleston, SC: Arcadia, 2013.
Johnson, Jan Simmons. *The House of Franciscus, 1710–2000 A.D.* Madison: University of Wisconsin Press, 1989.
Jones, Matt. "The Confederate President." *Collegiate Times,* www.collegiatetimes.com.
Judson, A. M. *History of the Eighty-Third Regiment Pennsylvania Volunteers.* Erie, PA: Lynn, 1865.
Kettel, Thomas Prentice, ed. *The United States Magazine and Democratic Review,* Vol. 22. New York, 1848.
King, Horatio C. *History of Dickinson College.* New York: American University, 1896.
King, Susan. George Francis Harbin Family Tree, https://records.myheritagelibraryedition.com/site-309336861/king-family-site-23andme.
_____. *Diary, 1854–1858.* MC 1999.9, Horatio Collins King Family Papers, Archives and Special Collections, Dickinson College, Carlisle, Pennsylvania.
Lapham, William B. *My Recollections of The War of the Rebellion.* Augusta: Burleigh & Flynt, 1892.
Latrobe, B. H. "Unfiled Papers and Slips Belonging in Confederate Compiled Service Records." *Civil War Service Records (CMSR)—Confederate,* NARA M347, RG 109, https://www.fold3.com.
Latrobe, Ferdinand C. *Iron Men and Their Dogs.* Baltimore: Drechsler, 1941.
Latrobe, John H. B. "Address of J.H.B. Latrobe." *Thirty-Seventh Annual Report of the American Colonization Society.* Washington: C. Alexander, 1854.
_____. *African Colonization: An Address.* Washington: H. S. Bowen, 1862.
_____. "Speech of J.H.B. Latrobe." *Thirty-Fifth Annual Report of the American Colonization Society* (1852): 54.
Latrobe, Osmun. *Diary of Osmun Latrobe.* Osmun Latrobe Papers, Virginia Museum of History and Culture, Richmond, Virginia.
Latrobe, Richard Steuart. Letter to Mrs. J. H. B. Latrobe, March 21, 1863. John H. B. Latrobe Papers, MS 0526, Maryland Center for History and Culture, Baltimore, Maryland.
Laven, Robert R. *Major General Philip Kearney.* Jefferson, NC: McFarland, 2020.
Lehmann, R. C. *Memories of Half a Century.* London: Chambers, 1908.

Letters Received by the Adjutant General, 1861–1870. Main Series, National Archives and Records Administration, M619, Washington, D.C., https://www.fold3.com.
Lincoln, Abraham. *Abraham Lincoln Papers: Series 1, General Correspondence, 1833 to 1916.* Library of Congress, https://www.loc.gov.
———. *Abraham Lincoln: Complete Works: Comprising His Speeches, Letters, State Papers, and Miscellaneous Writings.* New York: Century, 1894.
———. *Collected Works of Abraham Lincoln.* 8 vols., New York: H. Wolff, 1953.
Lockwood, John, and Charles Lockwood. *Siege of Washington: The Untold Story of the Twelve Days That Shook the Union.* New York: Oxford University Press, 2011.
Lowen, George Edward. *History of the 71st Regiment.* New York: Eastman, 1919.
Lyon, Samuel H. Letter to President Andrew Johnston, August 3, 1865. *Case Files for Former Confederates for Presidential Pardons*, NARA M1003, RG 94, https://www.fold3.com.
Lyon, William F., and Robert B. Lyon, Jr. *Wester Ogle National Register of Historic Places Inventory Nomination Form.* Washington: National Park Service, 1985.
Maddox, J. H. Letter to Secretary of War, September 7, 1862. *Index to Reports of Committees of the House of Representatives, 1876–77.* Washington: GPO, 1877.
Mahoney, Dennis A. *The Prisoner of State.* New York: Carleton, 1863.
Marriott, Joseph G. W. Letter to Secretary of War, December 3, 1862. *Letters Received by the Confederate Adjutant and Inspector General's Office*, NARA M474, RG 109, National Archives, https://www.fold3.com.
Martenet, Simon J. *Martenet's Map of Prince George's County, Maryland.* Baltimore, 1861, https://www.loc.gov/item/2002624036/.
Marvel, William. *Mr. Lincoln Goes to War.* Boston: Houghton Mifflin, 2006.
Marvin, Winthrop L. *The American Merchant Marine: Its History and Romance from 1620 to 1902.* 1916.
Maryland General Assembly. *Journal of the Proceedings of the Senate of Maryland, January Session, 1858.* Annapolis: Bull & Tuttle, 1858.
McClanahan, Brion. "Charles Carroll of Carrollton: The Southern Irish Catholic Planter." March 17, 2016, https://www.abbevilleinstitute.org/.
McClellan, George B. *George Brinton McClellan Papers: Correspondence II, 1823–1898,* Library of Congress, https://www.loc.gov.
McClellan, George B., and Sears, Stephen W., ed. *The Civil War Papers of George B. McClellan.* New York: Tickner & Fields, 1989.
McLachlan, James. "Civil War Diary of Joseph H. Coit." *Maryland Historical Magazine* 60 (September 1965).
McNamara, Pat. "Benjamin J. Keiley (1847–1925): Confederate Soldier, Catholic Bishop." McNamara's Blog, https://www.patheos.com/blogs/mcnamarasblog/2010/11/benjamin-j-keiley-1847-1925-confederate-soldier-catholic-bishop.html, November 2, 2010.
Melville, Herman. *The Confidence-Man: His Masquerade.* London: Longman, Brown, Green, Longmans and Roberts, 1857.
———. *Correspondence.* Edited by Lynn Horth. Evanston: Northwestern University Press, 1993.,
Meyer, Eugene L. *Maryland Lost and Found.* Baltimore: John Hopkins University Press, 1986.
Miers, Earl Schenck. *Lincoln Day by Day,* Vol.. 3, *1861–1865.* Washington: C. Percy Powell, 1960.
Miller, Oliver, ed. *Maryland Reports,* Vol. 11. Annapolis: Robert F. Bonsall, 1858.
Miller, Richard F. *States at War,* Vol. 4. Hanover: University Press of New England, 2015.
Minnix, Kathleen. *Laughter in the Amen Corner.* Athens: University of Georgia Press, 1993.
Mitchell, Charles W. *Maryland Voices of the Civil War.* Baltimore: John Hopkins University Press, 2007.
Mitchell, Charles W., and Jean H. Baker. *The Civil War in Maryland Reconsidered.* Baton Rouge: Louisiana State University Press, 2021.
Moore, Frank. *The Rebellion Record,* Vol. 2. New York: G. P. Putnam, 1862.
Moorman, John Jennings. *The Virginia Springs.* Richmond: J. W. Randolph, 1855.

Morgan, James A. III. *A Little Short of Boats: The Fights at Ball's Bluff and Edwards Ferry, October 21–22, 1861.* Ft. Mitchell, KY: Ironclad Publishing, 2004.
Mowrey, David L. *Cincinnati in the Civil War: The Union's Queen City.* Charleston, SC: History Press, 2021.
Myers, Frank M. *The Comanches: A History of White's Battalion, Virginia Cavalry.* Baltimore: Kelly, Piet & Company, 1871.
Myers, Thomas. *The Norris Family of Maryland.* New York: Clemens, 1916.
Nicholson, Isaac F. "The Maryland Guard Battalion, 1860–61." *Maryland Historical Magazine* 6 (June 1911): 121.
Nicolay, John G., and John Hay. "Abraham Lincoln: A History. The Announcement of Emancipation." *Century Magazine* 37 (1889).
Norris, Mrs. Mary. *Confederate Papers Relating to Citizens or Business Firms,* NARA M346, RG 109, National Archives, https://www.fold3.com/image/46474824.
"Obituary, John W. Selby." *The Dental Cosmos* 43 (1901): 961.
Oswandel, J. Jacob. *Notes on the Mexican War.* Philadelphia, 1885.
Owen, Kennedy. "September 14, 1814." *Maryland Historical Magazine* 11 (1916): 192.
Papenfuse, Edward C. "Ferrandini, Cipriano." *Archives of Maryland,* 2009, https://msa.maryland.gov/megafile/msa/speccol/sc3500/sc3520/014400/014473/html/14473bio.html.
Patton, W. W. *The American Board and Slaveholding* (1846).
———. *President Lincoln and the Chicago Memorial on Emancipation.* Baltimore: John Murphy, 1888.
Penepent, Brenda McCormick. "Family Tree of Nehemiah Hayward." https://records.myheritagelibraryedition.com/research/record-1-433543211-1-512912/, accessed September 11, 2023.
Pinkerton, Allan. *The Spy of the Rebellion.* New York: G. W. Carleton, 1883.
Pistelli, John. "Herman Melville, The Confidence-Man: His Masquerade." Blog, August 18, 2019, https://johnpistelli.com/2019/08/18/herman-melville-the-confidence-man-his-masquerade/.
Pohl, Robert. "Lost Capitol Hill: The DC Jail." June 24, 2010, https://thehillishome.com.
Pohl, Robert S., and John R. Wennersten, eds. *Abraham Lincoln and the End of Slavery in the District of Columbia.* Washington: Eastern Branch Press, 2009.
Pollard, Edward A. *Life of Jefferson Davis, With a Secret History of the Confederacy.* Philadelphia: National Publishing, 1869.
Postall, Rosa. Letter to Mrs. Baber, March 13, 1863. Baber/Blackshear Family Papers, Ms11, Hargrett Rare Book and Manuscript Library, The University of Georgia Libraries.
Protestant Episcopal Church. *Journal of the Seventy-First Annual Convention of the Protestant Episcopal Church in Maryland.* Baltimore: Joseph Robinson, 1854.
———. *Journal of the Seventy-Sixth Annual Convention of the Protestant Episcopal Church in Maryland.* Baltimore: P. E. Church, 1859.
———. *Journal of the Twenty-Ninth Annual Convention of the Protestant Episcopal Church in The Diocese of Alabama.* Mobile: Farrow and Dent, 1860.
Ramsdell, Charles W. "General Robert E. Lee's Horse Supply, 1862–1865." *The American Historical Review* 35 (July 1930): 758–777.
Raymond, James. *Political, or the Spirit of Democracy in 1856.* Baltimore: John W. Woods, 1857.
Records of the Columbia Historical Society, Vol. 52. Washington, D.C., 1989.
Renshaw, James A. "Major John B Prados: A Confederate Officer." *Louisiana Historical Quarterly* (1927): 241–248.
"Rev. Otis Henry Tiffany, D.D.." *The Dickinsonian* (November 1891).
Reynolds, Michael S. "The Protype for Melville's Confidence Man." *PMLA* 86 (October 1971): 1009–1013.
Rice, Allen Thorndike, ed. *Reminiscences of Abraham Lincoln by Distinguished Men of His Time.* New York: North American Publishing, 1886.
Robertson, James I., Jr., *Proceedings of the Advisory Council of the State of Virginia, April 21–June 19, 1861.* Richmond: Virginia State Library, 1977.
Rodkin, Dennis. "When a Chicago Street Mob Rescued a Fugitive from Slavery."

Chicago Magazine, June 24, 2019, https://www.chicagomag.com/chicago-magazine/june-july-2019/when-a-chicago-street-mob-rescued-a-fugitive-from-slavery/.
"Roger Brooke Taney." Dickinson College Archives, https://archives.dickinson.edu/people/roger-brooke-taney-1777-1864.
Rowland, Kate Mason. *The Life of Charles Carroll of Carrollton, 1737–1832*, Vol II. New York, G.P. Putnam, 1898.
Ruffner, Kevin Conley. *Maryland's Blue and Gray: A Border State's Union and Confederate Junior Officer Corps*. Baton Rouge: Louisiana State University Press, 1997.
Russel, Robert Royal. *Economic Aspects of Southern Sectionalism, 1841–1860*. New York: Noble, 1924.
Scharf, J. Thomas. *The Chronicles of Baltimore*. Baltimore: Turnbull Brothers, 1874.
Scharf, J. T. *The Chronicles of Baltimore*. Baltimore: Turnbull Brothers, 1874.
Schenck, Noah. *Rev. Mr. Schenck's Introductory Discourse in Emmanuel Church*. Baltimore: John D. Toy, 1860.
Schley, David. *Steam City*. Chicago: University of Chicago Press, 2020.
Sears, Stephen W. *George B. McClellan: The Young Napoleon*. Boston: Ticknor & Fields, 1988.
Semmes, John E. *John HB Latrobe and His Times 1803–1891*. Baltimore: Norman Remington, 1917.
Shaw, Donal. *London in the Sixties: One of the Old Brigade*. London: Everett & Co., 1908.
Shepard, Henry Elliott. *History of Baltimore, MD*. Baltimore: S. B. Nelson, 1893.
Slicer, Henry. "Journal." Lovely Lane Museum & Archives, Methodist Historical Society Collection, Baltimore, Maryland.
———. *Speech of Rev Henry Slicer*. Washington: H. Polkinhorn, 1856.
Slotkin, Richard. *The Long Road to Antietam*. New York: Liveright, 2012.
Smith, Tunstall. *Richard Snowden Andrews*. Baltimore: Sun, 1910.
Sodaro, Craig. *Civil War Spies*. North Mankato, MN: Capstone Press, 2014.
"Special Orders No. 191." National Park Service, https://www.nps.gov/mono/learn/historyculture/so191.htm.
Stanton, Frederic P. "Address of Frederic P. Stanton." *Thirty-Fifth Annual Report of the American Colonization Society*. Washington: C. Alexander, 1852.
Stedman, Laura. *Life and Letters of Edmund Clarence Stedman*, vol. 1. New York: Moffat, Yard & Company, 1910.
Steers, Edward. *Blood on the Moon*. Lexington: University Press of Kentucky, 2001.
Stegeman, John F. *These Men She Gave: Civil War Diary of Athens, Georgia*. Athens: University of Georgia Press, 2009.
Steuart, Richard D. "Henry A. Steuart—Rebel Spy." *Confederate Veteran* 16 (1908): 332–334.
Stewart, Charles W., ed. *Official Records of the Union and Confederate Navies in the War of the Rebellion*, II, Vol. 3. Washington: GPO, 1922.
Stone, Charles P. "Washington on the Eve of War." Robert Underwood Johnson and Clarence Clough Buell, eds. *Battles and Leaders of the Civil War*, Vol. 1. New York: Century, 1887.
Styple, William B. *McClellan's Other Story*. Kearney, NJ: Belle Grove, 2012.
Summers, Festus P. *The Baltimore and Ohio in the Civil War*. Gettysburg: Stan Clark, 1993.
Swords, Edward J. *Sword's Pocket Almanack, 1832*. New York: T. and J. Swords, 1832.
Syphur, Josiah Rhinehart. *History of the Pennsylvania Reserve Corps*. Lancaster: Elias Barr, 1865.
Tanner, Henry, *Louisville Directory and Business Advertiser, 1859–60*. Louisville: Maxwell & Co., 1860.
Thayer, William Roscoe. *John Hay*, Vols. 1 and 2. Boston: Riverside, 1915.
Thomas, Clarence. *General Turner Ashby: The Centaur of The South*. Winchester: Eddy, 1907.
Thomas, Dawn. *The Green Spring Valley: Its History and Heritage*. Baltimore: Maryland Historical Society, 1978.
Thomas, Emery M. *Bold Dragoon: The Life of J. E. B. Stuart*. Norman: University of Oklahoma Press, 1999.

"Thomas H. Harbin." MSA SC 5496-018954, Maryland State Archives, Biographical Series, http://www.msa.md.gov.
Thompson, Magnus S. "Col Elijah V White." *Confederate Veteran* 15 (1907): 158-160.
Thurston, George H., ed. *Directory of Pittsburgh and Allegheny Cities, 1862-63*. Pittsburgh: George H. Thurston, 1862.
Tiffany, Otis H. "Dr. Dempster as a Man of Progress." *John Dempster, Lectures and Addresses*. Cincinnati: Poe & Hitchcock, 1864.
Trout, Robert J. *They Followed the Plume: The Story of J. E. B. Stuart and His Staff*. Mechanicsburg, PA: Stackpole, 2003.
Tyler, Lyon Gardiner. *Encyclopedia of Virginia Biography*. New York: Lewis Historical Publishing, 1915.
Union Citizen Files. National Archives and Records Administration, M345, RG 109, Washington, D.C., https://www.fold3.com.
United States Catholic Magazine and Monthly Review 7 (January 1848): 224.
U.S. Adjutant General. *Official Army Register for August 1862*. Washington: GPO, 1862.
U.S. Army of the Potomac. *Index to the General Orders of the Army of the Potomac, 1862*. Washington: Blanchard & Mohun, 1863.
U.S. Congress, House of Representatives. House Select Committee on Alleged Corruptions in Government. *The Covode Investigation, First Session of the Thirty Sixth Congress, 1859-60*. Washington: GPO, 1860.
_____. *Index to Reports of Committees of the House of Representatives, 1876-77*. Washington: GPO, 1877.
_____. "Loyalty of Clerks and Other Persons Employed by the Government," *Reports of Committees of the House of Representatives, 37th Congress, 2nd Session, 1862*. Washington: GPO, 1862.
_____. *Report of the Joint Committee on the Conduct of the War*. Washington: GPO, 1863.
_____. *Reports of Committees of the House of Representatives of the Thirty-Fifth Congress*. Washington: James B. Steedman, 1858.
_____. *Reports of Committees of the House of Representatives, First Session of the Fifty-Second Congress, 1891-92*. Washington: GPO, 1892.
U.S. Congress, Senate. *Journal of the Senate of the United States of America*. Washington: A.O.P. Nicholson, 1856-57.
_____. *Reports of the Committees of the Senate of the United States*. Washington: GPO, 1862.
U.S. War Department. *The War of the Rebellion: A Compilation of the Official Records of the Union and Confederate Armies*, 70 Vols. in 128 books. Washington: GPO, 1880-1912.
Van Waes, Harrison S. "Together Again: Reuniting the Silver Tureens of Judge George Washington Dobbin." December 17, 2021, https://www.mdhistory.org/.
Venable, William Henry. *Centennial History of Christ Church Cincinnati*. Cincinnati: Stewart & Kidd, 1918.
Virginia General Assembly, House of Delegates. *Journal of the House of Delegates of the State of Virginia*. Richmond: Ritchie, 1862.
Volo, Dorothy Daneen, and James M. Volo. *Daily Life in Civil War America*. Westport: Greenwood, 1998.
Waller, Douglas. *Lincoln's Spies: Their Secret War to Save a Nation*. New York: Simon & Schuster, 2020.
Washington: City and Capital. Washington: GPO, 1937.
Welles, Gideon. *Diary of Gideon Welles*, Vol. 1. Boston: Houghton Mifflin, 1911.
Wells, Carol. "William Ross Postell, Adventurer." *Georgia Historical Quarterly* (Fall 1973): 390-405.
Whelen, Bernard, Philip Messing, and Robert Mladinich. *Case Files of the NYPD*. New York: Hachette, 2016.
White, Frank F., Jr. *The Governors of Maryland 1777-1970*. Annapolis: The Hall of Records Commission, 1970.
White, John G. *A Twentieth Century History of Mercer County, Pennsylvania*. Chicago: Lewis, 1909.

Wiggins, Kennard R., Jr, *America's Anchor*. Jefferson NC: McFarland, 2019.
Williams Cincinnati Directory and Business Advertiser, 1849–1850. Cincinnati: C. S. Williams, 1849.
Wilson, H. *Trow's New York City Directory, 1855/56*. New York: Trow, 1855.
Wingert, Cooper. "1850 Fugitive Slave Law," https://blogs.dickinson.edu/hist-wingert/uscommissioners/philip-a-hoyne/.
Woodruff, J. H., ed. *Cincinnati Directory Advertiser, 1836–37.* Cincinnati: Woodruff, 1836.
Woods, John W. *Woods' Baltimore City Directory*. Baltimore: Woods, 1860.
Worden, Amy. *Lawyers Hill Historic District, Howard County, MD*. Washington: National Park Service, 1992.
"Work of a Confederate Woman." *Confederate Veteran* 9 (1901): 321–325.
Wormeley, Katharine Prescott. *The United States Sanitary Commission: A Sketch of Its Purposes and Its Work*. Boston: Little, Brown and Company, 1863.
Yearns, Wilfred B., Jr. "The Peace Movement in the Confederate Congress." *Georgia Historical Quarterly* 41 (March 1957): 1–18.
Young, Frances G. *Edmund Clarence Stedman Papers*. Rare Book and Manuscript Library, Columbia University, in the City of New York.
Zellar, Paul G. *The Vermont Brigade in the Seven Days*. Jefferson, NC: McFarland, 2019.
Zevely, Douglass. "Old Residences and Family History in the City Hall Neighborhood." *Records of the Columbia Historical Society, Washington, D.C.* 6 (1903): 104–122.

Index

Abbott, Henry Livermore 83
abolition 30, 93, 95–96, 98, 153
abolitionists 34, 39, 57, 93, 123, 128
Acushnet 13
Albert, Augustus J. 149–150
Albert, Augustus J. Jr. 150
Alexander, George W. 47–48
Alexandria, Virginia 50–51, 62, 68
Alexandria Gazette 91, 136
Allen, Algernon Sidney 45, 133
Allen, Algernon Sidney, Jr. 45
Allen, Anne Boyd Owen 134
Allen, Aquilla R. 64
Allen, David Hume 45
Allen, Robert Owen 45
American Colonization Society 32–34, 43
American Guard 49–52, 89; *see also* 71st New York State Militia
Anacostia River 50
Annapolis, Maryland 38, 43, 50, 161
Andrews, Mrs. Richard Snowden 31
Andrews, Richard Snowden 33, 37, 39, 132, 151
Anglo-African American Institute 98
Appleton, George D. 8
Appleton's Bookstore 10–13
SS *Ariel* 17
The Aristocratic Monitor 22–24
Armageddon 124
Army of Northern Virginia 99, 101, 103, 105, 115, 135
Army of the Potomac 3–4, 6, 84, 89, 103, 107, 110–111, 121, 144, 154
Army of Virginia 90
Ashby, Richard 75
Ashby, Turner 73–76, 78; *see also* Seventh Virginia Cavalry
Aspinwall, William H. 102, 152, 154
Associate Reformed Church of Baltimore 95

Averitt, James Battle 72, 74–76, 137, 140–141; *see also The Old Plantation*
Avis, John 115

Babcock, Alexander G. 148
Bacon, Augustus O. 104–105
Baker, Edmund Dickinson 81–86, 109, 115
Baker, Lafayette 126–128, 150
Bakewell, Thomas 122, 158, 163
Ball, Dabney 46, 53, 57, 118
Baltimore, Maryland 5, 49, 53, 56–57, 74, 80, 95–96, 98, 116, 118, 123, 128, 134, 138–143, 145–146, 157–158, 166–167, 170, 175–176; Barney's roots in 16–18, 23, 58, 90, 103, 107, 156; Greene's in-laws 68–69, 126–127; secessionists in 27–44, 46, 135–136, 149–151, 159–161; smuggling from 47–48, 132–133
Baltimore American 75, 147
Baltimore County Horse Guards 76
Baltimore Daily Exchange 30
Baltimore Independent Greys 41
Baltimore & Ohio Railroad 29–31, 38–39, 41, 44, 74, 126–127, 131, 136, 141–144, 147–149
Baltimore Sun 48, 102
Barksdale, Ethelbert 130
Barlow, Samuel 155
Barney, John 20–22
Barney, Joshua 16–17
Barney, Maria "Rosa" (Mrs. William Ross Postall) 58, 108
Barney, Mary Chase 16–18, 21, 58
Barney, Samuel Chase 17–18, 21, 156, 175
Barney, William Bedford 16
Barney, William Chase 1, 4, 6, 16–27, 173, 175; as a peace ambassador 102–103, 106–112, 114, 120–121, 124, 132–133, 152–156; in Union service 49–52, 81, 85–92
Barnum's Hotel 29, 170
Barrett, James G. 61

219

"Battle Cry of Freedom" 98
Battle of Antietam 3–4, 6, 92, 101, 103–106, 119, 121, 129, 151, 156, 161
Battle of Ball's Bluff 73, 78, 80–83, 85, 89, 108, 115
Battle of Brandy Station 80
Battle of Buena Vista 123, 165
Battle of Bull Run (First) 52–54, 57, 60, 67, 88
Battle of Bull Run (Second) 90–93, 107–108, 116, 156
Battle of Chantilly 91, 105
Battle of Fredericksburg 119, 171–172
Battle of Gettysburg 145, 173, 176
Battle of Huamantla 62
Battle of Lewinsville 86, 90
Battle of Shiloh 96
Battle of Vicksburg 173, 175
Bayard, James A. 153
Beauregard, P.G.T. 54–55, 134
Bee, Barnard 52
Bel Air estate 139
Belmont, August 155
Benjamin, Judah P. 19, 42, 48, 132–136
Berford and Company 24
Berkeley, William N. 79
Biddle, Nicholas 35
Bladensburg, Maryland 49
Blair, Francis P. 90
Blanchard, Jonathan 130
Blue Jug (Washington County Jail) 60–62, 65–66, 72
Booth, Elizabeth 21–22
Booth, George Wilson 41, 43–44
Booth, James, Jr. 21–22
Booth, John Wilkes 71, 119
Bordeaux, France 17, 20, 25
Borland, Martha (Mrs. John W. Greene) 159, 164–166, 170
Borland, Phoebe 164–166
Bowen, Levi K. 17
Bowen, Walter 137
Boyce, William Waters 18–19, 25, 28, 116–117, 119
Breckinridge, John C. 27–29, 67, 149
Brevoort House Hotel 85, 91–92
Britton, Mrs. E.G. (Mrs. James S. Greene) 14
Brooklyn Atlantic Baseball Club 148
Brown, Albert Gallatin 18, 116–117, 119
Brown, George 36
Brown, John 73, 77, 176
Brown, Ridgely 138, 149
Brown Veil Club 44, 46
Bryan Hall 96–99
Bryantown, Maryland 60
Buck, John Nelson 143

Buck, Lucy 139
Buck, Thomas Horace 137–138
Buck, William A. 139–140
Buck, William Mason 139, 143
Buffalo, New York 164
Burnside, Ambrose 52–53, 111
Burrows, F.M. 68
Butler, Benjamin 38, 40–41

California Regiment 82–84, 86, 109
Calvert, Charles B. 42, 45
Cambridge, Maryland 47
Camp Tennally, Maryland 64, 66–67, 69–70; *see also* Tennallytown, Maryland
Camp Turner, Virginia 76
Camp Wilkins, Pennsylvania 65
Campbell, J. Mason 27–28
Capon Springs, Virginia 143
Carlisle, Maryland 56, 93–95
Carmichael, Thomas H. 48
Carr, Wilson C.N. 35, 37, 42
Carroll, Charles of Carrollton 32
Carroll, Henry J. 43
Carroll, James 27, 31, 33, 44–46, 136, 146
Carroll, Prudence Gough (Mrs. William T. Winn) 45
Carroll, Sophia Gough (Mrs. Thomas B. Sargent) 45–46, 146
Carskadon, J.H. 149
Cary, Hettie 44
Cary, Jenny 44
Cass, Lewis 20
Caulfield, Barnard G. 159–160
Centreville, Virginia 106–109, 156
Chadwick, James D. 65–67, 69
Chain Bridge 86–87, 108
Chambliss, James R. 109
SS *Champion* 96
Charlestown, Virginia 76
Charlottesville, Virginia 115
Chase, Hannah Kitty 21, 108
Chase, Salmon P. 28, 101–102
Chase, Samuel 16, 108
Chase & Co 25
Chesapeake and Ohio Canal 72
Chicago, Illinois 13–14, 27, 29, 31, 100, 123, 160, 169; Bryan Hall war meetings 96–99; Greene's visit to 128, 157–158, 176; Sanitary Commission 93, 96, 98
Chicago Times 97, 128, 156–158, 163, 167–168, 173
Christ Protestant Episcopal Church of Cincinnati 166
Cincinnati, Ohio 5, 13, 31, 66, 104, 130, 159–160, 164–167, 169–171
Cincinnati Commercial 5, 165, 170, 176
City Hotel, Chicago 128

Index

Claremont estate 39–40
Clephane, Lewis 64, 71
Clifton estate 45, 133–135, 139
Cloud, Daniel Mountjoy 5–6, 95, 134, 136–150, 159, 162, 175; *see also* Wilson, Horace N.
Cobb, Howell 105
cobbing 61–62
Columbia Methodist Episcopal Church 57, 118
Confederate Nitre and Mining Bureau 145
Confederate Signal Corps 144–145
Confederate Treasury Department 132, 135
Confederate War Department 69, 74, 76, 133
The Confidence Man: His Masquerade (Melville) 6–8, 14–15
Conrad, John S. 56, 67
Conrad, Nelson 56–57, 69
Conrad, Thomas Nelson 4–6, 36, 77, 95, 116, 145, 175; double agent 117–119, 131–132, 136–139; spy in Georgetown 56–57, 69–72
Conrad's Ferry 72, 79
Conrad's Store, Virginia 141
Cook, Asa M. 39–40
Copperheads 104, 128, 155, 160, 173
Corps of Observation 81
Cosmopolitan Art Association 11–13, 171
The Court Journal 23
Coutts Bank of London 20
Covode Committee 25
Crittenden, John J. 153
Cullison, Frances (Mrs. John Wesley Greene) 68, 160, 171
Cullison, James M. 47–48
Cullison, Jesse Marling 68, 122, 126, 128, 146–147, 167
Cullison, Micajah M. 68, 148–149, 176
Cullison Meeting House 68

Dashiell, John H. 146–147, 160–161, 167
Davidge, William H. 20
Davis, Jefferson 5, 27–28, 35, 55, 57, 71, 103, 135–138, 164–165; peace negotiations 105–108, 110, 122–125, 129–132, 152, 157–158, 172
Davis, Robert W. 35–36, 68
Davis, Thomas Sturgis 76–77
Dawson, Nathaniel 72, 74, 76
DeBow's Review 20
Delaney, Henry Rozier 46
Democratic Party 5, 30, 129, 155, 161
Dempster, John 97, 99–101, 123
Derby, Chauncy Lyman 12–13, 171

Dickinson College 56, 93–95, 97, 136–138, 146
Dix, John A. 42, 112, 117, 120, 150
Dobbin, George W. 36, 38–39, 143–145
Dobbin, Robert Archibald 144–146
Douglas, Stephen 27, 99, 159
Douglass, Frederick 93, 98
Draper, Joseph 165
Dunlap, John 122, 147, 158, 163–164
Dupont, Samuel F. 18
Durham, Thomas Wise 75
Duryee's Zouaves 91
Duvall, Amon 61, 63, 66

Eastern Penitentiary 168, 170
Eccleston, Samuel 90
Edward's Ferry 82
Eighth Louisiana Infantry 54
Eighth Virginia Infantry 78
Eldridge, G.H. 154
Elizabethtown, New Jersey 169
Elkridge, Maryland 32, 34, 38–39, 127, 144, 145
Elkridge Landing 141–143
Ellicott's Mills, Maryland 41, 127
Ellsworth's Zouaves 50–51
Elyria, Ohio 13, 171
emancipation 1, 5–6, 32, 97–102, 104, 123, 128, 130–131, 140, 143, 146, 148, 155, 160–161, 165, 167, 173; memorial for 99–100; proclamation 3, 101, 119, 124–125, 130–131, 156
Emerson, John S. 68
Emmanuel Protestant Episcopal Church 31–34, 36–37, 39–40, 46, 133, 143, 145–146, 160
Endsley, A.J. 122, 163
Essex Market Police Court 11–12
European Express 25
Evans, Nathan "Shank" 52, 77, 79
Evanston, Illinois 97, 99
"Ever of Thee" 27

Fair Haven, Maryland 48
Fairfax Courthouse, Virginia 52, 54
Faquir Mountain Rangers 73
Faulkner, Charles J. 54
Federal Hill, Baltimore 40
Ferrandini, Cipriano 29
SS *Fidele* 7, 15
Fifth Avenue Hotel 154
First Indiana Cavalry 115
First Maryland Cavalry 138, 145, 149, 175
First Maryland Infantry Regiment 41–42, 49, 132, 149–150
First Maryland Potomac Home Brigade 148

222　Index

First Methodist Church of Chicago 96
First Methodist Episcopal Church of Cincinnati 164
First Methodist Episcopal Church of Pittsburgh 164
First Michigan Infantry 50
First Virginia Cavalry 46, 53
Flower, Elizabeth Ada (Mrs. John Wesley Greene) 13, 171
Flower, Mary Jane (Mrs. Richard Tobias Greene) 13-14, 171
Foote, Henry S. 129
Forsha, Dr. S.A. 101
Fort Leavenworth 87, 89
Fort McHenry 48, 69, 145, 148, 176
Fort Sumter 30
Fortress Monroe 117, 120-121, 150, 152
Franciscus, Ada B. (Mrs. William Chase Barney) 23, 58
Franklin, Benjamin 17
Frederick, Maryland 44, 148
Free-soil Party 71
Friday Club 144
Front Royal, Virginia 139
Fugitive Slave Law 50, 119, 124, 157
fugitive slaves 40, 50, 124
Fuller, Richard 37

Garrett Bible Institute 97
Gatch, Thomas Benton 74
Gault, J. Emory 147
Geneva, New York 85
Georgetown, District of Columbia 56, 64, 69, 70
Georgetown Hospital 57, 67
Georgetown Institute 56, 70, 72
Gilmor, Harry 76-77, 138-139, 151
Gist, William H. 28
Gittings, Charlotte Ritchie 30
Gittings, John S. 29
Glen Ellen estate 76
Glenn, John 17
Glenn, William Wilkins 30, 34-35
Gordon, John Montgomery 44-45
Gordon, Rebecca Chapman 44
Gordonsville, Virginia 110
Grace Methodist Episcopal Church of Buffalo 164
Grace Protestant Episcopal Church of Elkridge 32, 34, 141, 143-144
Grayson, Eliza 157
Great Western Japanned Tin Ware Manufactory 165, 167
Greeley, Horace 3, 163
Greene, Herman Melville 13
Greene, John Wesley 1, 5-6, 164-167, 170-173, 175-176; ante bellum New York 10-15, 168-169; army chaplain 64-71; peace ambassador 122-133, 135-136, 138, 142-148, 152, 157-164; *see also* Greer, Benjamin F.
Greene, Richard Tobias 13-14
Greenhow, Rose O'Neal 54-55, 57, 60, 67
Greenland Gap, Virginia 149
Greer, Benjamin F. 8-10; *see also* Greene, John Wesley
Griffin, Charles 53, 86
Grogan, James J. 45
Grogan, Kennedy 149
Grogan, Robert Riddle 45

Hackensack, New Jersey 23
Hagan, Estcott & Moore 171
Hagerstown, Maryland 145
Halstead, Murat 5, 66, 130, 166-167, 176
Hampstead, Maryland 68
Han, Robert H. 41
Harbin, Thomas Henry 66, 137-138, 175
Harden, William 160-161
Harper, Kenton 38, 74
Harpers Ferry, Virginia 32, 38, 41, 44, 68-69, 73-74, 77, 157-158
Harrison's Island 73, 78-79
Hart, Bridget 18, 21
Harter, Thomas O. 115-116
Hatch, Ozias M. 111
Hay, David B. 75
Hay, John 4, 37, 104
Hayward, Henry P. 145
Herbert, James R. 41
Herr, J.D. 164
Hicks, Thomas H. 28, 47
History of the Pennsylvania Reserve Corps 123
House Committee on Naval Affairs 18
House Committee on Post Offices and Roads 19
Howard, Charles 27, 31, 37, 41
Howard, Charles, Jr. 135
Howard, Frank Key 30
Howard, John Eager 31
Howard, McHenry 35, 40-44
Howard, Mrs. Charles 160; *see also* Key, Elizabeth Phoebe
Howard, William 41
Hoyne, Philip A. 157, 160
Hull, John 20
Hume, Charles Connor 66
Hume, Frank 66, 175
Hunter, Robert M.T. 19
Hutton, Epa 79

Illinois Central Railroad 155
Imboden, John C. 149

Index

Ingersoll, Charles Jared 17
Irving House Hotel 153–154
Israel, Fielder 96

Jackson, Andrew 17–18
Jackson, William G. 141–144
Jackson Democratic Association 66
Jacobs, Curtis 33
Jennings, William 86
SS *John A. Warner* 112
Johns, Henry Van Dyke 46
Johnson, Daniel H. 25
Johnson, Jane Claudia (Mrs. Bradley T. Johnson) 44
Johnson, Phillip 77
Johnson, Reverdy 153
Johnston, Joseph E. 55
Joint Committee on the Conduct of the War 73, 85
Jones, Wesley Fletcher 161
Jones, William E., "Grumble" 149
Jordan, Thomas 55
Judiciary Square, Washington 60

Kane, George P. 35
Kearney, Philip 89, 91, 105
Keiley, Benjamin J. 105–106
Kelley's Island 75–76
Kerby, Joseph T. 150–151
Kerr, Orpheus C. (Robert Henry Newell) 173
Key, Elizabeth Phoebe 31, 145; *see also* Howard, Mrs. Charles
Key, Elizabeth Swan (Mrs. Robert A. Dobbin) 145
Key, Francis Scott 31
Key, John J. 121
Key, Mary Alicia Nevins (Mrs. Geoge H. Pendleton) 160
Key, Thomas M. 103–105, 107, 121
King, Horatio 56, 94–95, 137, 139–140
Know-Nothing Party 71, 94

Landstreet, John 46
Lanier Brothers and Co. 68–69
Lanier Guard 68
Lapham, William B. 77, 80
Latrobe, Benjamin H. 136
Latrobe, Henry B. 43, 132
Latrobe, John H.B. 31–34, 37–39, 43, 98, 132, 136, 141–145, 160, 171
Latrobe, Nora 31
Latrobe, Osmun 38, 106, 115, 171–172
Latrobe, Richard Steuart 145–146, 175
Laurel Brigade 149
Lawyer's Hill, Maryland 38, 40, 141, 144–145

Ledyard, Henry 20
Lee, John 126
Lee, Robert E. 4, 90, 102, 105–106
Leesburg, Virginia 72, 78, 80, 83, 141
Leonardtown, Maryland 69
Letcher, John 131
Libby Prison 110–111, 113–114, 116–117, 134
Liberia 32–33, 39, 43, 98
Liberty Street Methodist Episcopal Church, Pittsburgh 65, 123
Light Street Methodist Episcopal Church, Baltimore 170
Lincoln, Abraham 1, 3–6, 28, 30, 34, 54, 61, 81, 106, 110–111, 120–121, 139, 141–143, 156, 172–173, 175–176; emancipation 92, 98–104; Francis G. Young 83–85, 109; peace 36–38, 68, 122–130, 139, 152–153, 158–159; plots against 29, 58, 71, 116, 119, 160, 168
Lincoln, Edward Baker 81
Lincoln, Mrs. Mary 29–30, 84, 125, 177
Linton, John A. 18
London, England 20–21, 86, 88
Long's Hotel 20
Longstreet, James 34, 105–106, 115
Loudon Cavalry 77
Louis Phillipe I (king of France) 88
Louisville, Kentucky 170–171
Ludlow, William H. 88, 112, 120, 152
Lumbard, Frank 98
Lumbard, Jules 98
Lyon, James William 133
Lyon, Samuel H. 35, 45, 47–48, 133, 135, 175

MacKenzie, Alexander Slidell 30
Mahoney, Dennis A. 118–119
Manassas, Virginia 42, 53–55, 109, 150, 176
Manhattan 86, 153–154; *see also* New York City, New York
Mansfield, Joseph K. 49, 52, 68
Marriott, Joseph G.W. 149
Marriottsville, Maryland 148
Marshall, Charles 106, 150–151
Martin, Henry 52
SS *Mary Washington* 48
Maryland Agricultural College 45
Maryland Colonization Society 33
Maryland Flying Artillery 37, 132, 146, 150
Maryland Guard 41–42, 44
"Maryland, My Maryland" 33, 45, 146
Maryland Potomac Home Brigade 66, 148
Mason, James M. 58
Mason, John Francis 76

Index

Masonic Order in Maryland 31
Matsell, George W. 5, 168
SS *M.C. Stevens* 32
McCalmont, John S. 66–67
McClellan, George B
McClintock, John 93–95
McDonald, Angus 74, 76
McDowell, Irwin 52–53, 115
McKelvey, D.G. 58
Mechanicsville Bridge 105
Melville, Herman 6–8, 13–15, 163, 170; *see also The Confidence Man; Moby Dick; Typee*
Memminger, Christopher 132, 135
Mexican War 62–63, 75, 81–82, 123, 157, 164
Miles, William Porcher 133
Military Department of Washington 49
Millstone Landing, Maryland 41–43
Mississippi Rifles 124
Moby Dick 13
Monocacy Junction, Maryland 148
Monument Square, Baltimore 27, 29, 34, 37, 39, 44
Monument Street, Baltimore 30–31, 150; girls 44–46, 48, 146
SS *Monumental City* 24
Morris Chapel of Cincinnati 164
Moseby, John S. 133
Mount Airy estate 42
Mount Gilead, Virginia 78
Mount Vernon Place 29–30, 149–150
Mountain House Hotel 143
Mulberry Methodist Episcopal Church 9
Murray, William H. 42

Napoleon III (emperor of France) 88
National Police Gazette 5, 7–8, 10, 12, 168
National Republican Association of Washington 71
National Rifles 81
National Volunteers 27–29, 34
Native American Party *see* Know-Nothing Party
Naval Efficiency Board 18
Nevin, D.R.B. 109–110, 113–114
New Castle, Delaware 21–22
New Creek, Virginia 149
New Orleans, Louisiana 7, 13, 15, 17, 19–20, 25, 54, 116
New York and New Orleans Steamship Company 25
New York City, New York 4–5, 49, 100, 102, 104, 125; Barney ante bellum enterprises 17, 20, 22–25; Barney and Young's wartime return 84–85, 89–91, 108–109, 153–155; Greene's frauds 8–13, 15, 164–165, 168–171, 176; *see also* Manhattan
New York Fire Zouaves 53–54
Nicholson, Isaac F. 44
Nicholson, Rebecca 46
Nones, Joseph B. 23–24
Norris, Charlotte (Mrs. Charles B. Calvert) 45
Norris, Eleanor (Mrs. Thomas A. Spence) 45
Norris, Emma (Mrs. Frank Hume) 66
Norris, John E. 61, 66
Norris, Kennedy Owen 45
Norris, Mary Hawksworth Owen 33, 45–47, 133–136, 146, 149
Norris, William, Jr. 30
Norris, William Henry 27–31, 33–35, 37, 45–46, 48, 132–133, 135–136, 139, 144, 149
North Fifth Street Methodist Episcopal Church, New York 169

Old Capitol Prison 4, 43, 62–63, 112, 118–120, 133, 138
The Old Plantation (Averitt) 74
Oldfield, Catherine Barney 21, 108
Opequon Creek 52
Orleans' princes 87–89, 108
Oswandel, John Jacob 62
Ould, Robert 113
Owen, Rebecca (Mrs. James J Grogan) 45
Owen, Sarah 45

Pacific Mail Steamship Company 20
Paige, Nathaniel 103–104
Palmer, Innis N. 60
Panama 24–25
Paris, France 17, 20–21, 49, 58, 88
Patapsco River 38–40, 141
Patton, William Weston 98–101, 123
Patuxent River 41–43
Payne, Lewis 70–71
Pegram, Paynter and Davis 35, 68
Pendleton, Anna Pierce (Mrs. Noah Hunt Schenck) 166–167
Pendleton, George H. 31, 152, 159–160, 166–167, 176
Pendleton, Nathaniel G. 166–167
Pennsylvania Fairgrounds 65
Le Petite, Marie Felicite (Mrs. Willam Chase Barney) 17, 108
Phi Kappa Sigma 137
Phillips, George W. 61–62
Pinkerton, Allen 5, 29–30, 55, 58–59, 123, 150, 153–155
Piscataway, Maryland 138
Pittsburg Landing, Tennessee 96
Pittsburgh, Pennsylvania 1, 38, 65,

122–123, 125, 127–128, 130, 139, 142–143, 146–148, 158, 161, 163–164, 168
Plitt, Maximillian 148
Point Lookout 47
Point of Rocks, Maryland 44, 149
Pollard, Edward A. 129–130
Poolesville, Maryland 72–73, 77, 81, 84
Pope, John 90–91, 113, 115–116, 156
Pope's Creek 60
Potomac and Ohio Railroad 31
Potomac River 41–42, 46, 50, 57, 60, 72–81, 83, 99–103, 108, 118, 121, 130, 139, 145, 149
Powell, Lewis Thornton 71
Prados, John B. 54, 176
Pratt Street Riot 36, 45, 68, 76
Price, Birch & Company 50
Pride, Alexander H. 24, 50
Prince of Joinville 87–88

race war 34 3, 61, 173
Radle, William S. 126–128, 143
Randall, James Ryder 45
Randolph, George W. 131, 145
Reese, Thomas Sargent 146
Relay House 38, 126–127, 131, 141–143, 147
Reno, Marcus 115
Republican Party 27–28, 62, 71, 81, 85
Rhett, Thomas S. 31, 132–133
Rice, Nathan 130
Richmond, Virginia 4–6, 19, 42–44, 48, 69–70, 89–90, 137–138, 141, 143, 145, 150, 156–158, 164; Barney and Young mission to 102–103, 107, 109–112, 114–117, 119–121, 129, 132–135, 152–154, 156; Wood and Conrad mission to 112–113, 117–121, 123–124, 131–135, 175, 177
Rickett's Battery 53
Riddell, William C. 23–24
Ridgeley, Charles 76
Ritchie, Thomas 30
Riversdale estate 45
Roberts, Benjamin S. 149
Rogers, E. Law 48
Rogers, William H. 18
Romney, Virginia 75
Root, George F. 98
Rush, Benjamin 56
Russell, Charles W. 130

St. James College 145
St. John, Samuel 9–10
USS *St. Nicholas* 47; *see also* Zarvona, Richard Thomas
Salisbury, North Carolina 119
Sandusky, Ohio 171
Sandy Hook, Maryland 69

Sanitary Commission 90–91, 93, 96–98
Sargent, Henry Dorsey Gough Carroll 146
Sargent, Thomas B. 45–46, 146, 160
Selby, John W. 37, 68–69, 146, 161, 176
Schenck, Noah Hunt 31, 33, 36–37, 143, 146, 159–160, 166–167, 176
Scott, Winfield 49–50, 58, 119
Scoville, Joseph Alfred 3, 6, 54, 59, 87–89, 92, 101–103, 107–111
Secession 19, 28, 35, 39, 55, 57–58, 67, 117, 141, 146
Second U.S. Cavalry 60
Second Virginia Infantry 52
17th Mississippi Infantry 79
Seventh Virginia Cavalry 73–74, 137; *see also* Ashby, Turner
71st New York State Militia 49, 51, 53, 148; *see also* American Guard
71st Pennsylvania Infantry *see* California Regiment
Seward, Frederick W. 59, 86–87, 89–90, 107, 120, 152
Seward, William H. 28, 58, 88, 90–91, 99, 107–108, 120, 124, 143, 153
Shenandoah Valley 131, 134, 138–139
Sigel, Franz 115
Sing Sing Prison 8, 14, 168
Sixth Massachusetts Infantry 35–36, 68
slavery 32, 39, 63, 93, 117, 119, 124, 130, 155, 161, 173; critics of 6, 57, 71, 88, 97–99; Lincoln on 92, 99, 121; proponents of 5, 19–20, 27–28, 61, 67, 74, 77; tensions over 27, 57, 68, 95–96; trading peace for 104, 119, 121, 151
Slicer, Elizabeth Selby (Mrs. William Harden) 161
Slicer, Henry 161–162, 167
Smallwood, Ignatius 51, 54, 176
Smith, George W. 60
Smith, W.H. "Baldy" 4, 86, 104
Smith, William "Extra Billy" 55
smuggling: of horses 131, 149; of military supplies 44, 46–47, 73
South Mountain 105, 152
Southern Historical Association 136
Spence, Thomas A. 45, 47
Springfield, Illinois 81, 100
Stanton, Edwin M. 4–5, 62, 101–103, 112–113, 115–117, 119–125, 145, 150, 152, 158, 163, 177
"Star-Spangled Banner" 31
Stedman, Edmund C. 82, 115
Stein, Enoch H. 150–151
Steinmetz, B.H. 125, 127, 159
Steuart, George H. 38
Steuart, Harry A. 42–43, 132–133
Steuart, William Frederick 42

Index

Stewart, Charles 86
Stone, Charles P. 73, 78–79, 81–82, 115
Storey, Wilbur F. 97, 128, 159–160, 167, 169, 173; *see also Chicago Times*
Strawbridge Methodist Episcopal Church 37, 46, 68–69, 146; *see also* Trinity Methodist Episcopal Church South
Stuart, J.E.B. 46–47, 66, 116
Susquehana estate 43
Sykesville, Maryland 41

Taney, Roger 93
"Tannenbaum, O Tannenbaum" 46
Tennallytown, Maryland 167–168; *see also* Camp Tennally
Tenth Massachusetts Infantry 64
Tenth Pennsylvania Reserve Regiment 64–65, 67, 123, 176
Terry, William R. 52
Third Artillery 123, 157
Third Maryland Artillery 43, 132
Third New York Cavalry 82
Third Virginia Cavalry 72
Thirteenth Amendment 173
13th Virginia Cavalry 109
13th Virginia Infantry 68
35th Virginia Battalion 149; *see also* White's Comanches
39th Pennsylvania Infantry *see* Tenth Pennsylvania Reserve Regiment
Thomas, Edward M. 98
Thomas, George 41
Thomas, John 47
Thomas Viaduct 39
Thompson, William 12, 16
Thorn, Henry Culver 60
Tiffany, Otis H. 93–98
Tombs Prison 8, 12, 16, 24
Trimble, Isaac R. 31, 33, 37, 133
Trinity Methodist Episcopal Church South 146; *see also* Strawbridge Methodist Episcopal Church
Turner, Levi C. 115–116, 121
20th Massachusetts Infantry 83
25th Pennsylvania Infantry 35
21st Virginia Infantry 69
22nd Georgia Infantry 161
Typee, A Peek at Polynesian Life 13–14, 170; *see also* Melville, Herman

Union Bank 31, 44–45, 132
United State Catholic Magazine 23
United States War Department 56, 90, 117, 120, 122, 125

Vallandigham, Clement 160
Van Buren, John 153, 155, 172
Van Buren, Martin 153
Vanderbilt, Cornelius 25, 27
Viers, Mary Elizabeth (Mrs. Stephen Newton White) 77

Wadsworth, James A. 112, 120
Walker, Samuel H. 62
Wallace's Indiana Zouaves 75–76
Wallis, Severn Teackle 17, 30, 36, 47
Warren, Henry 73
Warren County Cavalry 137, 139
Washington, District of Columbia 5, 29–30, 43–44, 47, 66–69, 71, 91, 99, 115, 143, 168, 170, 176; Baker and Young 82, 84–86; Barney ante bellum enterprises 16, 18, 23; early defense of 34–36, 38, 49–50, 78, 81, 88–89, 116; Greene peace mission to 122–123, 126–127, 129–131, 142, 158–159; jails 60–61, 63–64, 137; rebel spies in 54–58, 72, 74, 80; secret missions from 102–103, 108–109, 112–113, 117, 120–121, 136–136, 152–153, 156; treason against 111
Washington, George W. 75
Washington Navy Yard 49–51, 54
Watson, Peter H. 123
Webb, W.B. 125, 158
Weddell House Hotel 128
Welles, Gideon 99, 121, 124
West Middlesex Methodist Episcopal Church 65
West Point Battery 86
West River, Maryland 42
Whig Party 44
White, Elijah 77–81, 149
White, Joseph J. 164–165
White, Stephen Newton 77
White Horse Tavern 60
White Sulfur Springs, Virginia 136
White's Comanches 80; *see also* 35th Virginia Battalion
Wilbur, A.D. 164
Wilkes, George W. 52
Willard's Hotel 85, 122, 125–126
Wilmington, Delaware 21
Wilson, Horace N. 123, 126, 128, 137–139, 143, 148, 150, 157, 161; *see also* Cloud, Daniel Mountjoy
Winans, Ross 27, 29
Winans, Thomas 41
Winchell, George D. 165, 171
Winchester, Virginia 72, 133, 139, 143, 150
Winder, Charles H. 58–60, 111
Winder, John H. 58, 111, 115–117, 119, 135
Winn, Ida B. 44–45
Winn, William T. 45
Winn, Prudence Gough Carroll 45

Wise, Henry A. 156
Wise, O. Jennings 156
Wistar, Isaac J. 83
Wolcott, C.P. 90
Wool, John E. 126
Wood, Fernando 4, 12, 104, 153, 155–157, 160
Wood, William P. 4–6, 60, 175; following Barney to Richmond 117–121, 131, 133–136, 141, 152, 155; as superintendent of Old Capitol Prison 62–63, 112–113
Woodward, W.R. 66
Wren, James 35

Wright, Alice 44
Wright, Robert Clinton 44

Yale College 30, 46, 132
Yates, Richard 96
YMCA 37–38, 68, 143
Young, Francis G. 82–86, 91–92, 106–109, 111–116, 153–154, 177
Young, Samuel C. 72–73

Zarvona, Richard Thomas 41, 47–49, 133–135

www.ingramcontent.com/pod-product-compliance
Lightning Source LLC
Chambersburg PA
CBHW032040300426
44117CB00009B/1136